The Ancient Constitution and the Origins of Anglo-American Liberty

The frontispiece to Edward Cook's 1682 *Argumentum Anti-Normannicum: or an Argument Proving, from Ancient Histories and Records, that William, Duke of Normandy Made no absolute Conquest of England, by the Sword; in the sense of our Modern Writers,* in which he presents a serious constitutional argument. Courtesy of the Huntington Library

THE ANCIENT CONSTITUTION
and the Origins of Anglo-American Liberty

John Phillip Reid

NORTHERN ILLINOIS UNIVERSITY PRESS

DEKALB

Published by the Northern Illinois University Press, DeKalb, Illinois 60115

Design by Julia Fauci

Library of Congress Cataloging-in-Publication Data

Reid, John Phillip.

The ancient constitution and the origins of Anglo-American liberty / John Phillip Reid.

p. cm.

Includes bibliographical references and index.

ISBN-13: 978-0-87580-342-5 (clothbound : alk. paper)

ISBN-10: 0-87580-342-3 (clothbound : alk. paper)

1. Constitutional history—England. 2. Law—United States—English influences.

I. Title.

KD3934.R45 2005

342.4102'9—dc22

2004030007

for

JOHN SEXTON

of NEW YORK UNIVERSITY

CONTENTS

The Ancient Constitution and the Origins of Anglo-American Liberty

Introductory Note

It has long been a matter of professional as well as academic discussion that there is an unbridgeable dichotomy separating the writing and discipline of history from the canons of the common-law methodology. When legal and constitutional points are being argued, history and law are not comfortable as joint participants. The common law, or more particularly common-law constitutionalism, both in England from the fifteenth to the nineteenth century and in North America from the eighteenth century to today, has been argued, proven, and sustained by evidence drawn from what the drawers said was history. History has particularly been the authority employed in constitutional contention by common lawyers to define, promote, and protect the concept of liberty and civil rights in general. Despite the purpose of lawyers and constitutionalists defending and, in fact, creating the principle of restrained, limited government controlled by the rule of law, their use of history has been frequently disparaged by professional historians. Indeed, the historians have instead lavished praise on the history used by the opponents of the lawyers and constitutionalists, that is, the abettors of prerogative rule and of the theory of the divine-right-of-monarchy. It is the purpose of the following chapters to explore this criticism by historians and to ask whether these critics were using the standards of the historical method practiced by professional, academic historians, to judge a legal methodology that is not history but advocacy and, therefore, should not be held to those standards; or, at most, if it is to be considered history, should be acknowledged to be a subdivision of history, that is, *forensic history*.[1]

The crossing of history with law is a mixture containing more snares than rewards, as it risks confusing rules of evidence basic to one profession with the canons of proof sacrosanct to another. True, there have been those who feel the mix takes well. For example, Alfred H. Kelly, a scholar of history thoroughly versed in constitutional law but who apparently had only a layman's knowledge of nonconstitutional law, thought the connection of methodology between law and history not only easily located but a fairly close match. They not only share intellectual substance, he pointed out, but the materials used in each are also the same. Writing for a legal publication in 1965, Kelly stated that

> [t]here is, after all, a fairly close relationship between the day-to-day methodology of the judicial process and that of historical scholarship. When a court ascertains the nature of the law to be applied to a case through an examination of a stream of judicial precedent, after the time-honored Anglo-American technique, it plays the role of historian. A historian might well say that in this process the court goes to the "primary sources."[2]

The implication—one that is shared by lawyers perhaps even more than by historians—is that there is a similarity between the methodology of law and the methodology of history. Indeed, the argument goes much further than process. It is not just techniques or procedure that the two disciplines have in common; they share substance as well. Certainly there are times when first-year law students think so. At least we must suspect that many would agree with the Chief Justice of the United States when he suggested in 1957 that in real property classes they are learning legal history. "All lawyers are, of course, in some sense students of legal history," Earl Warren contended. "The knowledge of medieval law, which is essential to the most elementary understanding of our land law, is an obvious example."[3]

What was obvious to Earl Warren could be quite obscure to other people. Warren would have been correct had he said that first-year law students often learn the name of old, even medieval judicial landmarks, such as the Rule in *Shelley's Case.*[4] They do not, however, learn what the decision stood for when first promulgated, and they certainly do not learn about it as an evolving and ever-changing legal doctrine.

Simply stated, the law student, the practitioner, or the law professor, when grappling with the Rule in *Shelley's Case,* is interested only in the latest interpretation of the rule—the last decision in the jurisdiction—and nothing else. Lawyers, to function as lawyers, do not have to learn anything of sixteenth-century law or of the rule's subsequent historical evolution. All that lawyers need care about is the net result of that evolution, the latest judicial, *nonhistorical* appraisal or interpretation of the rule.

The lawyer and the historian have in common the fact that they go to the past for evidence, but there the similarity largely ends. Some historians, such as Kelly, believe that common-law methodology requires the lawyer to play "the role of historian" and to go "to the 'primary sources.'" For such historians, Frederic William Maitland warned, there is a temptation "to mix up two different logics, the logic of authority, and the logic of evidence."[5] The differences in the logics are differences that Kelly missed. They are so basic that they make the ways that the two professions interpret the past almost incompatible. In discovering the past, the historian weighs every bit of evidence that comes to hand. The lawyer, by contrast, is after authority that will settle the case at bar.

The search for authority, the need to find "the law" or "the right law," is the main reason lawyers speak and think of the legal past in terms quite different from the historian's. J. W. Gough described how common lawyers

> look at the past from an unhistorical standpoint. In the English lawyer's view, a judge who applies a law to a fresh case elucidates what was always, potentially as it were, the law on that particular matter. One interpretation of the law may have been accepted for years, and then suddenly be reversed by a decision in a fresh case in a higher court, whereupon the new decision holds the field and the old interpretation is discarded as erroneous. Again, when a statute, let us say, has been applied over a long period of years, in changing circumstances, to a succession of cases, and has thus accumulated round it a whole nexus of judge-made law, the historian and lawyer will look at the original statute in a different light. The historian will want to know what the statute meant to the generation which enacted it, apart from the ways in which subsequent judges have adapted their interpretations of it to fresh circumstances. For the lawyer, on the other hand, these successive interpretations reveal the true meaning of the law. Not only, therefore, does the lawyer's business, unlike the historian's, lie not so much with what the statute originally meant as with what it means now, but he will be inclined, unless he is careful, to imagine that the statute always, at any rate potentially, meant what it has since come to be interpreted to mean.[6]

Our lesson is not that the lawyer is uninterested in the original meaning of the statute. Our lesson, rather, is that the lawyer *needs* another meaning. The concept of that other meaning—the legal, or what Gough called "the true meaning"—leads lawyers, unless they are on their historical guard, to commingle the current interpretation of the law with the historical interpretation. Common lawyers tend to be anachronistic, not merely because they are advocates, but because of the way they think and speak about the past.

To explore the legal methodology of forensic history, this study surveys the use made by lawyers, constitutionalists, and parliamentarians of the suppositive *ancient constitution* as the forensic tool with which to create, defend, and define the concept of liberty and of representative government.

The practice of ancient constitutionalism was the most persistent, long-lived use of forensic history by common lawyers. Sometimes called the gothic constitution, the ancient constitution was the putative aboriginal political structure of Anglo-Saxon governance, the origins of which are discoverable in the mythology of the forests of prehistoric Germany. It was the supposed norm of government for the Angles, the Saxons, and the Jutes when they were said by ancient constitutionalists to have been free people living under elected kings, vested with limited authority, and confined by the rule of customary law. For lawyers, constitutionalists, and parliamentarians of the sixteenth and seventeenth centuries, the ancient constitution provided a standard with which to argue against the actions, programs, laws, and decrees of contemporary government. The further that a government command deviated from the supposed model of the ancient constitution of liberty, the more it could be opposed as unconstitutional, or, at least, challenged as an act of "power" rather than an act of "right."

During the seventeenth and eighteenth centuries, in the American colonies[7] as well as in England and Great Britain, the ancient constitution generally was argued by lawyers and, if not by lawyers, by others more concerned with lawyerly questions than with history qua history. "Every Englishman who thought about the constitution," one historian has explained, "thought in some degree as a lawyer, and Coke's doctrines merely stated with the force of genius the lawyer's view of history."[8] Our question may well be whether there was a lawyer's view of history. Perhaps it was not the view or theory of history but the use—the lawyer's use of history, or forensic history—that was what gave the ancient constitution significance. After all, even the premier historian of ancient constitutionalism concedes that

> [t]he doctrine of the ancient constitution . . . was the work of common lawyers, and seems to have been shaped throughout by assumptions concerning the common law of England, deeply implanted in the mind of everyone trained in that study. These assumptions were first, that all the law in England might properly be termed common law [that is not correct]; second, that common law was common custom, originating in the usages of the people and declared, interpreted and applied in the courts; third, that all custom was by definition immemorial, that which had been usage and law since time out of mind, so that any declaration of law . . . was a declaration that its content had been usage since time immemorial.[9]

Although as long ago as the 1640s Sir Roger Twysden pointed out that the historian's law is different from the lawyer's law and, therefore, lawyer's history is different from historian's history,[10] there has been a tendency for British and American historians to evaluate forensic history by the canons of the historical method. The common lawyer's view of the past, when arguing premises based on the ancient constitution and immemorial law, has been described by phrases such as "incorrect,[11] "not always very accurate,"[12] "pseudo-historical literature,"[13] "propaganda,"[14] and, most frequently, "ahistorical myth"[15] or "mythology."[16] It is not necessary to dwell on these comments. What is important is to realize the degree to which scholars trained in the historical method have been critical of seventeenth-

and eighteenth-century practitioners of forensic history. In order to appreciate the extent of the dichotomy between the approaches of the two professions, it is also worth noting that criticisms have not always been consistent. Among other charges that have been made against the practitioners of forensic history, it has been said that they misled "real" historians into accepting their "history." Herbert Butterfield, for example, learned that

> what he had called whig history was really lawyers' history, justifiably practised by them when thinking about the law in which the latest meaning of an event is the only meaning to matter, and in which new opinion abolishes its predecessor—neither of which is true in historians' history. To a lawyer the doings of the past signify only inasmuch as they persist into and have life in the present. All very fine for them, but this teleological preoccupation, which ruins genuine history, they had imposed on the historians. What Butterfield had been attacking, though it took him some time to find it out, was the readiness with which from the seventeenth century onward historians had accepted the lawyers' interpretation of the history of law, government and constitution.[17]

The argument has been carried to rather extreme lengths. The lawyers, it has been complained, "popularized" the "opinions of Edward Coke" "in such a tendentious manner that it became almost impossible to undertake a study of the Norman Conquest in a proper spirit of historical inquiry."[18] They did so even though the history they wrote was history that real historians knew was "bad" history.[19] That is, they "played havoc with history,"[20] perhaps unconsciously;[21] did not heed the lessons of historians;[22] and, of course, lacked training in the canons of writing proper history,[23] an unpardonable fault even though what they wrote, forensic history, was the history they were trained to write.[24] Sometimes the complaint verges on nonsense. "Lawyers," it was charged in 1983, "had played a large part in eroding the foundations of the throne, especially through a fundamental misreading, authoritative in tone, of the history of the common law by men like Coke and Selden (a misreading that was to skew the thinking of Thomas Jefferson and other, lesser men for a long time)."[25]

Finally, when reading the chapters that follow, keep in mind that, despite the arguments made and the theories expressed by the writers who are quoted, this study is not about how history should be written or about the canons or methodology of history. This is a study of ancient constitutionalism. It is a topic that has long deserved the attention of constitutional scholars and historians. Together with the other main forms of forensic history—contractarianism and original intentism—ancient constitutionalism was the instrument that lawyers, constitutionalists, and parliamentarians used over several centuries to neutralize arbitrary power by placing a rein on discretionary decision making. By helping to limit prerogative and executive discretion, the forensic history of ancient constitutionalism both reinforced the rule of law and protected law itself from the politics of an arbitrary state.

CHAPTER ONE

Forensic History

During the late spring of 1779 Brigadier General Francis McLean, commanding the British forces at Halifax, established a post of six hundred men on the site of the present town of Castine, Maine. Proclaiming the reinstitution of royal jurisdiction, McLean called for the support of all inhabitants who "are well affected to his Majesty's person, and the ancient constitution under which they formerly flourished, and from the restoration of which they can alone expect relief from the distressed situation they are now in." Later that year, a Massachusetts expedition arrived in Penobscot Bay to reduce the British fort. Countering McLean's proclamation, Brigadier General Solmon Lovell announced the reestablishment of American authority, which, he said, meant rule by the very same ancient constitution that had been McLean's rallying point. "I have thought proper to issue this Proclamation," he explained, "hereby declaring that the allegiance due to the *ancient constitution* obliges to resist to the last extremity the present system of tyranny in the British Government."[1]

The event was isolated—a small scrimmage on the marchland of empire to fix the line between the future province of New Brunswick and the future state of Maine. That both sides appealed to the ancient constitution, however, placed the battle within the mainstream of the revolutionary controversy. The ancient constitution had been a central element of the prerevolutionary debate from its beginning with the passage of the Stamp Act to its conclusion with the Declaration of Independence. At one time Patrick Henry was under the mistaken impression that the Virginia Resolves against the Stamp Act, the initial formulation of the American legal case that he drafted, had asserted that without the principle of taxation only by representation "the ancient Constitution cannot subsist."[2] The Declaration of Independence was first published in book form as part of a collection by George Bryan or "Demophilus" entitled *The Genuine Principles of the Ancient Saxon, or English Constitution.* That book was printed in Philadelphia, where the readers of the *Pennsylvania Gazette* had recently been urged to compare the defects of their state's constitution "to the English constitution in its original purity, before the Norman invader had abolished as many of the free customs of the people as he possibly could."[3] What Pennsylvanians should do, "Demophilus" urged, was return to the ancient Saxon constitution. "This Colony, having now but one order of freemen in it; and to the honor of Pennsylvania, but very few slaves, it will need but little argument to convince the bulk of an understanding people, that this ancient and justly admired pattern, the old Saxon form of government, will be the best model, that human wisdom, improved by experience, has left them to copy."[4]

Nothing new or particularly American was being said, yet there were observers in the mother country who seemed to think either that what colonial whigs said was unusual or that they overargued the ancient constitution. "Upon the whole," a writer for London's *Critical Review* complained, "we cannot help thinking that the American advocates deal too much in references to ancient and prophane history."[5] The point was not well taken. During the eighteenth century the ancient constitution appears to have been more widely cited and defended in Great Britain than in North America. That should not be surprising. The doctrine of the ancient constitution was then considered the original theoretical basis for English law and for English constitutional principles that constituted the concept of liberty as liberty has come to be defined over the previous three centuries. The ancient constitution was the cornerstone of the arch supporting the various rules, rights, maxims, and dogmas that, collectively, can best be summarized as the *jurisprudence of English and American liberty.* The fact that is surprising and is surely difficult to understand in the twenty-first century is that most practitioners of ancient constitutionalism in the eighteenth century believed that they espoused a constitution that had existed *unchanged* since time immemorial. "It is curious to remark," the Earl of Abingdon noted in 1777 and 1780, "that the Constitution and Form of Government established by our wise Forefathers in America, was precisely, in Principle, the Constitution and Form of Government of the Saxon Heptarchy."[6]

By the time Abingdon wrote, the Americanization of the ancient constitution had become an assumed fact. The dispute about whether the ancient constitution ran in the colonies was now much less intense than it had been earlier in the century.[7] When the question arose in Parliament as to whether the appeal of felony[8] lay in the colonies, John Dunning, the Chatham party's lawyer in the Commons, expressed outrage. "I cannot sit silent when it [appeal of felony] is proposed to be taken away, or suspended with regard to America," he protested. "We must suppose it is an existing right in America. . . . I have heard it reckoned as the remnant of ancient barbarism that ought not to stand. I wish the constitution could be made more palatable to those who have it in their power to destroy it. Gothicism is almost every part of the constitution. Every part of the constitutional history is gothic. Is it to be understood, that we are to have a macaroni constitution in the room of it?"[9] Solicitor General Alexander Wedderburn, who thought appeal of felony "a remnant of ancient barbarism," did not know if it was part of American criminal procedure but with apparent regret admitted that an appeal, with its attendant trial by battle, might still be legal in England and Wales. "The law of England admits of no limitation of time beyond a very distant period indeed," Wedderburn pointed out. "Whatever was the law of England continues to be the law of England."[10] By contrast Edmund Burke rejoiced that neither the appeal of murder nor the trial by battle had been abolished by legislation. "Men have gone upon [the practice] of delivering in their rights to the hands of the state," Burke lamented. "In proportion as they have given up, they have established this kind of government called absolute, or arbitrary in proportion as they have given up [rights]." It was better not to tinker with ancient practices, not even the anachronistic right to appeal by battle. "It is a thing totally agreeable to the old law. If you destroy this, you will destroy the whole system of jurisprudence. This country has left these two together, meaning to keep up government and liberty."[11]

Burke was speaking within the mainstream of eighteenth-century British constitutional thought. Trial by battle "was superstition and barbarism to the last degree,"[12] yet liberty might be imperiled if there was a power in government that could abolish the appeal by mere command. Retaining appeal, even as a dormant anachronism, furthered liberty by preserving liberty's most tenacious support, the authority of custom and the authority of ancient immemoriality. The jurisprudential reason—a major theme to be developed in this book—was that legislative deviations from the ancient law could be promulgated only if arbitrary authority superior to "law" was constitutional. A more political, less legal explanation was that liberty had been more nearly perfect during ancient than in more recent times, making Gothicism and Saxonism standards for measuring the liberty of currently existing government institutions. In 1764, James Otis of Massachusetts Bay outlined the theory's most generally accepted historical premises:

> Few people have extended their inquiries after the foundation of any of their rights, beyond a charter from the crown. There are others who think when they have got back to old *Magna Carta* that they are at the beginning of all things. They imagine themselves on the borders of chaos (and so indeed in some respects they are), and see creation rising out of the unformed mass or from nothing. Hence, say they, spring all the rights of men and of citizens. But liberty was better understood and more fully enjoyed by our ancestors before the coming in of the first Norman tyrants than ever after, till it was found necessary for the salvation of the kingdom to combat the arbitrary and wicked proceedings of the Stuarts.[13]

The same year that Otis wrote, Robert Lowth, bishop of London, making much the same point, pushed the origins of the ancient constitution back to even before the Saxons. "Our Civil Constitution was from the first founded on the liberty of the People," he told the judges and lawyers attending the Durham assizes. That liberty had been "an essential part of the form of government, that universally prevailed among the northern nations, and was transplanted hither with our Saxon ancestors. The people had their acknowledged rights, and the obligation was reciprocal between them and their governors. These were legal kings, not arbitrary tyrants: they were bound and restrained by the laws of the community, framed with the people's participation and consent."[14] Whether the constitution had evolved first among German tribes or later with the Anglo-Saxons after they had conquered the Britons was irrelevant to eighteenth-century constitutional thought. What mattered was that it was the same constitution—then and now. "[T]he present civil constitution of England," Otis concluded, derived "its original" from the Saxons. "This government, like that from whence they [the Saxons] came, was founded upon principles of the most perfect liberty."[15]

There is no need to rely on provincial lawyers and established clergymen. British scholars and judges also embraced the ancient constitution without qualification. In 1766 Sir William Blackstone, who would serve as Vinerian professor of law at Oxford, member of Parliament, and puisne on the Court of Common Pleas, insisted "that the liberties of Englishmen are not (as some arbitrary writers would represent them) mere infringements of the king's prerogative, extorted from our princes by taking advantage of their weakness; but a restoration of that antient constitution, of which our ancestors had been defrauded by the art and finesse of the Norman lawyers, rather than deprived by the force of the Norman arms."[16] As late as a decade before the parliamentary reform act, at least one writer was still defending "the genuine unchangeable English constitution."[17] The operative concept—really a probative concept, as we shall see—was of a timeless constitution of unchanging general principles. As understood in the eighteenth century, this timeless or ancient constitution proved "that our Government was always *Legal;* that the People had their *Rights,* as well as the Kings their *Prerogatives;* and had *Representatives* too, to assert those Rights; that our Kings were not *arbitrary,* nor our Monarchy *absolutely* Hereditary."[18]

The timeless constitution gave English and British lawyers of the seventeenth and eighteenth centuries a jurisprudential instrument with which to maintain the privileges of Parliament and the autonomy of the common-law courts against the pretensions of prerogativism—or, as they saw it, the rule of law against arbitrary government. In the 1760s and 1770s, American whigs resorted to the same ancient constitution for the same purpose, turning against Parliament the legal theory that had made Parliament supreme over the crown. With reluctance they had concluded that Parliament rather than the monarchy had become the potential institution for arbitrariness in imperial government.[19] "Our most ardent Desire," the freeholders of

Virginia's Hanover County told their representatives in 1774, "is, that we and your latest Posterity may continue to live under the genuine unaltered Constitution of England."[20] They meant the same timeless constitution to which Sir Edward Coke had turned in 1628 and on which parliamentary lawyers had relied in 1641. As another Virginian, Richard Bland, had explained just eight years before, it was "a Fact, as certain as History can make it, that the present civil Constitution of *England* derives its Original from those *Saxons* who, coming over to the Assistance of the *Britons* . . . made themselves Masters of the Kingdom, and established a Form of Government in it similar to that they had been accustomed to live under in their native Country."[21]

But what was the ancient constitution in the eighteenth century? There may be no better discussion than that of the *Craftsman,* the newspaper promoting the opposition politics of the faction led by Viscount Bolingbroke. "From the earliest accounts of time," the *Craftsman* explained, "our ancestors in Germany were a free people, and had a right to assent or dissent to all laws; that right was exercised and preserved under the Saxon and Norman Kings, even to our days."[22] The Saxons, before they had invaded Britannia, had been a free people, living under a constitution of liberty.

> When They were settled, according to their Liking, They form'd a Government upon the same Model; That is, their *Leader,* or *General,* was appointed the *chief Magistrate,* though with much less Power than our *modern Kings;* the *other great Men,* or *Officers of the Army,* held the next Rank in the Commonwealth, like our *Lords;* and the *Body of the People,* who follow'd Them, had a third Share in the Government. These *three Orders* composed what is now called the *Legislature.* . . . This is what We mean by our *ancient Constitution;* and though it hath been often interrupted, or depress'd, by Conquest, Usurpation, and arbitrary Power, the *Stamina* of it have been still preserved, and transmitted down to us thro' all Ages and Changes of Government.[23]

The eighteenth-century ancient constitution bestowed on the fortunate Britons a tenacious spirit of liberty, a spirit molded in the German forests and toughened during Tudor and Stuart constitutional battles, "[a] Spirit of *Liberty*" which, "transmitted down from our *Saxon Ancestors,* and the unknown Ages of our Government, preserved itself through one almost continual Struggle, against the Usurpations of our *Princes,* and the Vices of our *People.*"[24]

> Though it must be confess'd that our *old Saxon Constitution* hath undergone many violent Convulsions, since the *Conquest,* I think the whole Series of our History, as far as We can discover it through the Gloom of Antiquity, is one continued Proof that the Foundations of it were never intirely overturn'd; and though various Alterations have been made the *Form of our Parliaments,* the *Essentials* have been preserved, and the *People* were never totally deprived of their Share in *those Assemblies.*[25]

The Legal Perspective

It is worth stating here a proposition that will be repeated over and over in this study. The doctrine of ancient constitutionalism was a method of legal argumentation. For some seventeenth- and eighteenth-century writers it may have been an explanation of actual historical happenings. For most, certainly for most common lawyers, it was not.[26] Of the contrasting points of view from which we can study the history of liberty, perhaps the one that is overlooked more than any other is the legal perspective. The "ideology of the Ancient Constitution," the leading scholar of the subject has contended, was an "elaborate set of historical arguments by which it was sought to show that the common law, and the constitution as it now stood, had been essentially the same since pre-Conquest times and—if the argument were pressed home—since time immemorial, or at least since an unrecorded beginning in the woods of Germany."[27] One need not quarrel with that conclusion to suggest that another dimension can be added. If we find the ancient constitution a puzzle of historiography because the concept of a timeless, never-changing rule of law seems ahistorical, it may be that we are thinking about historical methodology when it would be more helpful to think about forensic argument.

Unless we are willing to dismiss as "unscholarly" the theories, writings, and values of most seventeenth- and eighteenth-century constitutionalists, it does seem that the use and abuse of the concept of the ancient constitution deserves to be considered from the perspective of those who used and abused it, and not just by the canons of the historical method as practiced by twentieth- and twenty-first-century historians. It is not an unimportant question if we agree with Professor Pocock that "[t]hroughout the seventeenth and eighteenth centuries, every major piece of either historical or political thinking involved, if it did not consist in, the adoption of an attitude towards the 'ancient constitution.'"[28] We should stop and ask ourselves what it is that we learn when we are told that by using the term *ancient constitution* Sir William Blackstone was "apparently locating himself within one of the major currents in seventeenth-century historical thought."[29] Blackstone was concerned with legal thought, not historical thought or its "currents." When evaluating Blackstone's arguments, our perspective of judgment should be Blackstone's, not that of some discipline he was not practicing; nor should we hold him to a standard that he would not have thought relevant had it been explained to him. It does not do to measure usefulness by the historical alone, to say that the "juridical nationalism" of Fortescue and Coke may have been "useful . . . for the rights and privileges of the propertied classes" but "was a serious impediment to any kind of historical understanding."[30] The question should not be whether juridical nationalism was good history but why it was a concept that Fortescue and Coke believed useful, how they attempted to utilize it, and whether it did serve or could have performed the role expected of it by its common-law practitioners.

Perhaps we have gone too far down a road of professional separation. Is it possible that historians and lawyers can no longer understand one another because they are asking different questions based on different assumptions? It has been said, for example, that we should understand that "the so-called Brady controversy" was a "debate concerning the English legal past taking place during the last years of Charles II's reign."[31] Those who participated in the debate would have been more likely to say that it concerned the English legal present as it then existed during the last years of Charles II's reign. As Glenn Burgess has recently made quite clear, debates about an "ancient constitution" in the seventeenth century were actually debates about the contemporary, seventeenth-century constitution.[32]

Consider the contention that the common lawyer's way of looking at the past was "traditional" rather than "historical."[33] Admitting that it was not "historical," we might better understand what those lawyers were about if we probed a bit deeper and asked whether their way of looking at the past was more "forensic" than "traditional," or, if traditional, whether it was traditional within the dynamics of constitutional advocacy, with lawyers making arguments they thought would sustain the constitutional doctrine that they favored, not explaining what they understood to be accurate historical interpretation.

There is one other question to be asked and one further point of precise terminology to be raised. The question is: if seventeenth- and eighteenth-century students of the ancient constitution were not writing history, what were they doing? The answer usually given is politics. The ancient constitution, it is said, was "a political weapon."[34] That answer is certainly correct, but does it go deeply enough? In the context of a constitutional controversy, the adjective *political* may not be as accurate as we would wish.

To free troops to fight in America in 1775, the British ministry, without parliamentary approval, hired Hanoverian soldiers for garrison duty at Gibraltar and, perhaps, Ireland. A debate over whether the hiring was constitutional without Parliament's approval erupted in the House of Commons. During the debate Edmund Burke complained that, when defending the administration, the attorney general "had ransacked history, statutes, and journals." Lord North replied by asking "whence the proofs and authorities of a point of law could be better drawn, than from history, statutes, and journals."[35] We would do well to mark North's choice of nouns. Unlike almost all our recent commentators on the ancient constitution, he did not say "point of politics," that is, he did not ask "whence the proofs and authority of a point of politics could be better drawn." To assert that "law" is a more accurate word than "politics" is not to contend that history, statutes, and journals could not be relevant to politics. They are, however, the essence of legal argumentation. That is one reason Lord North's word is more "accurate" than the language of those who use the adjective *political* to describe debates about the ancient constitution. However political they may have been, they were even more "legal" or "constitutional."

The distinction may strike some scholars as mere semantics, but we are concerned with the ancient constitution and, more significantly, with how the ancient constitution was used and argued. The best answer is that the ancient constitution was not argued as will, choice, decision, or policy. It was, rather, argued as precedent, analogy, principle, and forensic history.[36] The ancient constitution in the eighteenth century was not a political program for the sovereign to implement but a constitutional apparatus of forensic advocacy to propagate what were claimed to be ancient forms of restraint upon the current sovereign.

Nationality may make a difference as to how we see the distinction. A historian who is British could be less disposed than an American to recognize that something which is constitutional is not necessarily "political." Consider a Briton who is a historian of the eighteenth century and is writing of the Wilkes election controversy, of the laws discriminating against Catholics, or of the unprecedented Stamp Act with which Parliament attempted for the first time to tax a geographical group of British subjects, none of whom elected representatives to the Commons. That historian might reasonably describe each of those events equally as "political." An American historian, by contrast, might more readily think them constitutional if for no other reason than that under the American legal system they posed issues that would be referred to the courts for solution rather than settled in the legislature.

It may be, too, that the distinction is worth pursuing as it could help avoid confusions that have contributed to imprecise or inaccurate history writing. To think, that is, of arguments about the ancient constitution as "legal" or "constitutional" rather than as "political" or "historical" should clarify what was said by focusing attention on the forensic reality rather than on the standards of historiography. By way of illustration consider the following paragraph from Sir John Fortescue's *De Laudibus:*

> The Realm of *England* was first inhabited by the *Britons,* afterwards it was ruled and civilized under the Government of the *Romans;* then the *Britons* prevailed again; next, it was possessed by the *Saxons,* who changed the Name of *Briton* into *England.* After the *Saxons,* the *Danes* lorded it over us, and then the *Saxons* prevailed a second Time; at last, the *Normans* came in, whose Descendants obtain the Kingdom to this Day: And, during all that Time, wherein those several Nations and their Kings prevailed, *England* has nevertheless been constantly governed by the same Customs, as it is at present.[37]

Thinking of this statement in terms of history or, perhaps, politics rather than as law, a recent commentator expressed surprise "that Fortescue should have taken this abstract and unhistorical view of law since later on he relates the growth of the English jury system, with remarkable penetration, to the social structure of the country."[38] It may be, rather, that Fortescue is less surprising than consistent. From the perspective of legalism he was, in both instances, on the "liberty" side of constitutionalism against governmental power. By arguing that the ancient constitution remained the same through the invasions of the Romans, Saxons, Danes, and Normans, he was saying that constitutional law—not just in those ancient times but in his own day—was based on the authority of custom and the rule of law and, by implication (although this is an issue for a later period), that it was not the command of a sovereign. By delineating how the constitution had changed to permit the growth of the jury he was supporting the same constitutionalism. Common lawyers thought of the jury as they did the ancient constitution—a timeless, changeless, immemorial protector of liberty. Of course they knew that the jury's function as judge of proof was constantly changing, not only in how it determined facts, but by its encroachment upon other methods of proof through the expansion of writs such as *trespass*. Between the sixteenth and the eighteenth centuries the English and American people as well as the common-law bar would come to cherish the jury as their chief institutional defense against arbitrary state prosecution.[39] To evaluate Fortescue's argument as history leads to the conclusion "that Fortescue retained an essentially static view of society."[40] To think of it as constitutional law, however, could lead to the conclusion that Fortescue, like Coke, Selden, and John Adams, espoused a dynamic interpretation of law in which the ancient constitution was an analogy, or precedent, or body of fundamental principles that could be cited to resist and repel whatever new guise arbitrary power might assume.

CHAPTER TWO

The Advocacy of Lawyers

That last conclusion goes against the accepted grain. There is an idea currently rife among scholars of English history that the ancient constitution was not a dynamic device spurring the growth of liberty but a static shield for preserving the status quo. Put another way, it was an argument for conservative constitutionalism.[1] If this is a misunderstanding, the cause may again be vocabulary. It is a fact, we are told, "that the common lawyers, holding that law was custom, came to believe that the common law, and with it the constitution, had always been exactly what they were now, that they were immemorial."[2] Perhaps the terminology employed by common lawyers has been taken too literally. At least it does seem that some scholars of historiography have given undue weight to the word *immemorial*. "All the common-lawyers right through the [eighteenth] century," it was contended in 1958, "believed that the constitution they were so proud of was literally so old as to be without origins: 'immemorial' in the legal sense because eternal in the chronological sense."[3] The implication, often stated explicitly,[4] has been that lawyers should have known better. This accusation has even been applied to Sir William Blackstone. Although in the 1760s he was a somewhat better historian than most of the seventeenth-century common lawyers, he is still said to have gotten his history wrong.

> The ancient feudal constitution contained the origins of English liberties and also of the mechanisms by which, in Montesquieu's analysis, those liberties had been preserved. Properly understood, it was a rational structure that made sense in terms of modern political science. Blackstone appears to be the first writer to

> have attempted a historical account of the English constitution based upon such a synthesis of Spelman, Hale, and Montesquieu; the result, while not entirely convicing, is a major improvement on what had gone before.[5]

Again it may be that we are not asking the most useful question. That question is not why a lawyer like Blackstone was untutored about historical dynamics. The question, rather, is why he ignored what he undoubtedly knew.

Of course common lawyers,[6] even Coke,[7] and certainly constitutionalists arguing in the eighteenth century,[8] knew that changes had occurred in the "immemorial" law throughout Saxon, Norman, English, and British history. There were, to be sure, some writers who seemed to say that the ancient constitution had been unchanged down through the centuries,[9] just as there were others who scorned the entire notion of an ancient constitution.[10] But there is little evidence from either side of the Atlantic that members of the bar in general did not appreciate that today's ancient constitution incorporated yesterday's innovations or that today's statutes could become tomorrow's ancient constitution.[11] To acknowledge time, transmission, and change, however, did not require eighteenth-century constitutionalists to abandon the ancient constitution or the concept of immemorial law. Certainly John Fortescue-Aland did not think so when he wrote the preface to a 1714 edition of *De Laudibus*.

> Thus, Sir, we find the Stream of the Laws of *Edward* the Confessor, flowing from a *Saxon* Fountain, and containing the Substance of our present Laws and Liberties, sometimes running freely, sometimes weakly, and sometimes stopped in its Course; but at last, breaking thro' all Obstructions, both mixed and incorporated it self, with the great Charter of our *English* Liberties, whose true Source the *Saxon* Laws are, and are still in being, and still the Fountain of the Common Law. Therefore it was a very just Observation of my Lord *Coke,* who says, that *Magna Charta,* was but a Confirmation, or Restitution of the Common Law of *England;* so the Common Law really is an Extract of the very best of the Laws of the *Saxons*.[12]

Surely we have here a clue of how the eighteenth century conceptualized the ancient constitution: the common law was the "best" of Saxon laws. Not all Saxon laws were incorporated in the current constitution; only those laws that were the "best" had survived. The best laws of the Saxons surviving in the immemorial ancient constitution were laws that in the eighteenth century were identified with "liberty." Liberty—or constitutional restraints on governmental power—was the connecting link across the centuries. It is barely possible that the elements of liberty in Saxon times were the same as the elements of liberty in the eighteenth century. It is, to be sure, more likely that eighteenth-century Britain projected its own liberty concepts back to Anglo-Saxon England and what it looked for it found. Had the question been put to most eighteenth-century common lawyers they would have said that it was immaterial how changes in constitutional law had occurred, or how they were explained. Retention of liberty, Viscount Bolingbroke believed, was reason enough for Britons to cling to the mystique of the ancient constitution.

> [O]ur *Constitution* is a System of Government suited to the Genius of our Nation, and even to our Situation. The Experience of many hundred Years hath shewn that by preserving *this Constitution* inviolate, or by drawing it back to the Principles, on which it was originally founded, whenever it shall be made to swerve from them, We may secure to ourselves, and to our latest Posterity, the Possession of that *Liberty,* which We have long enjoy'd. What would We more? What *other Liberty* than This do we seek? And if We seek no other, is not This mark'd out in such Characters as He, that runs, may read? As our *Constitution* therefore ought to be, what it seldom is, the *Rule of Government;* so let us make the Conformity, or Repugnacy of Things to *this Constitution* the Rule, by which We accept them as favourable, or reject them as dangerous to *Liberty*. They, who talk of *Liberty in Britain* on any other Principles than Those of the *British Constitution,* talk impertinently at best, and much Charity is requisite to believe no worse of Them.[13]

Bolingbroke's perspective was not unique. During the very last year of the eighteenth century, John Reeves, judge, law writer, legal historian, and political reactionary, was still explaining why the substance of the ancient constitution remained the same even while its premises were constantly changing. Like Bolingbroke, Reeves's measure of continuity was liberty.

> That our Constitution is not precisely the same that it was in the Reign of Ja[mes] I, I am the last man to deny; because it is one of the strongest persuasions I have, about its excellence, that it is capable of, and is continually receiving, improvements, either by the accession of new benefits, or by the attainment of new securities to protect original rights. Many of these have accrued since the time of James I. There was the Petition of Right, which rather secured old Rights than gave new ones; the abolition of the star Chamber was a new benefit; the Habeas Corpus Act was a new benefit; the Bill of Rights was rather a new security to old Rights, except in the circumstance of a protestant King. . . . All these, without enumerating others, were improvements in the Constitution, and nothing can be clearer, than that the Constitution is not now, in all its circumstances, though it is in substance, and in principle, the same that it was heretofore.[14]

That substance was both immemorial and current. It was immemorial because the constitution always supported liberty against arbitrariness, a task requiring only a few general principles, not a detailed code.[15] It was current because the liberty preserved was forever up-to-date.

This notion of immemoriality may not be so easily explained away as Reeves once thought. It seems to have meant one thing to eighteenth-century lawyers and quite another to twentieth-century historians of ancient constitutionalism. The lawyers may have been largely to blame for any misunderstandings. Again consider that they may not have expressed themselves as clearly as twenty-first-century scholarship expects. In line with their professional training, eighteenth-century lawyers tended to explain their understanding of the ancient constitution in lawyer's terms, suitable perhaps for addressing other lawyers but containing the seeds of misunderstanding when interpreted from the perspective of another discipline. An example is analogy, a way of reasoning that those who do not use it may not look for when seeking understanding. Because analogy was a common lawyer's way of reasoning about law, analogies drawn to the ancient constitution deserve our attention. Come now four instances of the technique that, although agreeing in substance, used different analogies to make the same point. The first was argued by the magistrate and novelist Henry Fielding. It was wrong, he contended, to think of "something uniform and permanent, as if the Constitution of *England* partook rather of the Nature of the Soil than of the Climate, and was as fixed and constant as the former, not as changing and variable as the latter."[16] The second was written by the great Restoration jurist Sir Matthew Hale. He thought the argonauts' ship an analogy more apt than soil and climate.

> So that Use and Custom, and Judicial Decisions and Resolutions, and Acts of Parliament, tho' not now extant, might introduce some *New* Laws, and alter some *Old,* which we now take to be the very Common Law itself. . . . But tho' those particular Variations and Accessions have happened in the Laws, yet they being only partial and successive, we may with just Reason say, They are the same English Laws now, that they were 600 Years since in the general. As the Argonauts Ship was the same when it returned home, as it was when it went out, tho' in that long Voyage it had successive Amendments, and scarce came back with any of its former Materials; and as Titius is the same Man he was 40 Years since, tho' Physicians tell us, That in a Tract of seven Years, the Body has scarce any of the same Material Substance it had before.[17]

In 1725, the analogy of language also occurred to George St. Amand of the Inner Temple:

> It may seem an extravagant Position to say, that the present Constitution of our Legislature is built on the same Principles, and has undergone no other Change than what the Alterations of Time have wrought in our Circumstances, made necessary to preserve its Fundamentals; as that in old *Germany* was, if not from the first planting of that Country, at least from the first accounts we have of it, which are sixteen hundred Years old: but as to this, the Constitution may be compar'd with our Language, the present

> Dialect being so widely different from what it was so many Ages since, 'tis scarce credible that it has receiv'd no other Changes but what such a Length of Time necessarily works in all: And yet, whoever will, gradually ascending, read Books of every Age to the oldest of our *Saxon* Monuments, will not be sensible of the Change. So fares it as to the Constitution in general . . . when the Times and Causes of the several Changes that have happen'd in it, come to be ranged in due Order . . . all appears . . . easy, coherent, and natural.[18]

The final example is an analogy later repeated and made famous by Blackstone—a building. It had been employed at least a generation before Blackstone. "[I]f the Foundations, the main Pillars, and Corner Stones of this ancient, noble Building are still standing," Fortescue-Aland contended in 1714, "tho' it should happen to be fitted up and adorn'd with other Materials now, yet it will bear the Name of the old Fabrick, and properly be accounted the same Identical Building."[19]

The evidence to be developed here is that for lawyers of the seventeenth and eighteenth centuries the ancient constitution was not so much the legal substance of the case being argued and defended as it was an argumentative model of what the English and British constitution in fact was, or, certainly, should be. They used the ancient constitution not to prove something concerning history but to strengthen the vision they were promoting of current liberty and civil rights. The law they taught was not law locked in a changeless time but immemorial law constantly reaffirmed both by usage and by redefinition.

The last point may be illustrated by considering the arguments of two English barristers who wrote during the period of the American Revolution. Referring to the Saxons as "the persons who formed the embryo of our constitution,"[20] Edward King of Lincoln's Inn summed up the subsequent history of the Saxon constitution as a history of changes that were, from the perspective of liberty, "improvements."

> When I say this, however, I mean not to reflect on times past; as if a tolerable form of government never prevailed 'till these our days: nor to insinuate that the present constitution is so totally different from what was heretofore established, as to be quite void of any support from precedent and prescription. I am persuaded, on the contrary, that the ancient constitution during different periods was *such* as we may reasonably suppose to have been most fit and expedient for the nation at those times; and also *such,* that it is an easy matter to shew how the present form of government regularly, lawfully, and even necessarily, arose from it.[21]

It did so "lawfully" because the ancient constitution was a program for liberty, and as the nation progressed to improvements in liberty it was guided by the law of the ancient constitution. Or, as Edward Wynne said two decades later, "Freedom was always of its very essence; but its freedom has been improved."[22]

Richard Wooddeson used a somewhat different measure of "progress" than King when he wrote of "advances towards restoring the pristine laws and constitution" of the Anglo-Saxons.[23] "[T]he English constitution," Wooddeson contended, had "immemorially been in substance much the same" as it was in 1777, when he first lectured students as Oxford's third Vinerian law professor. Although insisting that the immemorial constitution "remains a venerable fabric, which has well withstood the decays of time, and the ravages of faction," Wooddeson did not mean that it had been unchanged. "[T]he English constitution has immemorially been in substance much the same, or has at least borne a strong resemblance to the present system," he explained,[24] in part because all changes had been by consent of the people, implied by the acceptance of custom. "[C]hanges are gradually and imperceptibly introduced, which, deriving a sanction from time and universal acquiescence, are matured into fundamental laws, or principles of the constitution. . . . Since history and reason alike teach us, that the finished fabric of a well-ordered constitution is to be the work of succeeding generations, and gradually to be improved by progressive experience."[25]

That the Vinerian professor of law put such stress on a progressive immemorial sameness suggests that the ancient constitution played a larger role during the latter decades of the eighteenth century than has been realized. We might better appreciate that role if our adherence to the canons of the historical method did not make it so difficult for us to take seriously the concept of evolving permanence or to accept the possibility that those who could conceive of a timeless constitution did not have to mean a changeless constitution. Timeless change need not imply changeless time. The notion of adaption within the immemorial ancient constitution does not have to be accepted, but it deserves serious attention as a cue to seventeenth- and eighteenth-century constitutional thought. Changing immemoriality was not the eccentric fantasy of lawyers and law professors such as Wooddeson. The thesis of an ever-altering timeless law was articulated by many other people besides barristers in the eighteenth century. Samuel Squire, a bishop of the established church, stated the general understanding when he explained why the ancient constitution could add improvements while remaining unchanged. It was that the ancient constitution had always been a constitution of freedom and that the liberty of the Saxons was the liberty of eighteenth-century Great Britain.

> Our ancestors were born free, lived under a free government in their first settlements, brought freedom with them into Britain, and handed it down to us inviolate, at the expence of all that was near and dear to them, their lives and fortunes. . . . Our present constitution cannot so truly be said to have been changed or altered, as improved and perfected by time. Where then was that hereditary indefeasible right of princes; where that omnipotent and uncontroulable power of kings, which men of slavish principles were wont to talk so much of? Our earliest forefathers knew nothing of it, we feel nothing of it at present.[26]

Uses of the Ancient Constitution

The uses of the history of the ancient constitution during the eighteenth century were the uses of forensic history. In addition, ancient-constitution scholarship shared the uses to which most history was put in the eighteenth century. That century was a time when history was used to instruct by example, to instill moral lessons, and to educate the public about government, law, and society. "History well wrote is the *easiest* and most *effectual* Teacher of *Moral* Science," the *London Journal* explained in 1732.[27] The American chief justice, John Jay, stated the theme at its simplest: "The history of Great Britain," he wrote in one of his contributions to the *Federalist Papers,* "gives us many useful lessons."[28] A Scottish example is provided by Gilbert Stuart, a leading eighteenth-century Scots advocate. He used the ancient constitution to teach people about the then extant British constitution of 1768. To make his case, Stuart limited his evidence to the laws of prehistorical Germany and the laws of Anglo-Saxon England. "If," he explained, "I have made it appear, that the parts which compose our constitution arose more immediately from the forests of Germany, I have answered my intention."[29] John Reeves claimed that the ancient constitution had "written" its own lessons about *current* constitutional law—lessons of law not history. As proof, Reeves traced legal principles back to what he claimed were their origins. "I thought this the only true way of obtaining, what is called constitutional knowledge;—It was studying the Constitution in the History which itself had written for our Instruction—its own Acts delivered down to us, in its own language."[30]

Instruction for the sake of instruction was seldom enough. Usually the purpose was to get across a practical lesson, such as warning that the norms of the ancient constitution were no longer so well respected as they had been in some known or prehistoric past. Unless the young nobility and gentry "are instructed in what is our Original Constitution," Francis Gregor argued, "what are the Ancient Rights and Privileges thereof, they can never be able to defend it, as they ought, against those who make it their protest Business to cry it down."[31] Virginia's Arthur Lee cited more recent history when putting the history-as-warning technique to work for the American whig cause during the prerevolutionary controversy in 1775. The plan for the crown to pay salaries to colonial judges, Lee contended, alarmed American whigs more than any other grievance, because "[t]he political history of their parent country had taught them the evils their ancestors had experienced from the conduct of Judges so circumstanced."[32]

Another eighteenth-century use of history sometimes emulated by students of the ancient constitution was history-as-pride. In a history of the Gothic constitution, for example, Thomas Rymer surveyed countries such as France and Germany where the ancient constitution once had force, reaching the satisfying conclusion that "[i]t is in *England* onely that the ancient, generous, manly Government of *Europe* survives, and continues in its original lustre and perfection."[33]

The most celebrated practitioners of ancient-constitution history during the eighteenth century were the American founding fathers. There is a general consensus that they argued "scientific" history at the Constitutional Convention, expecting to uncover neutral principles and universal rules applicable to all nations and all ages to guide the future governance of the United States. "It can be shown," according to the claim frequently made, "that the use of history in the debates both in the Philadelphia Convention and in the state ratifying conventions is not mere rhetorical-historical window dressing, concealing substantially greedy motives of class and property. The speakers were making a genuinely 'scientific' attempt to discover the 'constant and universal principles' of any republican government in regard to liberty, justice, and stability."[34]

Without stretching matters too far, it is possible to argue that the founding fathers at Philadelphia objectively used the science of history according to the historical method.[35] That conclusion, however, has been too often simply assumed, rather than proven. The evidence should be reexamined by asking to what extent the history used at the convention differed from the history used by Sir Edward Coke and other common lawyers whose writings the founders knew so well.

There is a second doubt that should be raised. It concerns the assumption that, during the eighteenth century, history and law were related disciplines.[36] It is just not true that in colonial America "[t]o study law was to study its history."[37] History was only marginally necessary for a knowledge of law and not at all needed to practice law. It may have been true that to practice *constitutional* law was to argue forensic history, but that is the type of history historians skeptical of the ancient constitution disparage or say is not history. Nor is it correct to think that law led "directly to history,"[38] although again it could be claimed that *constitutional* law led directly to forensic history. The question is not so much how history was used as the nature and methodology of that history. When examined closely it will quite often turn out to involve evidence from the past selected to support an argument rather than an investigation of evidence of the type generally described as "scientific" history. That is, it is forensic history.

Forensic history, in recent years, has been given other names: "lawyer's history," "law-office history,"[39] and "magisterial historiography."[40] These terms are contumelious labels fastened by its critics onto the style of historical adjudication practiced by the United States Supreme Court from the 1960s into the twenty-first century. The standards of judgment, however, are too negative and too narrowly confined to the historian's professional canons, judging as history a use of the past that is not history but advocacy. Forensic history or lawyer's history could as aptly be termed a form of historical utilitarianism and judged favorably by its adjudicatory aspects rather than unfavorably on its pseudo-historical trappings.[41]

In the eighteenth century the uses of practical or purposeful history were much wider and more scholarly than the lawyer's history associated with brief writing or the historical adjudications of the United States Supreme Court during the past half century. Its reach was often subtle, and one must look carefully or it can be mistaken for history written to explain the past. Sometimes it appears under the guise of the historical method, as in a 1732 London newspaper:

> A Faithful and Judicious History, or, a true Registry of the *Actions* of Men, and the Springs or *probable* Occasions which produced them, is of the greatest Use and Service to Mankind; for, it lays before us, not only our *Actions,* but the *Connection* of those Actions with our *Happiness* or *Misery,* and so is a kind of *visible* or *sensible* Morality; it teaches us by *Facts,* what Philosophers and venerable Sages teach us by *Reason,* with this Difference, That we *see* and *feel* in the One, what we only understand in the Other: We have *Sense* and *Experience* for our Guides, which generally conduct us safer to our Journey's End, than *cool* and *abstract* Reason.[42]

This writer respected history. He wanted, so he said, "Faithful and Judicious History." But he also wanted history to serve a practical purpose, to enlist in the struggle to prevent analytical rationalism from determining the course of eighteenth-century progress. The purpose should not be confused with John Dickinson's famous admonition to the Constitutional Convention. "Experience must be our guide. Reason may mislead us."[43] It is not just, as Dickinson would have it, that history may be a safer or more conservative guide than speculation or rationalization. History should also be the weapon with which the instrumental fends off the analytical. The distinction to be underlined is utility. The forensic historian, in contrast to the nonforensic or "scientific" historian, searches the past for material applicable to a current issue. The purpose of the advocate, unlike that of the historian, is to use the past for the elucidation of the present, to solve some contemporary problem or, most often, to carry an argument. It is the past put in the service of winning the case at bar.

During the sixteenth, seventeenth, and eighteenth centuries lawyers were not the only persons to put the past to work. It was often called on to support not only law and government but religion as well.[44] Indeed, it was the bishop of St. Davids who contended in 1745 that not just history in general but the ancient constitution in particular could legitimately be used to resolve contemporary political disputes.

> [T]he history of the civil constitution cannot be too carefully studied, or too minutely enquired into, especially in such a country as ours is, divided into parties, and where each party confidently appeals to the antient constitution of the kingdom for the truth of the opinions it maintains, and pretends to make that the measure of its political principles, by which alone it is ready to stand or fall.—Can it then be deemed an useless and an unnecessary undertaking to describe what this ancient constitution of our kingdom was by the

> incontestable evidence of history, and to delineate that primitive form of government thro' all its several branches, which our Anglo-Saxon ancestors first established in this island?[45]

There were many other pragmatic, political, and constitutional uses to which evidence from the past was put in the seventeenth and eighteenth centuries. It would serve no purpose to delineate each of them except to note that history was used to propose as well as oppose alterations in the constitution. It was a tactic of constitutional argumentation that Edmund Burke, at least, warned could be abused as well as used. "It is always to be lamented," he told the House of Commons in 1780, "when men are driven to search into the foundations of the commonwealth. It is certainly necessary to resort to the theory of your government, whenever you propose any alteration in the frame of it, whether that alteration means the revival of some former antiquated and forsaken constitution of state, or the introduction of some new improvement in the commonwealth."[46] Burke's lament has been echoed in more recent times. "Let us then come to a preliminary finding," John Clive concluded in 1989, "to the effect that the past lends itself all too readily to use by those who have a political axe to grind. Nothing works better to further a cause—good or bad—than to lend it legitimacy by supplying it with a long heritage."[47] Of course, that was not the criterion for seventeenth- and eighteenth-century common lawyers. For them "a long heritage" was not the substance of constitutional legitimacy. It was only part of the evidence of constitutional legitimacy.

Of more immediate interest for understanding the uses of the ancient constitution in the seventeenth and eighteenth centuries is the most frequent and most significant use that eighteenth-century lawyers and parliamentarians made of the past: to serve their concept of liberty. The past was used for liberty in two ways: to define the current meaning of liberty (not a historical meaning) and to defend the contemporary constitutional right to liberty.[48]

As a general matter, Lord Hervey of Ickworth noted in 1734, when opponents of Robert Walpole complained of "the Loss *of Liberty,*" they usually talked "of *the Liberty of Old England* in Comparison with, or Opposition to *That* now subsisting in this Country."[49] One of those opponents, Viscount Bolingbroke, urged Britons to keep up "the spirit of liberty" by continuing to make that comparison. "Let us justify this Conduct, by persisting in it, and continue to ourselves the peculiar Honour of maintaining the Freedom of our *Gothick Institution of Government,* when so many other Nations, who enjoyed the same, have lost theirs," Bolingbroke wrote.[50] "I need not descend into more Particulars to shew the Perpetuity of free Government in *Britain.* Few Men, even in this Age, are so shamefully unacquainted with the History of their Country, as to be ignorant of the principal Events and signal Revolutions, which have happened since the *Norman Æra.*"[51] After all, Henry Fielding pointed out to the Westminster grand jury, what would the history of England teach but the defense of liberty when that history was itself primarily the story of the English and British people's struggle "to maintain and preserve to themselves and their Posterity, that very Liberty which we now enjoy."[52]

Fielding was saying something we no longer comprehend but which would have been readily understood by British people in the seventeenth and eighteenth centuries. To use history to show that liberty had been fought for and had been defended successfully was to make a constitutional point about the English and British people's right to liberty. Those ancestors who struggled for liberty against arbitrary power not only had won it for themselves but by their sacrifice had purchased it for their descendants. The fact that that price had been paid conferred one of the title deeds by which English constitutional theory before the nineteenth century vested individual citizens with "ownership" of liberty. Not only liberty but civil rights as well had vested in the current generation in part by being purchased by the blood of earlier generations.[53]

This concept of the ownership, the possession, the fee-simple to civil rights and to liberty, is essential to understanding the common lawyer's use of forensic history and the seventeenth and eighteenth century's recurrent citation of the ancient constitution. Laity as well as lawyers, Irish as well as English, knew that more was involved than respect for antiquity or finding greater wisdom through the survival of the immemorial over the novel.[54] It was, rather, a matter of authority: the authority for the common law, the authority for the constitution, the authority for liberty. This perspective of authority is a recurring eighteenth-century emphasis that could easily be overlooked if we do not pay close attention to the words that were used. What may pass as rhetorical flourish in the twentieth century could have been the substance of the argument in the eighteenth. Reflect, for example, on why Viscount Molesworth translated Francis Hotman's *Franco-Gallia*. He did so, he explained, to show that during the era of the ancient constitution on the Continent, most of Europe had possessed liberty. By 1711, when he wrote, the people of Great Britain alone enjoyed it. "Therefore," Molesworth went on, "a sincere Desire of Instructing the only Possessors of True Liberty in the World, what Right they have to that Liberty, of what great a Value it is, what Misery follows the Loss of it, and how easily, if Care be taken in time, it may be preserved, has induced me to Translate and send Abroad this small Treatise."[55] What we in the twenty-first century can easily miss is one clause in Molesworth's statement containing a legal doctrine that ceased to be part of Anglo-American constitutional law in the nineteenth century. He said he was teaching "what Right" the English people had to liberty.

It was the right to current liberty that concerned students of the ancient constitution in the seventeenth and eighteenth centuries, not whether the ancient constitution was historical fact or still existed in 1711, as it supposedly had existed in Gothic Europe. Constitutional law was their discipline of learning, not historiography.

CHAPTER THREE

The Authority of the Past

We must go back to the basics of an abandoned jurisprudence. It is necessary to be on guard that the nineteenth-century concept of law as the command of the sovereign does not cloud our vision. For most of history English law was not command, but the opposite of command. Law, at least constitutional law, blunted the force of command. Even as late as the age of the American Revolution, the essence of law was that it, law, was "right" as opposed to "power."[1] The theory was of a legality that we have forgotten, and for that reason it would be well to start with the elementary. The most rudimentary legal principle of ancient constitutionalism was the authority conferred on constitutional law by antiquity. That authority, keep in mind, served liberty primarily by being a restraint on power.

Authority for law was the reason Fortescue-Aland in 1714 still found legal substance in the boast of his ancestor of three centuries earlier "that neither the Roman nor Venetian, which are esteem'd very ancient, can claim so great Antiquity as ours."[2] It was also the legal theory behind a challenge from John Wilkes to Samuel Johnson in 1770. Johnson had defended the constitutionality of Wilkes's expulsion from the House of Commons. "Go back," Wilkes replied, "to the first establishment of representation; trace the claims of the representative body thro' the long records of successive parliaments."[3] Wilkes was doing what members of Parliament had always done, what Sir Dudley Digges, for example, did when he spoke for the Commons at its crucial conference with the Lords on April 3, 1628. He was commanded by the Commons, Digges said, "to shew unto your Lordships in general: That the Laws of England are grounded on Reason more ancient than Books, consisting much in unwritten Customs; . . . and so ancient, that from the Saxon dayes, notwithstanding the injuries and ruines of time, they have continued in most parts the same."[4]

It is true that some appeals to mere antiquity were so extravagant that occasional eighteenth-century critics poked fun at the practice;[5] nonetheless, we should be impressed with how frequently and intensely appeals were made.[6] Even more to the point is the importance that the eighteenth century attached to the mere attribute of being ancient. An example is provided by Francis Gregor's boast that Fortescue had proved "that the *Common Law* is the most rational, as well as the most antient in Europe."[7] Today it is difficult to tell if Gregor took greater pride in the common law's rationality or its antiquity. It may come as a surprise, but most of his contemporaries would have put more stock in antiquity.[8]

What was the attraction of the past? While considering that question it would be well not to be misled by platitudes such as that of the seventeenth-century constitutionalist Edward Cook suggesting that age made the law "the more venerable, and gave an addition of honour to it,"[9] or that of Lord Keeper Finch, who spoke of an English constitution "made Glorious by Antiquity."[10] Nor should we be taken in by the supposition of recent scholars that "history could legitimize certain institutions,"[11] that change was "generally suspected . . . because change did threaten the character of the state,"[12] or that time, experience, and usage were argued to "legitimate" actions.[13] That last idea is close to seventeenth- and eighteenth-century constitutional theory. It was, however, custom, not history, that was the legitimatizing agent. The problem is with the word *legitimate.* Time did more than make a rule of law legitimate.[14] It was time that converted a rule from a standard of conduct into coercive law. As Maurice Shelton charged the Suffolk County grand jury at Bury St. Edmunds in 1726, "After an Use and Practice of our Laws, time out of mind, then they are taken to be the Common Law of *England,* and not before; nothing but Time immemorial making any thing Part of our Constitution."[15]

That charge at Bury St. Edmunds explained the jurisprudential significance of time, of antiquity, and of the law's appeal to the past. That appeal was not just a mustering of evidence proving what was law. It was one of the processes that vested law with its authority to command obedience. Shelton did not exaggerate when he said "nothing but Time immemorial making any thing Part of our constitution," for he did not mean "Time immemorial" as twentieth-century scholars have assumed but as it was understood at law. Moreover, when he said "nothing but Time" he probably was not saying that custom was the only authority for constitutional law. Most other authorities for constitutional law—the original contract, prescription, ownership, sacrifice of ancestors, and sometimes even nature—depended on the same evidence—custom and the passage of time—for proof.

We must not forget the problem of the meaning of legal time or immemoriality in constitutional law, but for the moment we are concerned with the question of authority and why the ancient constitution was almost exclusively a matter of law, seldom of historiography. Of course there were observers in the eighteenth century who brought up the issue of historical dynamics, complaining that constitutionalists defended the "English" constitution not on grounds of fitness or utility, but by the authority of custom alone. "One would suppose," the *Critical Review* objected, "they thought it was to be defended on no other principles, than those of its having been established in nearly the same form wherein it now exists, for ages immemorial. A fact which some have with great labour and difficulty endeavoured to render probable; but of which there is much reason to suspect the truth."[16] Even though we in the twenty-first-century agree with the argument's historical theory, we should hesitate before embracing its jurisprudential implications, at least for the seventeenth and eighteenth centuries. From the perspective of those times, the *Critical Review* was not raising neutral objections, but wading in on one side of the then current debate about the nature of the constitution—on the side of arbitrary power or anticonstitutionalism. The other side—the side that won in seventeenth-century England, lost in the eighteenth century, and then won again in America at Yorktown—located "right" in the rule of law rather than in the command of the sovereign. And the authority for law was in the past, in the ancient constitution, as George Lawson said when going back to the Saxon kings and to Edward the Confessor's time to find evidence of authority. "What the power[s] of these [Saxon] Parliaments, and of these Kings were, is the great Question," he explained. "For that once known, the Constitution will be evident."[17] He did not mean the Confessor's constitution. He meant the constitution of 1689.

In order to illustrate the ancient constitution as authority for law, our investigation can be limited to one issue: the jurisdiction of the houses of Parliament. Francis Hargrave was explaining constitutional authority when he discussed a dispute between the Lords and the Commons over the Lords's jurisdiction in civil cases. That dispute was settled, Hargrave pointed out, "under the supposition of a primitive and inherent right in the lords, attached to their order by the law and constitution of the kingdom."[18] The controversy had occurred during the reign of Charles II, over a century before Hargrave wrote. John Somers, future lord chancellor of England, was offering a solution to a constitutional crisis of his own time, the 1680s, when he devoted 13 pages to instances of early Saxon "parliaments" electing kings or deciding the succession to the throne. For Somers those elections were evidence proving a point of current constitutional law: "That it hath been the constant opinion of all Ages that the Parliament of *England* had an unquestionable power to limit, restrain and qualify the Succession as they pleased, and that in all Ages they have put their power in practice."[19]

Sir Robert Atkyns, a contemporary of Somers's who served as a judge on the court of Common Pleas and as lord chief baron of the Exchequer court, was explicit when explaining why the House of Commons enjoyed powers and privileges by inherent right and not by grace and grant of the crown. "I shall clearly prove," he contended, "that these Powers and Priviledges were indeed their ancient Right and Inheritance. Which they cannot be unless that House, or the Commons by their Representative, have been ever from the beginning of the Government a part and member of the Parliament." He then "proved" the Commons had been part of Parliament since the beginning of relevant time by marshaling the selective evidence of forensic history. Lord Coke, for example, was quoted for the evidence that tenants on the ancient demesne had always had a privilege "[n]ot to contribute to the Wages of the Knights of the Shire."

> Now the Priviledge must be as Ancient as their Tenure and Service, for their Priviledge comes by reason of their Service, and their Service is known by all to be before the Conquest, in the time of *Edward* the Confessor, and in the time of the Conquerour. And it is expressly said by this Learned and Reverend Judge [Coke], That these Tenants, in the Ancient Demesn[e], claimed this by Prescription; and it could not be so, if the Wages of the Knights of the Shire had begun within Memory of Man, or of any Record. Therefore it clearly follows, That Knights of the Shire to serve in Parliament, and the paying Wages to them for their Service, has been Time out of Mind, and did not begin 49 H[enry] 3 for that is within Time of Memory in a Legal Sence.[20]

Reading this argument, today's critics of ancient-constitution history will readily conclude that it is nonsense, unsupported by historical evidence. But Judge Atkyns said he was calling on the evidence of history in a "Legal Sence." He said nothing of being interested in the evidence of history in a historical or scientific sense. Atkyns used the Saxon constitution not to prove a historical point but, as he said, "clearly [to] prove" as a matter of constitutional law in 1689 that the House of Commons possessed its powers and privileges by inherent right, not by royal grant.

Three decades earlier, William Prynne had encountered a similar legal controversy and had enlisted the same constitutional proof—evidence from the ancient constitution—to establish the constitutional authority of the other house of Parliament, the Lords.[21] The House of Commons had proclaimed itself "the only Supream Judges and Judicature of the Realm, paramount [to] our Kings, Lords, Laws, Liberties, Great Charters, and all other Courts of Justice, having an absolute, arbitrary, unlimited power, to act, vote and determine what they please, without appeal or consult."[22] The Lords, the Commons voted, was not an inherently equal branch of parliament because its members sat "only by Patent, by the *Kings will, Tenure or descent;* not by the Peoples free Election . . . ; That they represent themselves only not the Commons [the people]; and are the Sons only of Conquest, of Usurpation; (brought in by the Conquerour,) not of Choice and Election."[23]

"To this I answer," Prynne wrote, turning directly to the authority of the ancient constitution, "That our *Lords, Dukes, Earls, Barons, Nobles* (yea *Archbishops, Bishops, Abbots, Priors* too who held by Barony) sate antiently in all our General National Councels and Parliamentary Assemblies, many *hundreds of years before the Conquest,* both in the *Britons* and *Saxons* reigns, by right of their Peerage and Tenures, as now they doe."[24] It was a matter of right established by law, and law in this case was found in the custom of the realm. Public officials, be they "Kings, Magistrates, Judges, Ministers, Peers or Members of Parliament," need not be elected if they hold their positions by other valid customary procedures; procedures that vested their offices with "a general implicit or tacit consent." This constitutional principle is especially valid "when the antient Laws of the Land, continuing still in full force, and the custom of the Kingdom time out of mind, requires no such ceremonie of the peoples particular election or call."[25] In England *"the antient Laws, Statutes, and Customs of the Kingdom"* conferred jurisdiction on the Lords differently than on the representatives of the common people. The Lords enjoyed parliamentary privileges *"without any election of the people,"* but members of the Commons were elected. If, however, custom had been otherwise, and the king from time out of mind had appointed the knights and burgesses to Parliament, then they would sit in the Commons constitutionally by royal pleasure and they would not need to be elected, because crown appointment would be "a Law and usage" sanctioned by the consent of popular acquiescence.[26]

That the Commons's tenure by election was from time out of mind, that is immemorial, did not mean it was so ancient it had no known origin. The Lords's jurisdiction rested on that degree of immemoriality, not that of the House of Commons. Its beginning could be traced to the reign of Henry III. The ancient constitution stretched back only as far as relevant time.

> By, and in the very primitive constitution of our *English Parliaments,* for many hundred years together there were no Knights nor Burgesses at all, but only *the King and his Nobles:* after which, when elected Knights gestes were first sent to Parliament about 49 H. 3 it was granted by the Kings grace, and unanimously agreed by the kingdoms, peoples general consents, that our Parliaments should alwayes be constituted and made up, not by Knights and Burgesses only, . . . but likewise *of the King* . . . and of the Lords . . . who ought of right to sit, vote, make Laws, and give Judgement in Parliament by vertue of their Peerage, Baronies, Offices, without any election of the people.[27]

The Commons's jurisdiction came from royal command, popular consent, and usage unbroken for the duration of relevant time out of mind. The authority of this jurisdiction vested the Commons with constitutional security from interference by the king[28] but did not vest it with superiority over the Lords, whose constitutional tenure ran to even more anciently relevant time. As there had never been a period when the Lords were not part of parliament, their right was of greater immemoriality. They held it by immemorial custom and by consent that was at least implied if not expressed. "This right of theirs is confirmed by *prescription* and *custom,* from the very first beginning of Parliaments in this kingdom till this present, there being no president to be found in History or Record of any Parliament held in this Island since it was a kingdom, without the King . . . or without *Lords and Peers.*"[29] The legal conclusion was not that the Lords had a higher, more constitutional jurisdiction than the Commons but that if the Commons had a right to sit in Parliament, the Lords could not be denied co-jurisdiction, as the legal authority upon which their right depended, though no greater than that of the Commons, was more constitutionally demonstrable:

> Their sitting, voting, judging therefore in Great Councils, Parliaments, being so antient, clear and unquestionable ever since their first beginnings til[l] now; and the sitting of Knights, Citizens, Burgesses by the peoples election, in our antientest Great Councils, Parliaments, not so clearly evident by *History or Records* as theirs: we must needs acknowledge, subscribe to this their Right and Title; or else deny the Knights, Citizens, Burgesses rights to sit, vote in our Great Councils, Parliaments, rather than theirs, who have not so antient nor clear a Title or right as they, by many hundreds of years.[30]

Summarizing the authority for the Lords's jurisdiction (and *not* the extent of that jurisdiction), Prynne cited four sources, one of which most interestingly was the consent of all previous Houses of Commons. "This Right and Privilege of theirs is vested legally in them by the very *Common Law* and *Custom* of the Realm, which binds all men," Prynne explained. "By the unanimous consent of all our Ancestors, and all the Commons of *England* from age to age assembled in Parliament, since they sat in any Parliaments; who alwaies consented to, desired, and never opposed the Lords sitting, voting, power or Judicature in Parliament; and by *Magna Charta.*"[31]

The legal doctrine must be obvious. Although the past in the form of constitutional custom was researched for proof of the source of law and as evidence of law, it was primarily cited as authority for law. Custom (which must not be confused with history) was the authority making law binding on government as well as upon subjects. It still was considered law's authority by as late as the year of the American Declaration of Independence by Matthew Robinson-Morris, second baron Rokeby, when he asserted that there still existed a popular legislative power which was of higher authority than parliament.

> Our ancestors formerly assembled and resolved upon their laws and their measures in their collective capacity: their princes and their leaders were as evidently commissioned in the execution of them, as one private person is by another: the power then reverted to the body and on occasion issued from it

> again. This was the first origin of our form of government; where we are to seek, where we shall find and by which we shall comprehend its real, original nature and essence. Whatever changes or variations have through necessity and the mutability of things since been made or happened in its outward form and circumstances, these have all referred and related to its primitive inherent principle.[32]

Allan Ramsay made much the same point, also during the American Revolution, when he questioned the "power" of Parliament to have constitutionally promulgated the Septennial Act of 1716, destroying "the annual elective power of the people."

> [T]his annual elective power, the first principle of our constitution, is a right of inheritance, which was brought into England by our Saxon forefathers, at the first establishment of the Saxon mode of government, in this island; and which the people, hold by the ancient, common law of the land. And which they had enjoyed, from generation to generation, for twelve-hundred years, before the reign of William the third. And therefore this elective power of the people, may be truly called, their constitutional right of inheritance. An inheritance that can no more be taken from them, or restrained, justly, than any estate, in land, can be taken from the right owner.[33]

Ignore Ramsay's "bad" history. Think instead of the implications of his legal thesis: writing in London in 1771 he was arguing that the ancient constitution was a higher authority than the legislative command of the sovereign parliament.

The Theory of the Past

It is necessary to be precise. We are discussing law, not history, and the issue is why the authority of law to command obedience could be established by appealing to the past. It is not quite accurate to say that English law, "being customary, relied for authority on the presumption of its own continuity."[34] It was not continuity but consent that vested authority, and the legal doctrine dominating seventeenth- and eighteenth-century customary law was not presumption but prescription. "Every Priviledge is by Prescription," Judge Robert Atkyns stated in 1689. "[I]t is held, That a man cannot prescribe to an Incident or Appendant, nor indeed to any Power or Authority where the Principal Thing hath not had a perpetual continuance." Atkyns overstated the principle, however, when he added, "[W]here the beginning of a thing is known, there can be nothing belonging to it by Prescription."[35] Time and unchallenged exercise of the right or of the enjoyment of the property prescribed were necessary to prove prescription, not immemoriality alone. Edmund Burke was closer to the mark when he wrote, "Prescription is the most solid of all titles, not only to property, but, which is to secure that property, to government."[36]

The doctrine of prescription told people that they owned a privilege or had, by time, acquired a right. The doctrine of consent was different. It had more to do with explaining why time vested a rule of conduct with the coercive force of law. With legislation, consent was established by direct vote or representation. With custom, the proof of consent was acceptance over time of the custom or rule by the population. Consent to law, Oxford's Vinerian professor Richard Wooddeson told his students in the 1770s, could be proved by "long and uniform custom [which] bestows a sanction, as evidence of universal approbation and acquiescence."[37]

The theory of consent played two roles in seventeenth- and eighteenth-century constitutional law. First, it reenforced the individual citizen's civil and property rights by adding a theoretical justification for the rule of prescription. In the eighteenth century, H. T. Dickinson has explained, people understood "that much English law was based on custom, precedent and prescription rather than on the deliberate conscious decisions of an absolute monarch or a sovereign legislature. They also knew that many property rights were based on possession and long prescriptive right rather than on legal documents. Thus, in both the field of common law and the sphere of property rights, it was recognized that an appeal to prescription could make good a lack of documentary legal evidence."[38] If anything, what Dickinson said was even more true for the seventeenth century.

Second, the doctrine of consent strengthened public liberty by providing a popular basis for the privileges the British government possessed and, by implication, restraining its power, including the power of Parliament to promulgate coercive legislation. As Wooddeson explained to his Oxford students:

> However the historical fact may be of a social contract, government ought to be, and is generally *considered* as founded on consent, tacit or express, on a real, or *quasi,* compact. This theory is a material basis of political rights; and as a theoretical point is not difficult to be maintained. For what gives any legislature a right to act, where no express consent can be shewn? what, but immemorial usage? and what is the intrinsic force of immemorial usage, in establishing this fundamental or any other law, but that it is evidence of common acquiescence and consent? Not that such consent is subsequently revocable, at the will even of all the subjects of the state, for that would be making a part of the community equal in power to the whole originally, and superior to the rulers thereof after their establishment.[39]

If we say that the implied consent of custom, not history, vested unwritten law with its authority, we must not forget that custom was also law. "General customs, which are the universal rule of the whole kingdom," John Adams observed in 1773, "form the common law in its stricter and more usual signification." A striking instance of the doctrine was England's "four superior courts of record, the chancery, the king's bench, the common pleas, and the exchequer." Their authority to bind individuals to judgment had not been promulgated "in any written statute or ordinance" but depended "merely upon immemorial usage, that is, upon common law," for its support.[40]

We should be especially impressed by what John Adams said about the binding force of custom when we consider that the issue he was discussing was judicial tenure. The rule that custom was law that had to be obeyed restrained him from arguing for the constitutional principle we know he favored. As an American whig, Adams wanted judges independent of the royal prerogative, serving securely for life at good behavior. Colonial judges, however, did not have tenure for life, and the reason was not just royal charter or gubernatorial instructions, but that immemorial English custom ordained that they serve at pleasure. "[T]he office of chancellor of England," Adams quoted an English barrister arguing in a common-law court, "could not be granted to any one for life. And why? Because it never was so granted. *Custom and nothing else prevails, and governs in all those cases*." Adams had to agree with that barrister. "[C]ustom was the criterion, and that alone," he admitted. "So that, if the king should constitute a baron of the exchequer during pleasure, he would have an estate for life in his office, or the grant would be void. Why? Because the custom had so settled it. If the king should constitute a judge of the king's bench, or common bench [Common Pleas], during good behavior, he would have only an estate at the will of the grantor. Why? Because the custom hath determined it so. And that custom could not be annulled or altered but by act of parliament."[41]

The certainty that custom gave to nonstatutory constitutional law in the seventeenth and eighteenth centuries is further illustrated by a quotation Adams dismissed; a quotation he might have cited to argue that judges should have life tenure. "If," another barrister had told an English court, "any judicial or ministerial office be granted to any man to hold, so long as he behaves himself well in the office, that is an estate for life, unless he lose it for misbehavior." Adams agreed only if the granted position was "an office that by custom, that is, immemorial usage, or common law, . . . or by an express act of parliament, . . . has been granted in that manner, but not otherwise."[42] Here in stark outline was the basic constitutional function of custom as authority. It did not purport this or that form of government so much as government by the rule of law or law that was a restraint on arbitrary power. It was a barrier against the will and pleasure of governmental capriciousness. In English and British constitutionalism it was primarily a barrier against the will and pleasure of the crown. Much as an American whig might wish that high-court judges served at life tenure, that tenure, to be constitutional, would have had to have been based on custom or colonial statute; it could not be ordained by the discretion of the royal prerogative.

It will not do to make much of a prerogative threat in the eighteenth century. Few voices were then raised on behalf of royal sovereignty over law, and although almost every constitutionalist who wrote of the dangers of arbitrary government wrote that the danger was prerogativism, it is impossible to tell how many believed that threat was real.[43] The jurisprudents of custom may have used the crown as their straw man, but their true fear was unrestrained power and their objective was preservation of the rule of law.[44] Still, they make it seem that the king was the threat, and one reason, as indicated by John Shute Barrington, a barrister of the Inner Temple and first Viscount Barrington, was the legacy of the ancient constitution, which had originally been designed to keep royal power in its place.

> All that we learn of our *Saxon* Ancestors from History, is, that, before their Coming here, Things of great Consequence were determin'd by all the Freemen, and the lesser by the principal Persons; and when upon their Coming here, they had such a standing Officer as a King, his Power was so limited, that he could do nothing without the Consent of the one or the other . . . ; and the greatest of the *Saxon* Kings acknowledge[d], that they owe[d] their Crown to the Election of the Nobles and People.[45]

Barrington was putting the ancient constitution to its most basic eighteenth-century use—to craft the bulwarks of constitutional restraint. The chairman of the Suffolk County quarter sessions was also thinking of restraint when he recounted to the grand jury instances from the history of the ancient Britons as well as the Saxons demonstrating that government power had anciently been limited. The same limitations, he was saying, held in 1726.[46] Thirteen years later, William Petyt's *Jus Parliamentarium* was published by an editor hoping to spread the word of restraint and ancient constitutionalism. Petyt, he explained, possessed an

> uncommon Penetration into the Knowledge of our ancient Records and legal Antiquities; more particularly those which give a true Idea of the Frame and Constitution of this limited Monarchy: A Government which consists in the Execution of Laws dictated by Reason and Experience, and receiving their binding Force from the Consent of the People governed; not flowing from, or depending upon the misinformed Judgment, or capricious Will of One, or a few.[47]

Whether or not he thought he was publishing a study of history, Petyt's editor certainly thought he was publishing a study of constitutional authority.

In the hands of some lawyers, the jurisprudence of constitutional custom was a theory of authority that not only checked power but never served power. Custom was authority for liberty only; it was not authority for arbitrariness or even, perhaps, for ordinary government power. William Jones explained the theory in 1768. "In questions of private right, precedents are law," Jones contended. "But in questions that regard the Constitution, they lose a principal part of their force, *what has been,* is by no means to be considered as the invariable rule for *what should be.*"[48]

> In many cases, rights at first imperfect and infirm acquire strength from age, they are confirmed by the exercise of them; but it is not so with the powers of government; they derive their force from their intrinsic merit alone; originally bad, no prescription, no usage, however inveterate, can protect them. The rights of the individual, of the church, of the crown may have their respective limitations, but against those of the Constitution "no time can run."[49]

"Respect for the sentiments of our ancestors," Jones argued, should be a criterion for "maintaining the original rights of mankind"; it should not be "employed in confirming the usurpations against them."[50] Or, as James Burgh contended, the past could not be authority for rules of arbitrary power. "The longer grievances have continued, the more reason for redressing them."[51]

Jones's jurisprudence was extremist and, although commanding some respect among constitutional theorists, was devoid of practical application. It is revealing for our purposes, however, for it illustrates one of the salient aspects of eighteenth-century ancient constitutionalism: its usefulness to opponents of arbitrary power.

Due perhaps to our emphasis on the historical method rather than on common-law argumentation, the ancient constitution's role in combating medieval arbitrariness—and, of course, as a defense of liberty as liberty was defined in the seventeenth and eighteenth centuries—has not always been credited by recent scholars. The ancient constitution, it was suggested in 1965, "was supposed to be immemorial, and its merit consisted in the antiquity of its usage rather than in any rationalization of its principles."[52] Seventeenth- and eighteenth-century constitutional jurisprudes would have been puzzled by that statement. They would have agreed, of course, that the reasonableness of the ancient constitution was not in the principles it contained. Its rationalization or reasonableness was in the authority that the ancient constitution bestowed on principles which the party utilizing and citing the ancient constitution was defending or espousing. The "merit" of the ancient constitution was not in the antiquity of its usage but in the degree of security from governmental whim and caprice that antiquity provided current, existing civil rights. We would be unwise to underestimate the significance of security. In the customary jurisprudence of an unwritten constitution there is no element more essential to liberty than security against arbitrariness.

But what was the concept of arbitrariness in the seventeenth and eighteenth centuries? To understand the answer to that question it is necessary to rid ourselves of twenty-first-century thoughts about arbitrariness having something to do with despotism, tyranny, or cruel government. The concept of "arbitrary" may have such connotations today, but that was not the legal definition in the eighteenth century. Then it was not the harshness of power, the brutality of power, or the certainty of the exercise of power that made government arbitrary. It was, rather, the possession of power unchecked.[53] Tyrannical power was abuse of power; arbitrary power was power without restraint.

In eighteenth-century parlance, arbitrary was the difference between liberty and slavery, right and power, constitutional and unconstitutional. To the eighteenth-century legal mind, knowing what was arbitrary delineated the concept of the rule of law. "For it is certain," Jared Eliot reminded Connecticut's lawmakers in 1738, "*That to the Constitution of every Government, Absolute Sovereignty must lodge somewhere.* So that according to this Maxim, Every Government must be Arbitrary and Despotick. The difference seems to be here; Arbitrary Despotick Government, is, When this Sovereign Power is directed by the Passions, Ignorance & Lust of them that Rule. And a Legal Government, is, When this Arbitrary & Sovereign Power puts it self under Restraints, and lays it self under Limitations."[54] It was, Viscount Bolingbroke agreed, a matter of power and not of the type and structure of government. Whether power was vested in a single monarch, in "the *principal Persons of the Community,* or in the *whole Body of the People,*" was immaterial. What matters is whether power is without control. "Such Governments are Governments of *arbitrary Will,*" he concluded.[55]

Just as the eighteenth-century concept of arbitrariness should not be confused with cruelness or terror, for it could be benevolent, mild, and materially beneficial, so it should not be confounded with absoluteness. "[E]ven *absolute Power,*" John Locke pointed out, "where it is necessary, is *not Arbitrary* by being absolute, but is still limited by that reason, and confined to those ends, which required it in some Cases to be absolute," such as martial discipline which vests an army officer with power to order a trooper to die but cannot "command that Soldier to give him one penny of his Money."[56] Law was the distinction. If the officer acted within the parameters of law, his absolute orders were not arbitrary. That element—law—was all-important to eighteenth-century constitutional thought. For "court whigs," Reed Browning has pointed out—and also, it should be added, for most other educated Britons and Americans—there were "but two types of government: arbitrary and lawful,"[57] or as John Arbuthnot explained in 1733, "what is not legal is arbitrary."[58]

Law is one of three legal concepts by which the eighteenth century measured arbitrariness. The other two were liberty and constitutionalism. Arbitrary power was the antithesis of liberty and the opposite of constitutionalism.[59] These points and counterpoints were concisely summarized by George Campbell, preaching in Aberdeen, Scotland, on the fast day commemorating the American rebellion.

> [W]hen men are governed by established laws which they know, or may know, if they will, and are not liable to be punished by their governors, unless when they transgress those laws, we say they are under a *legal government.* When the contrary takes place, and men are liable to be harassed at the pleasure of their superiors, tho' guilty of no transgression of a known rule, we say properly they are under *arbitrary power.* These are the only distinctions I know between *free* and *slavish, legal* and *arbitrary,* as applied to governments.[60]

Or, as Connecticut's Jared Eliot added, a government under the restraint of law "is what we call a Legal Limited & well Constituted Government. Under such a Government only there is true Liberty."[61]

Arbitrariness and people's fear of arbitrary power were why the ancient constitution and immemorial law were tools of constitutional advocacy during the seventeenth and eighteenth centuries. The authority of custom was then the most viable alternative to rule by the will and pleasure of sovereign command. Immemorial law was not argued to block judicial judgments or (except in rare instances such as by American whigs during the prerevolutionary controversy) to restrict parliamentary legislation. The ancient constitution was a standard of reference for seventeenth-century antiprerogativists and for eighteenth-century constitutionalists opposed to arbitrary power. They argued the evidence of ancient constitutionalism when seeking either to prove the authority of a legal principle or to preserve liberty's security through the rule of law.[62] What seventeenth- and eighteenth-century constitutionalists sought from ancient-constitution advocacy and the concept of immemoriality was the security of governance by law.

CHAPTER FOUR

The Advocacy of the Past

It has recently been suggested that "the attraction which the concept of the ancient constitution possessed for lawyers and parliamentarians probably resided less in whatever ultimate principle provided its base, than in its value as a purely negative argument." The explanation is that "a truly immemorial constitution could not be subject to a sovereign: since a king could not be known to have founded it originally, the king now reigning could not claim to revoke rights rooted in some ancestor's will."[1] That theory was the essence of seventeenth-century constitutionalism, and at that time the "argument" was not thought negative. It was, rather, both positive and dynamic constitutional doctrine, as likely to be employed to create and redefine rights as it was to be used to defend existing rights or just to maintain the status quo.[2]

A seventeenth- and eighteenth-century constitutionalist usually did not argue immemorial law negatively by saying, for example, that the crown was forbidden to command some result, such as to abolish jury trial, because jury trial was immemorial and had never been ordained by the will and decision of a known sovereign, a predecessor of the present king. That seventeenth- or eighteenth-century constitutionalist would have been more likely to argue that the people had a right to trial by jury because it had existed by immemorial custom from time out of mind. The right to trial by jury, like any other right attributed to the ancient constitution, was positive; it was real, material, tactile, concrete, and existed independently of creation, will, caprice, or pleasure. Law was thought of and spoken of as an entity, separate from command or promulgation, the conceptionalization of the abstract into the tangible in a way that we no longer comprehend. When Sir Edward Coke said that "no man ought to be wiser than the law,"[3] he was thinking of an autonomous reality that humans could manipulate but was altered only by internal evolution.

We cannot say that the autonomy of law was a concept believed in by those who espoused it. At worst its validity had to be accepted, because the concept of an autonomous law was essential for constitutional government as constitutionalism was then conceived. The law, which was the seventeenth and eighteenth centuries' custodian of civil rights, had to be independent of sovereign command or else liberty would have been no more secure than was any ordinary revocable grant.

"Are not the Liberties of the People settled upon as sure a Foundation from the Concessions of our Princes?" an anonymous writer asked in 1734. "Are they not indeed upon a surer Foundation than *Original Contract;* since these Concessions are to be seen, and the *Original Contract* not to be seen?"[4] For constitutionalists of customary restraints the answer was unreservedly "no." Rights that were grants rather than entrenched in timeless custom were rights without security, the same as being not rights at all. Liberty depended on the supremacy of law over power. "[I]f ever you set the King above Laws," the grand jury of Chester was instructed during the 1690s, "then it must necessarily follow, that the King derives his *Title* to the Crown of *England* not from the *Laws of England,* but from something else."[5] That something else was what seventeenth- and eighteenth-century constitutionalists could not concede, or there would have been no English constitutionalism. Not only did individual rights have to come from "law" rather than the king's grace, but so did the king. For students of the ancient constitution the legal formula had to be "That *the Law makes the King.*" That was how in 1694 William Atwood, sometime chief justice of New York, stated what was probably the most fundamental legal doctrine for seventeenth-century constitutionalists.[6] "The Office of the King," Samuel Johnson added that same year, "depends wholly upon the Law both in its making and in its being."[7] "This High Office and Dominion was given him by Law, and all his Powers which are very Great, and give him an Opportunity of doing a world of Good, are all stated by Law; for else how should we know they are his? and they are butted and bounded by Law, or else they might be pretended to be Infinite. We find it thus in the first Constitution of this Monarchy."[8] It was, Johnson explained, entirely a matter of law: "And again all Englishmen that have any tolerable knowledg[e] of the Constitution are sensible, that the Office of the King depends upon the Law both in its making and in its being, that a King as he is Impowered by Law must act by Law; and therefore they must needs know at first sight, that a King whose Authority is Antecedent to the Law, Independent of the Law and Superiour to the Law . . . is an invented and studied King, whom the English law knows not."[9]

The law that made the king was the ancient constitutional autonomous law, not the legislation of Parliament, for, although Parliament could alter, amend, and reorganize that law, it, like the king, was the product of the same law and received its authority from that law. Just as the king was king because the customary, prescriptive law of the ancient constitution made him king, so Parliament was Parliament due to the same law.[10] The concept of sovereign, demiurgic law was explained in 1610 by Thomas Hedley, long before there were notions of either parliamentary supremacy over the king or parliamentary sovereignty over the law. He was addressing the House of Commons.

> But then you will say, the parliament, which is nothing else in effect but the mutual consent of the king and people, is that which gives matter and form and all complements to the common law. No, nor that neither, for the parliament hath his power and authority from the common law, and not the common law from the parliament. And therefore the common law is of more force and strength than the parliament. . . . But from logic to law, the king by his prerogative may dispense with a statute law, so he cannot with the common law. Also, the common law doth bind, and lead or direct the descent and right of the crown. But whether a statute law may do so or no, it hath been doubted. But you will say the parliament hath often altered and corrected the common law in divers points and may, if it will, utterly abrogate it, and establish a new law, therefore more eminent. I answer set a dwarf on a tall man's shoulders, and the dwarf may see farther than the tall man, yet that proves him not to be of a better stature than the other. The parliament may find some defects in the common law and amend them (for what is perfect under the sun), yet the wisest parliament that ever was could never have made such an excellent law as the common law is. But that the parliament may abrogate the whole law, I deny, for that were includedly to take away the power of the parliament itself, which power it hath by the common law.[11]

It will be said that Hedley's theory of sovereign law was superannuated by the time of the American Revolution, which occurred eight decades after the Glorious Revolution when Parliament did what he said it could not do, change the descent and right of the crown. But, in fact, the Glorious Revolution changed perceptions about autonomous law much less than has been assumed. How else do we explain the shocked reactions of so many contemporaries to Blackstone's discovery that by the 1760s Parliament had become omnipotent? If Blackstone was right, the Earl of Abingdon protested, the ancient constitution was a dead letter and to "that *arbitrary Power,* against the Introduction of which, *separately,* we have been contending from the Saxon Era to the Era of George III, *conjunctively,* we must now submit; though attended, in this Form, by a State of Slavery, tenfold more oppressive, than any other Form could possibly inflict."[12] *Slavery* was also the word that American whigs used after Parliament passed the Stamp Act. If Parliament could tax the colonies internally, they were "slaves," as it meant that Parliament, and not the "law" was to be their rule.[13]

Except for *arbitrary* there was no word that practitioners of ancient-constitution jurisprudence put to such frequent use as *slavery*. Slavery and its opposite concept, liberty, need close scrutiny, for they reveal much about why we should not be thinking of history and historiography; they show why the legal concept of custom, not the historical method, was what guided the selective research and the selective polemics of ancient constitutionalists. In the seventeenth and eighteenth centuries forensic historians used the ancient constitution for three purposes: proof of authority, establishment of consent, and avoidance of slavery. If we were to sum these up in one concept it would be said that the object of seventeenth- and eighteenth-century ancient-constitutional advocacy was to preserve the contemporary version of liberty through the rule of law.

This is not the place to discuss the theory of legal and constitutional custom. The concept of custom should not be treated as it is treated here, as a side aspect of ancient-constitution jurisprudence. It was, in fact, more important to the development of Anglo-American liberty than was the ancient constitution, and deserves a separate study. The best we can do, if we must treat custom briefly, is to object to those historians of the ancient constitution who insist that the "philosophy of custom" was "a view of institutions as based purely upon immemorial usage and experience, with no conscious beginnings and nothing more to justify an institution than the presumption that, being immemorial, it must on innumerable occasions have proved satisfactory."[14] We must resist arguments that confound historical "immemorial" with legal "immemorial." True, some practitioners of ancient constitutionalism used the word *history*, but, as with Bolingbroke in the following sentence, the appeal was generally to custom: "When I say *that Parliaments were intirely built on the same general Principles, as well as directed to the same Purposes, as they still are,* I shall be justfy'd by the whole Tenor of our *History*, and of our *Law*."[15] Legal custom was less a presumption of satisfaction with institutions that had no beginnings and was more like Sir Matthew Hale's argonauts' ship, a constant flow of change, a process of preservation rather than experimentation, of securing liberty through reinvigoration of the rule of law. Custom, as understood by lawyers before the eighteenth century, Fritz Kern explained, "quietly passes over obsolete laws, which sink into oblivion, and die peacefully, but the law itself remains young, always in the belief that it is old. Yet it is not old; rather it is a perpetual grafting of new and old law, a fresh stream of contemporary law springing out of the creative wells of the sub-conscious."[16]

The concept of custom should also be kept in mind when considering the ramifications of the authority of the past. The principle that concerns us is the authority *for* law not the authority of history. History in the seventeenth and eighteenth centuries did not bestow coercive authority, although practitioners of forensic history sometimes assumed that it did. If we wish to be exact, we should associate authority or "power"[17] with custom rather than history. Custom was one of law's authorities.

Custom was almost as important to existing law for the consent that it implied as for the authority that it conferred. Immemorial usage was "evidence of common acquiescence and consent," Vinerian law professor Wooddeson emphasized in the late eighteenth century. "Laws ratified by custom, are generally the most ancient, and esteemed highly sacred, having been approved by the experience of ages."[18] Just about a century earlier, Judge Atkyns had explained the doctrine of implied consent by invoking a remarkable instance of the timeless concept of law, one that was repeated so often we must assume that it made sense to common lawyers of the late seventeenth century. "We our selves of the present Age," he wrote, "chose our Common Law, and consented to the most ancient Acts of Parliament, for we lived in our Ancestors a 1000 Years ago, and those Ancestors are still living in us."[19] Before protesting this idea, reflect that Atkyns was speaking of legal consent, not of a physical fact. You may say he was employing a legal fiction, but you would be wrong. As was said in 1769 of the *"ancient and approved laws"* of "the British, Roman, Danish, Saxon and Norman times," "if they had not been liked by these people, they would have been altered."[20] The consent is implied or constructive, not actual and direct.

The principle of implied consent was not intended to strengthen the authority of law qua custom by giving it a popular base, but to strengthen customary law or ancient constitutionalism against the onslaughts of other types of law such as prerogative law, Star Chamber law, or civil law. The argument that common law and custom were laws popularly consented to would later anger Thomas Jefferson and Jeremy Bentham, but in the seventeenth and eighteenth centuries it was a contention that reenforced the jurisprudential pretensions of constitutionalism and customary liberty.[21]

Resistance to prerogative law, however, was not the chief jurisprudential function performed in the seventeenth and eighteenth centuries by the concept of an autonomous law based on the authority of custom and popular consent implied from acquiescence in the ancient constitution. Its prime function, rather, was to fend off law by will and pleasure, whether that law was based on paternalism, nationalism, divine right, reason, efficiency, or nature. This was a losing battle, of course, at least in Great Britain after about 1740 because the law that it opposed was the law that had the future before it, the law that would dominate the nineteenth century in the form of parliamentary sovereignty. The contest as understood in the seventeenth century was summed up by William Prynne when he boasted that one of his forensic-history books concerned "My *Antiquity triumphing over Novelty*."[22] It was a telling forensic strategy. A proponent of customary constitutionalism could oppose any constitutional innovation or reform by insisting that constitutional custom was grounded on something more secure than political choice, on, for example, as Edmund Burke insisted when opposing extension of parliamentary representation, "the peculiar circumstances . . . and . . . habitudes of the people."[23]

As long as you had no quarrel with the status quo, customary constitutionalism provided a higher sense of security and, therefore, a more certain degree of secured liberty, than did prerogative, parliamentary, or democratic discretion. The artificial reason of immemorial custom was perceived as safer, certainly less risky, than the analytical or natural reason of even the wisest men. Recently, Charles Gray explained the distinction:

> The artifice [of artificial reason] is simply the law: there are cases for which a lawyer can draw a solution from positive legal sources. Such a legal solution will be better than the solution an ideally wise person would reach with only natural reason to depend on. That is true because the law is a collective product, a repository of many wise men's thinking about related problems over a long stretch of time. The value of a correct legal solution will sometimes not be evident to a critic whose cognitive and moral acuity, however distinguished, are only his. It is permissible to toy a bit with language here and say that what seems reasonable to one person, or one age, will not typically be as rational as the law, whose rationality is not fully visible in any single perspective. When one has laid hold of this truth and presumed in favor of the law's rationality, one will of course begin to see it.[24]

Philosophical reason could not make better law, according to ancient constitutionalists, for the best law came from timeless change through centuries of experience, popular consent, and uncountable judicial and human decisions.[25] American whigs believed that they well knew the difference, for they had experienced it. They had wanted to remain in the British Empire governed by the customary ways of the eighteenth-century imperial constitution. They had watched from afar as the logic of sovereignty persuaded the ruling faction in Great Britain that despite tradition, experience, and a hundred and fifty years of constitutional custom, Parliament had both the constitutional right and the legal power to legislate directly for the colonies.[26] American whigs resorted to civil war rather than risk the constitutional insecurity of a law of absolute legislative command that would brook no restraints from the ancient constitution.

The threat of sovereign discretion was not an American fear alone in the last half of the eighteenth century. A surprisingly large number of people in the mother country were apprehensive that the old safety of customary liberty was fast losing ground to the capricious rationality of law by legislative command. The bishop of Worcester was concerned enough in 1760 to warn that any enquiry about the British constitution was "a question of FACT; that must be tried by authorities and precedents only; and decided at last by the evidence of historical testimony, not by the conclusions of philosophy or political speculation."[27] That was the traditional theory of constitutionalism, the old methodology that William Dowdeswell, member for Worcester and chancellor of the exchequer, outlined when he argued that even the House of Commons, if acting as a court of judicature, did not have the legal right to be arbitrary. Rather than promulgate commands according to the dictates of caprice or arbitrary choice, the House should be controlled by taught, nondiscretionary, common law standards of decision, the most important of which was usage.

> When this usage is collected from *antient, uniform, and uninterrupted* practice of Parliament, we have the custom of Parliament; and that *custom* is the *law of Parliament.*
>
> These restraints therefore do not stand solely on the decision of the House, or the judgment of a court having competent jurisdiction in the case: they are much better founded in the *previous usage,* and the *repeated acquiescence* of those who are affected by them. They are also similar to the like restraints at common-law, except in those very few instances in which the clear undisputed usage of Parliament, not deduced from one, but established by many precedents and the general tenor of parliamentary proceedings, may have, for very good reasons not adopted, the practice of other courts. So that an incapacity at common-law to be elected into the House of Commons stands in need of the following conditions. It must be similar to the like incapacity established and declared at common-law in similar cases; it must not be repugnant to common-sense; nor contradicted by the usage of Parliament.[28]

There was, of course, a more basic principle at stake than common-law methodology. Eighteenth-century constitutionalists clung to the old constitutionalism of rights buttressed by appeal to the past rather than the new constitutionalism of rights established by appeal to abstract principles, because they did not want to lose governance by the rule of law. As late as 1823 the polemicist who is remembered as the "dean of the radical reformers"[29] demonstrated how comfortably and effortlessly eighteenth-century radicalism had been able to assume a guise of antiquity as he urged Britain to return to the old constitutionalism that by then existed only in the United States. What the old breed of constitutionalists had been opposed to, John Cartwright explained, was "a Constitution which can be twisted and moulded into any form, to agree exactly with the whims, the caprices, and the despotic views of the Ministers for the time being."[30] In other words, the old breed of constitutionalists—which included the ancient constitutionalists—had been opposed to the constitutionalism that would become the rule of the British constitution of the nineteenth, twentieth, and twenty-first centuries.

Waging Forensic History

There have been two main arguments made up to this point. First, the ancient constitution was not primarily an institutional framework for a broad model of government such as mixed monarchy. It was, first and foremost, a defense of governance by the rule of law. Second, the purpose of the ancient constitution was advocacy, not history.[31] The next question is whether practitioners of ancient-constitution advocacy in the seventeenth and eighteenth centuries intended to argue forensic history rather than impartially to investigate the past. The evidence leaves little doubt that they understood they were pleading a constitutional cause.

Our evidence starts with the generation after Coke and Selden, which means that it starts with Nathaniel Bacon. Puritan, zealous parliamentarian, and Cambridge University's member in the Long Parliament, Bacon made no bones about the cause for which he was writing: "A Private Debate concerning the right of an *English King* to Arbitrary rule over *English Subjects,* as Successor to the *Norman Conquerour,* (so called) first occasioned this Discourse," he explained in the "advertisement" of his first "history." With that purpose, he had "necessarily fall'n upon the *Antiquity* and *Uniformity* of the *Government* of this *Nation*."[32] Bacon included an appendix in another book entitled "A Vindication of the ancient way of Parliaments in England." He wrote it, he explained, "because some mens Pens of late have ranged into a denyall of the *Commons* ancient Right in the Legislative power; and others, even to annull the Right both of Lords and Commons therein, resolving all such power into that one principle of a King, *Quicquid libet, licet,* so making the breach much wider than at the beginning."[33]

Bacon used the forensic history of ancient constitutionalism to question the Stuart concept of monarchy, saying "of the *Saxon* Commonwealth," for example: "Afar off it seems a Monarchy, but in approach discovers more of a Democracy," "a beautiful composure, mutually dependent in every part from the Crown to the Clown; the Magistrates being all choice men, and the King the choicest of the chosen: election being the birth of esteem, and that of merit."[34] People on the other side of the controversy, not liking what he was doing, took steps against Bacon's books, as explained by the printer of a fourth edition of his history, published the year after James II was driven into exile by the Glorious Revolution.

> This *Book* at its first *Publishing,* which was shortly after the Death of *King Charles the First,* had the ill fortune to be coldly received in the world, by reason of the Circumstances of those times; but after *K. Charles the Second* was possest of the *Crown,* and endeavoured to advance the *Prerogative* beyond its just bounds, the *Book* began to be much enquired after, and lookt into by many *Learned Men* who were not willing to part easily with their *Birth-Rights,* so that in a short time it became very scarce, and was sold at a great rate; this occasion'd the private Reprinting of it in the year 1672, which as soon as the Government perceived, they Prosecuted both the *Publisher* and the *Book* so violently, that many hundreds of the Books were seized and burnt; that, and the great want of the *Book* since occasioned the Reprinting of it (without any *Alterations* or *Omissions*) in the year 1682, when the Press was at liberty by reason of the ceasing of the Act for Printing, but *Prerogative* then getting above the *Law,* it met with a new Persecution, and the *Publisher* was Indicted for the Reprinting of it.[35]

During the Restoration, Edward Cook anonymously published a book that has in recent years been criticized as bad history. It may have been bad by the standards of historical scholarship, but it is by no means certain that Cook intended it to be history, or even thought of it as history. Surely his title suggests that it was not history, or, if history, it was, at best, forensic history: *Argumentum Anti-Normannicum: or an Argument Proving, from Ancient Histories and Records, that William, Duke of Normandy Made no absolute Conquest of England, by the Sword; in the sense of our Modern Writers.*[36] The question Cook was disputing, to be discussed below, was the most bitterly argued point of constitutional law during the seventeenth century. Just a few years earlier Peter Heylyn, a Laudian theologian, had enlisted on the other side of that debate, when he stated as the operative doctrine of English constitutional law that "the power of *making Laws* . . . is properly and legally in the King alone." And "for the proof thereof," he claimed, all he had to do was show that William of Normandy had become king of England by conquest following a war in which the Anglo-Saxons who opposed him were defeated. "When the *Norman* Conqueror first came in, as he wonne the Kingdom by the sword, so did he govern it by his power: His *Sword* was then the *Scepter,* and his *will* the *Law*. There was no need on his part, of an Act of Parliament; much less of calling all the *Estates* together, to know of them after what form, and by what Laws they would be governed."[37] A fact pointed out by Quentin Skinner, but too often forgotten, is that "this strand of systematic and unashamed absolutist theorizing spanned the Interregnum years, a decade before gaining its full articulation by Hobbes, a generation before gaining its full historical dress from Dr. Brady."[38]

A second fact too often discounted is that the stakes for this history seemed incredibly high for those participating in the debate. They were nothing less than the governance of England and of Great Britain. If Heylyn's "history," and with it the constitutional law it supported, was to prevail, James Tyrrell warned, "all the Liberties and Priviledges we now enjoy, being at first derived from the Concessions of Kings (and those in great part wrested from them by Force) their successors may, whenever they shall think it conducing to the greater safety of the Kingdom (of which they are to be the sole Judges), resume them."[39] It was that use of forensic history, to prove the constitutionality of royal legislation, that led Sir Robert Atkyns to attack as "Innovating Writers" those "historians" who, by dating the House of Commons from the reign of Henry III, "would destroy Foundations, and remove our Ancient Land-marks, and the Ancient and Just Limits and Boundaries of Power and Authority."[40] It is revealing of the grip that these historical theories held on lawyers at that time, that Atkyns actually argued this same "history" in an important criminal prosecution, when he claimed that the "Powers and Privileges" of the House of Commons, "were indeed their ancient Right and Inheritance." But, he added, the rights and privileges of the house could not be "ancient" "unless the House, or the Commons by their Representatives have been ever from the beginning of the

Government a part and member of the Parliament."[41] Atkyns was arguing for the defense of Sir William Williams who was being prosecuted, at the instigation of Lord Chief Justice George Jeffreys, for licensing (when speaker of the Commons) Thomas Dangerfield's libelous *Narrative.* Atkyns was so confident of his historical thesis that, as counsel, he even assumed the burden of historical proof, saying that the power and privilege of the House of Commons "have ever been a part of parliament, and that they were long before 49 H[enry] 3." Otherwise, he admitted, "they are but precarious in their power and privileges, and enjoy them but of grace."[42] Although bold, Atkyns was not foolhardy. It is indicative of how seriously this school of forensic history was taken by the Stuart courts that he did not publish his argument until after the Glorious Revolution.

William Prynne, whose work as a historian has been questioned by the historiographers of ancient constitutionalism, also spelled out the fact that it was not historical scholarship but current constitutional liberty that motivated his research.[43] He was, Prynne wrote, explaining and defining rights immutable "against those *traiterous* late published Pamphlets, which professedly deny it, and endeavour, a *totall abrogation* of all *former Lawes,* to set up a *New modell* and *Body* of the *law,* to rule us for the future, according to their pleasures." Prynne was not objecting to any particular laws but to a way of looking at law, a definition of authority—law as command. He was defending the definition of "law," asserted by the title of his book, "the Good, Old, Fundamentall Liberties, Franchises, Rights Laws, of all English Freemen."[44] In truth, he never attempted to disguise the fact that the "history" he wrote was forensic. In the "Epistle" of the book defending the inherent jurisdiction of the House of Lords, Prynne stated that he was writing as an "advocate" for the Lords. The "seditious *Design*" of the Commons to legislate without concurrence of the upper House "has engaged me (the unablest of many) out of my great affection to *Royalty and real Nobility,* and a deep sence of the present and tottering *condition* of our *Kingdom, Parliament* (the very *Pillars* and *foundation* whereof are now not only *shaken,* but almost *quite subverted*) voluntarily, without any Fee at all, to become your Honors *Advocate,* to plead your Cause, and vindicate your undoubted hereditary right of *sitting, voting, judging in our Parliaments.*"[45]

During the 1650s, the years of the Long Parliament and Oliver Cromwell, a rival school of jurisprudence had become more vocal, rejecting the good old law and claiming "*That to plead for these and other fundamental laws and liberties, as unalterable,* (though the only Bulwarks & Badges of our Freedome) is nothing else, *but to enslave the Nation.*" What that new legalism could mean, Prynne warned, was that "people do not only lose their Liberty, but are brought under such a kinde of Tyranny, out of which AS BEING WORSE THEN THE EGYPTIAN BONDAGE there is no hope of deliverance." He was rallying his readers against the new theorists of rational nationalism, including the Levellers, "who," Prynne asserted, "shall endeavour by force, fraud, or flattery to compell or perswade them, to sell, resign, betray, or give up these their *Ancestrall* Priviledges, Inheritances, Birthrights to them."[46] Lest there is any doubt that Prynne was fully aware of the argument, consider that in the introduction of an earlier book he had written: "I *here present thee with* Truth Triumphing over Fals[e]hood, Antiquity over Novelty; *to settle both thy Judgement and Practice, in these unset[t]led* times, *wherein the very* Foundation *of* Parliaments, States, Churches, Government, *are shaken and subverted.*"[47] Surely it is evident that Prynne knew that he was not just writing, he was, in fact, *waging* forensic history.

To turn back those whom he called enemies of "our *Hereditary, fundamentall laws, liberties, rights, franchises,*" which were "their own, and every other *English Freemans* best *inheritance* and *security,*"[48] Prynne adapted the most effective jurisprudential weapon at his command, the ancient constitution. Marshaling his evidence in a totally timeless context, he wrote a classic summary of ancient-constitution jurisprudence, outlining the argument and stating its fundamental purpose.

> I shall in a *Chronological* way tender you a large *Historical Catalogue of National, Parliamental, civil and military* Contests, Votes, Declarations, Remonstrances, Oathes, Vows, Protestations, Covenants, Engagements, Excommunications, Confirmations, Evidences, Statutes, Charters, Writs, Records, Judgments and Authorities in all ages, undeniably evidencing, declaring, vindicating, establishing, perpetuating these *Fundamental Hereditary Rights, Liberties, Priviledges, Franchises, Customs, Laws,* and abundantly manifesting the extraordinary *care, industry, zeal, courage, wisdome, vigiliancy of our Ancestours,* to defend, preserve, and perpetuate them to posterity, without the least *violation* or *diminution.*[49]

Prynne sought the principles of restraint—principles he wanted secured as inherent in the constitution of Cromwellian England—by claiming that before the Roman conquest "the *British* Kings were obliged to governe their subjects justly, and righteously, according to the established Lawes of those times, which secured their Liberties, Properties, Goods, Lives against all violence and arbitrary Tyranny, Rapines, Taxes,"[50] and that centuries later, the "English *Saxons* from the first Settlement of their Kingdomes and Monarchies, had no Soveraign Power at all to make, alter, or repeal Lawes, impose Taxes . . . but onely by common consent in General Parliamentary Councils, much lesse to imprison, condemn, exile, out-law any mans person, or to deprive him of his Life, Lands, Goods, Franchises, against the Law."[51]

Prynne's law of the power of taxation can be put into an historical perspective about which he never could have imagined. For his theories would be echoed by American whigs one hundred and ten years later. Writings of the crown's authority to tax in Celtic British times, he asserted, that "it is clear, That Taxes and Tribute not granted and assented to in Parliament, though imposed by a *Conquering Invader,* binde not the *Nation.*"[52] On taxation during Saxon times, he argued that "the ancient *English Saxon Kings* at and from their primitive Establishment in this Realm, had no power nor prerogative in them to impose any publike Taxes . . . on their people without their Common Consents and Grants in their Great Councils of the Realm."[53] Of course, we have long known that there were no Celtic or Saxon parliaments, but is that the standard by which we should judge Prynne's "history"? A much more important point is that his "history," like that of the American whigs in the next century, reshaped constitutional law.[54]

Any thought that the constitutionalism of American whigs is irrelevant to the legal dogmas of Atkyns, Prynne, and the other seventeenth-century constitutionalists of limitations should be dismissed. Government by the rule of law not only was the legal ideal of seventeenth-century constitutionalists but also was the legal ideal for which the Americans fought. That creed was summed up at the end of the first decade of the next century when a writer cast it in terms of grades of supremacy with restraint higher than command—the autonomy of sovereign law over the discretion of prerogative power. "Whenever the Crown," it was said, "in any Cases, issues any Grants or Commissions contrary to Law, they are void; which shews the Superiority of the Law over the Regal Power. And that Power cannot extend it self in any Instances beyond the Bounds of the Common or Statute-Laws, in which 'tis solely founded."[55] This positioning of autonomous law was not confined to royal command. By implication it applied to all command that in time would come to be identified with the concept of sovereignty in British constitutional law. It expressed a formula from the past, not the rule of the future, yet as long as it remained a viable explanation of British constitutional theory, the forensic history of ancient constitutionalism was a major factor shaping the contours of constitutional debate—which does not mean it had much influence in determining the result.

Throughout the eighteenth century the British constitution was in a remarkable state of contrariety—not a state of transition, it is always in such a state, but a state of polarity. Constitutional theory in Great Britain was torn between competing constitutional doctrines that, without tearing the nation into impotency, existed side by side, each supported by tenable, familiar, aggressive legal theories. Indeed, the eighteenth century can be called an epoch of two constitutions in both Great Britain and the American colonies, with the mother country eventually falling under one constitution and the American states consciously selecting the other. If we wish to summarize the development in two sentences, we might say that the British who opposed the American version of the constitution were "looking ahead," away from the ancient constitution, to government by consent, to a constitution of parliamentary command, in which government was entrusted with arbitrary power and civil rights were grants from the sovereign. The Americans were "looking backward," not to government by consent but to government by the rule of law, to a sovereign that did not grant rights but was limited by rights, a sovereign that was, like liberty, created by law, the guardian of liberty. Perhaps they were not looking back to the ancient constitution, but they were looking back to the constitution of Sir Edward Coke, to the constitution that had triumphed over Charles I and James II.[56]

Ranged in opposition to the constitution of supreme, immutable autonomous law in the eighteenth century was a school of legal theorists who, in the late seventeenth and early eighteenth centuries, were thought of as "anticonstitutionalists." In more recent times they have been called absolutists, modernists, Filmerians, Bodinians, Austinians, or rationalists. For the moment—that is for most of the eighteenth century—parliamentarians, satisfied with having established supremacy over the crown, had not sensed the potential of sovereignty over law and the extreme ground among the jurisprudes of arbitrary power was held by a small minority of royalists. The constitution they wanted was summed up by the claim that "Parliaments owe their Being to him [the king], but he his own to Birth-Right."[57] This was a theory of constitutional law that could be stated as a straight principle of pragmatic jurisprudence but sometimes was advanced in the dress of history, usually in the form of an attack on ancient constitutionalism. The chief exponent of this school of law in the period covered here was Robert Brady, who wrote several studies of contemporary constitutional theory that he cast in historical contexts.

By the twentieth century Brady had become somewhat of a historian's folk hero, the lonely prophet of a darker, less enlightened age, who had the vision and the intelligence to be the good historian courageously but in vain exposing the misconceptions and misrepresentations of those bad historians, the ancient constitutionalists. He has been proclaimed "a pioneer in modern historiography,"[58] the "most advanced historian of his day,"[59] the seventeenth-century scholar who helped expose "the politically disastrous consequences of anachronistic thinking,"[60] who wrote "with a rigorous devotion both to scholarship and the interests of the royalist cause,"[61] and whose "enlightened idea had wonderful royalist potential."[62]

No one disputes that Brady wrote better history than his opponents, the adherents to ancient constitutionalism. To the extent that he wrote better history he probably should also be called a better forensic historian—or a better historian who wrote forensic history—for he was no less an advocate than the ancient constitutionalists, a fact about which he openly boasted. "I have written these *Tracts*," Brady said, explaining the history he published, "to *undeceive* the People, and to shew them, That really they were not *possessed* of these *Peices* [*sic*] of *Sovereignty* and *Empire* antiently, nor of such *share* in the *Government*, as these *Unquiet, Tumultuous* Men endeavour to make them believe they had, and still ought to have."[63]

What separated Brady from the seventeenth- and eighteenth-century lawyers who wrote "history," aside from the fact that he wrote to oppose them, was that he had less reason than they to depart from what are today recognized as the canons of historical methodology. In most other respects he was like them. He was writing on one side of the current constitutional controversy, he was a royalist bent on demythifying the ancient constitution, and he was just as ready to select and manipulate historical facts as any of the forensic historians whose writings have been more sharply criticized in the twentieth century.[64] Indeed, he has been commended for his success. "No omnipotent parliament and elective crown could threaten the Stuarts when the idea of the ancient constitution was proved to be so erroneous," Isaac Kramnick has said of Brady's history.[65] It is striking how historians who (unlike David Douglas and J. G. A. Pocock) acknowledge Brady's constitutional advocacy judge him primarily by the canons of professional historians, even when indicting him for practicing forensic history. Consider just one, Corinne Weston, who said, "Every bit as rigid in his own way as the whig historians, Brady likewise was guilty of present-mindedness and hence anachronism in his account of the English past though his skilful and rigorous use of Spelman's *Glossary* made this less obvious in his case. In sum, Brady's examination of early English history was always subservient to the larger cause of placing a legal sovereignty based on the sword in the Stuart kingship."[66]

Brady was surprisingly open about the forensic and polemical purpose of his "history." It was the advancement of a constitutional theory that had never been dominant in English constitutionalism a legal theory that repudiated not just the ancient constitution but the principle of limited government, the doctrine of mixed monarchy, the rule of law, and the authority of custom.

> *First,* That not only all Government, but particularly *Monarchy* does owe its immediat[e] Foundation and Constitution to God Almighty.
>
> *Secondly,* That by the Law of God, Nature and Nations the Crown ought to descend according to Priority of Birth, and Proximity of Blood.
>
> *Thirdly,* That if an Act of Parliament were obtained to exclude his *R. H.* [the duke of York, it] would be unjust, unlawful, and *ipso facto* void, as contrary both to the Law of God and Nature; and the known Fundamental Laws of the Land.[67]

There was no need to rely on the logic of patriarchy. History going back to Roman times, once cleared of ancient constitutionalism, demonstrated "*That all the* Liberties *and* Priviledges *the People can pretend to, were the* Grants *and* Concessions *of the* Kings *of this Nation, and were Derived from the Crown.*"[68] Brady was attempting much more than what a twentieth-century admirer has termed enhancing "the power of the crown by situating it in a context of incessant change."[69] He was less interested in historical dynamics than royal absolutism. Brady's forensic history was driven by the legal theory that, as Isaac Kramnick suggests, "[n]o omnipotent Parliament and elective Crown could threaten the Stuarts if the claim that the ancient constitution had accorded power to Parliament was erroneous."[70]

It may be wondered why Brady's history has earned such praise from recent historians who have otherwise been so sharply critical of forensic history when practiced by constitutionalists. He was not much honored before the twentieth century. His own contemporaries, in both the seventeenth and the eighteenth centuries, had strong objections both to his work and to his advocacy. In 1725, George St. Amand fastened on Brady the most disparaging term a constitutionalist could, at that time, apply to an opponent when referring to him as "the very learned Advocate for Slavery." Three years later, in a charge to the Westminster grand jury, he was called one of the "Advocates for Arbitrary Power," perhaps the second worst thing that a constitutionalist could say about someone.[71] In the year of the battle of Lexington, the Scots lawyer Gilbert Stuart described Brady as "a writer who is known to have disgraced excellent talents, by . . . giving a varnish to tyranny," and even as late as 1796 Francis Hargrave still thought it worthwhile to remind readers that Brady was "arbitrary" and to refer to him as "the learned but bigoted Dr. Brady."[72] These men in the eighteenth century were still fighting the controversy that New York's future chief justice, William Atwood, had joined in 1681 when he summed up Brady's argument by stressing conclusions that today are apparently considered to have been the discoveries of good history, but which Atwood and his contemporaries thought blatant forensic politics.

> For according to him [Brady] the Tenents *in Capite* were the only *Members* of the Great Council before 49 H. 3. and if others were after, 'twas by Usurping upon the Rights of Tenents *in Capite,* who and not others, when the *new Government* was *set up, began to be Represented* by *two Knights for every County, out of their own number,* and they *at first,* that is then, *Elected* their own Representatives; and yet these Tenents *in Capite* might be set aside if the King and his Council pleased, nor was any power given to others to chuse till 10 H. 6. c. 2 which gave no new power, and the Lords depend upon the Kings pleasure.[73]

More than a century after Atwood published this comment John Reeves explained "the Cause of [Atwood's] warmth." It was, of course, the constitutional issues that were at stake. Brady's opponents used the ancient constitution against him because "it would set the Privileges and Pretensions of the Commons upon a higher footing, if they could be proved to be of very remote Antiquity; and that so late a period, as that of Henry III. and Edward I. and the rebellious proceedings that were the immediate Cause of their being summoned to Parliament, gave them a very low origin in point of time, and something very like usurpation in point of Title."[74] The warmth, therefore, was caused by a dispute about legislative jurisdiction, and at stake was everything they thought important. In one seemingly unpolitical conclusion, Brady contended that not only was the House of Lords anciently summoned only at the crown's discretion, but also it was discretionary for the king to decide which members were to be summoned at each session. Atwood understood precisely what Brady was saying, and, somewhat surprisingly, he spelled it out, not trying to hide any of the implications. "*[T]he making this to have been* the Constitution of the House of Lords, *and maintained in* Practice ever since, *is as much as to say, the* Rights *of that Order of men, are not set[t]led at this day.*"[75]

Brady's retelling of the House of Commons was equally contentious. And for Atwood's contemporary, Judge Robert Atkyns, it did not matter if his history was proven scientific history. To accept his evidence that the representatives of the Commons were first called to Parliament by Henry III could mean in law that "all the Power and Priviledge the House of Commons claims, is not by Prescription, but that they depend upon the King's Royal Will and Pleasure, and had their Original by his meer Concession, and not by Ancient Inherent Right, nor Original Constitution, and therefore may be resumed at Pleasure."[76] No matter what twentieth-century admirers of Brady might claim, his contemporaries, who championed the independence of the Commons, said the controversy concerned parliamentary autonomy and that it was purely forensic. "As on Mr. *Petyts*, and my side," Atwood wrote, "the *design* can be no other, than to shew how deeply rooted the Parliamentary Rights are; So the Doctors [Brady's] in opposition to ours, must be to shew the contrary, (a *design* worthy of a Member of Parliament) and 'tis a Question whether he yields these Rights to be more than *precarious*."[77] Atwood also complained of a book by Brady, which, he asserted, was written "against Mr. *Petyt* and my Self," that it "not only treats us with Pedantick Scorn . . . but it seems, to trample on the best Constitution, our Government it self, under Colour of its being *New* in the 49th of Hen[ry] 3."[78]

It is a wonder how we in the twenty-first century have come to think that these controversies were solely disputes about history. Despite Atwood's clear assertion that he was discussing the seventeenth-century constitution, his argument just quoted has been called, without any intention of anachronism, "the Whig interpretation of English history."[79] In the seventeenth and eighteenth centuries it was not lawyers alone who knew these disputes turned on other matters than the canons of historiography. Just consider the attitude of a clergyman, Samuel Johnson, commenting on a *History* by another clergyman, Abednego Seller. "[W]hen I had discover'd of what Stamp the Historian was," Johnson observed, meaning that Seller was a Jacobite or what Johnson termed "a King *James*'s Man," "I needed no great sagacity to understand the Design and Drift of the History. It is this plainly, to thrust out the present Government, by leaving no Room for it, and by telling us that the late Tyranny was Sacred and Irresistible."[80]

Everyone also understood that no matter the premises of the debate, whether about the origins of a house of Parliament or the antiquity of the constitution, there was one fundamental issue at stake: whether the magistrate was the creature of the law or the law the command of the magistrate. That was the reason why the editor of one of Petyt's books noted that during the reign of Charles II "[t]hen it was that the Body of Mercenaries undertook to maintain several extraordinary Points; they would prove, That the Laws are the King's Laws; that from him they receive their binding Force; that Parliaments owe their very Essence to the Royal Favours; that they are only for Counsel; that they are not very ancient; that the Commons are not anciently a constituent Part of Parliament."[81] The constitutional theory was that the law would remain safely superior over the magistrate only as long as it was perceived older and not of his creation. "To support the Power and Priviledge of the House of Commons, as being an essential part of the Parliament," Atkyns insisted, "it is absolutely necessary to make it out against these Innovators, that the House of Commons have ever been a part of the Parliament, and that they were long before 49 H. 3." Otherwise, he warned, "they are but precarious in their power and priviledges, and enjoy them but of Grace."[82]

Atkyns's scholarship is challenging. Like other ancient constitutionalists, he put the burden of proof on his own side of the controversy. But, because he assumed such a heavy burden, his jurisprudence appears extreme. To prove "the transcendent Power of the High Court of Parliament," Atkyns said that he had to maintain "[t]hat the House of Commons was originally, and from the first Constitution of the Nation, the Representative of one of the three Estates of the Realm, and a part of the Parliament."[83] What should be marked is that the burden may have been less, even much less, than it appears when first thought about. After all, it rested on forensic, not "historical," proof.

"Nemiesis awaited Brady," R. J. Smith has complained. "The Revolution [of 1688] robbed him [Brady] of place, and, for over two hundred years, of recognition of his true stature."[84] In fact, as Isaac Kramnick has pointed out, Brady did not have to wait until the nineteenth century for professional vindication, as he had some disciples even in the eighteenth, the century of constitutionalism.[85] A distinction, however, must be made between disciples of his better history and those of his new law. Most eighteenth-century writers citing him seem to have embraced his conclusions of law, writing against the ancient constitution[86] and the "myth" of Magna Carta.[87] They appear, in other words, to have been more interested in questioning the authority of customary constitutionalism than in pursuing scientific history. It was a rare person in the eighteenth century who thought it possible to accept Brady's history and reject his law. "For tho' I agree with *Brady* in many of his *Facts,*" a newspaper correspondent wrote in 1735, "and think them *undoubted Records* and *True Testimonies;* yet I agree with him *in none of his political Principles,* nor *in the Use* he designed to make of *his facts.*"[88] To take his history wholeheartedly, one almost had to accept his constitutionalism—at least until the nineteenth century. That could have risks. John Reeves, for example, reacted so strongly against the French Revolution that he embraced Brady completely and was prosecuted by the Commons for saying that the king was supreme in British law.[89]

Not only the dispute over the evidence but the constitutionalists' reaction to Brady continued into the eighteenth century. Arbitrary government was still the fear, and the legacy of the ancient constitution remained so strong that well into the 1770s unlimited power, or law as command of the sovereign, was described as new constitutional theory that had only recently "sprung up amidst the decaying Forms of *Gothick Policy*."[90] As late as the year of the Stamp Act, when Parliament decided to impose the "new" law of command on the colonies, Brady's history was labeled "insufficient."[91] On both sides of the Atlantic in the 1760s the forensic habit of arguing "historically" lingered on, as did the concept of immemoriality as a shelter for immutable civil rights.[92]

Perhaps the most telling indication of the significance for the eighteenth century of the jurisprudence associated with the ancient constitution was the fact that there were in Great Britain several prosecutions (and much talk of other prosecutions) against people who published pamphlets doubting either the antiquity of the House of Commons or Parliament's coordination with the crown.[93] British officials willing to go to the trouble of seeking indictments in these situations thought something serious was at stake, a perception that has not always been understood by later generations. Discussing the House of Commons's expulsion, fining, and imprisoning during Elizabeth's reign of a member for writing that the House was the new person in the trinity of king, Lords, and Commons, Sir John Ernest Neale in 1953 observed, "To the precedent-quoting, wishful-thinking House of Commons of Elizabethan times, whose fantastic notions about the antiquity and powers of Parliament were the prop of their adolescent egoism, it was lese-majesty."[94] More recently a scholar has suggested that the reason the Commons prosecuted this case was its "enhanced prestige."[95]

Neither egoism nor prestige was at stake. Constitutionalism was, and constitutionalism was such a fragile growth that it needed constant vigilance. When James II was on the throne, Brady's opponents had felt it wise to remain silent.[96] Later it was thought necessary to silence Brady's disciples to preserve the constitutional settlement and the Protestant succession.[97] One hundred and ten years after Brady published his *Complete History of England,* Parliament spent part of at least four days debating what was described as a "Libel on the British Constitution." The offensive book had been written by John Reeves, who espoused not only Brady's history but, more importantly, his constitutional law as well. Reeves's book, the Earl of Albemarle complained, contained "doctrines directly hostile to the spirit of our constitution, and tending to alienate from the minds of the people their affection for it." Reeves was accused of propagating five constitutional principles: "1. That the king alone makes laws. 2. That the other branches of the legislature are derived from the king. 3. That our liberties were grants from the king. 4. That the only object of the Revolution was to secure us a Protestant king. And 5. That the verdict of juries went for nothing."[98]

In the ensuing parliamentary debate, the libel came down to a matter of John Reeves against the ancient constitution, and ancient constitutionalism prevailed. At issue was the mixed limited constitution of 1795, but discussion turned on forensic history, which meant, of course, that even the Saxons were relevant. One member of the Commons, a serjeant-at-law, protested that he could never "admit that it was historically correct, that the monarchy of this country was at any time antecedent to its constitution."[99] It was probably immaterial whether the fact could be proved historically. It could not be admitted constitutionally. "To assert that the Lords and Commons derived all their functions from the crown was most unconstitutional doctrine," John Courtenay warned the House of Commons. "Not under the Saxon or even the Norman line had any such doctrine prevailed; during the latter period, the English always claimed the rights they enjoyed under the Saxon government, though they were not always successful in their claims."[100] Courtenay did not have to offer historical proof, for he was talking of law and the proof was in the existing constitution. The House of Commons voted an address to the king that the attorney general be directed to prosecute John Reeves.[101]

It would be better for our knowledge of seventeenth- and eighteenth-century liberty if intellectual historians would give some thought to the purpose of forensic history. To ignore eighteenth-century constitutionalism is to make certain that we do not understand it. At the very least it should be considered that potentially there was an ultimate sovereignty vested in the king, who could commit no illegal act. Today we know that this potential sovereignty was harmless theory, but the eighteenth century did not enjoy our perspective, and for many people then it seemed constitutionally vital to have a counter theory of limitations upon the king's power. The constitutional imperative, therefore, arose not due to the inherent merits of ancient constitutionalism but from fear of the alternative—a fear Dr. Brady had said was groundless.

> In the name of God let the English People enjoy all their *Just, Due, Legal Rights, Liberties* and *Privileges,* and let them never be *disturbed* in the present Establishment of more Freedom to them, than all the Subjects in the World do enjoy . . .; Let them enjoy every thing whereto the KING or His *Antecessors* have given their *Consent,* and that hath been *Allowed* and *Owned* by *Usage* and *Practice* many *Centuries* of Years, and found *Agreeable* to the *Interest* of *Prince* and *People.*[102]

Brady's law makes sense in twenty-first-century Great Britain, for (if you substitute *Parliament* or *cabinet* for *king*) it is nineteenth-, twentieth-, and twenty-first-century British law. It had little appeal, except with a monarchist, in the seventeenth and eighteenth centuries when liberty rested on customary grounds. Brady, Judge Atwood objected, was asking the English to trust sovereign will and pleasure, unchecked even by theoretical limits.

> Perhaps 'twill be said I injure this *good man* in imputing to him a *design* in relation to the present Government; Since he owns that the *most excellent great Council* [Parliament] . . . received *its perfection from the Kings Authority, and time.* But 'tis obvious that *its Perfection,* must be meant [must mean] of such *its Perfection,* as his Book allows, and he would make *evident,* but what is that? That Lords should . . . be Summon'd to Parliament, or past by, at the King's pleasure, and that if the King pleas'd he might Summon *one Knight for a County, one Citizen for a City, one Burgess for a Burgh, and those nam'd to the Sheriff.*[103]

Atwood was not saying that prerogative discretion of such extremes was inevitable if Brady's constitutional theory became law. What he and other constitutionalists said was that if the forensic history of ancient constitutionalism were repudiated there would be no theoretical defenses against prerogativism, or, to use a twentieth-century expression, the security of mixed monarchy would "lose all credibility."[104]

What especially deserves to be marked is the fact that the same argument was being made late in the eighteenth century. Similar to Atwood, but exactly one hundred years later in 1781, another barrister attacked an anticonstitutionalist argument that had been made by Dean Josiah Tucker:

> The intention of these misrepresentations is sufficently apparent. They evidently tend to invalidate the existence of political and indeed of civil liberty beneath the feudal government, except in the instance of the Barons. To reduce the husbandmen and the tradesmen to a state of villenage. To deny the existance of the rights we at present enjoy, till they were wrung from the crown by the arms of its vassels, and disseminated by similar usurpations of the commons. And finally, by these insidious deductions to strengthen the author's attack upon the privileges we feel, and the constitution we revere.[105]

It was for the same forensic reason that the Irish law professor Francis Stoughton Sullivan, in the year of the American Declaration of Independence, urged in the second edition of his *Lectures* that students study the ancient constitution and the Gothic forms of government.

> From hence only shall we be able to determine whether the monarchy of England, as is pretended, was originally and rightfully an absolute royalty, controuled and checked by the virtue of the prince alone, and whether the privileges of the subjects, which we are so proud of, were usurpations on the royal authority, the fruits of prosperous rebellion, or at best the concessions of gracious princes to a dutiful people. . . . The question is of a matter of fact; for on the decision of the fact, how the constitution of England antiently stood, the question of the right solely depends.[106]

Sullivan stated what is today an incredible theory of law. We must, therefore, be impressed that we do not find it in some extreme polemical tract of ancient constitutionalism, but in lectures intended to teach law students the common law. On both sides of the Irish Sea during the American Revolution the two university professors entrusted with the task of teaching the common law of England were, in fact, teaching the ancient constitution of Sir John Fortescue, Sir Edward Coke, and Sir Matthew Hale. Reject Brady and follow William Petyt, Richard Wooddeson instructed his Oxford students, adding with a confidence that only a common lawyer could place in forensic history, "that among the [ancient] Britons there existed legislative assemblies of the democratical kind."[107] Sullivan told his students in Dublin to study the constitution of *contemporary* Great Britain by going back in time, to as far as the Roman Empire and the forests of prehistoric Germany.

> This research will be of use, not only to understand our present constitution, which is derived from thence, but to make us admire and esteem it, when we compare it with that which was its original, and observe the many improvements it has undergone. From hence, likewise, may be determined that famous question, whether our kings were originally absolute, and all our privileges only concessions of theirs; or whether the chief of them are not originally inherent rights, and coeval with the monarchy; not, indeed, in all the subjects, for that, in old times, was not the case, but in all that were *freemen,* and, as all are such now, do consequently belong to all.[108]

Sullivan's history may be nonsense to twenty-first-century intellectuals, but it had been the very essence of seventeenth-century constitutionalism, and, for the Irish professor of constitutional law, it remained the essence of eighteenth-century constitutionalism. For Sullivan, living in the final decades of the eighteenth century, customary constitutionalism was the only pillar strong enough to support liberty.

CHAPTER FIVE

Forensic Techniques of Ancient Constitutionalism

Arguments should not be misconstrued. The claim made here is not that advocates of the ancient constitution understood law better than their opponents or that they always argued correct legal principles. Constitutional law was much more uncertain during the seventeenth and even the eighteenth century than it would be in Great Britain after 1850 or in the United States after 1803. In both England and the colonies the law of Selden, Coke, Somers, Bolingbroke, and James Otis was at least as doubtful as the law of James I, Strafford, Jeffreys, Walpole, and Thomas Hutchinson.[1] What is contended is that exponents of ancient constitutionalism were generally arguing for restraint on government power and did not want government acting capriciously toward life or property. And the reason was not because thinking of the past led them to champion restraint but because the ancient constitution was a convenient, pragmatic, contemporary, and forensic way of arguing restraint by those already converted to that side of the constitutional paradox.

If we accept the premise that students of the ancient constitution in the seventeenth and eighteenth centuries were arguing the contemporary constitution, not history, we will better understand what they were saying and why they said things in certain "unhistorical" ways. It was not just common lawyers but everyone arguing against arbitrary power in those centuries who tended to look at the past from what recent critics have termed an ahistorical standpoint. Of course the learned, accepted method of thought about the common law makes the perspective even more pronounced. Even today, a lawyer trained in common-law methodology thinks that a judge who rules on a question in litigation is stating the law as it has always been. If the judge reverses a previous decision and states a new rule in its place, lawyers are aware that the law has changed, but the new rule is thought of by lawyers less as being new than as having always been *potentially* the law on that particular matter. What to a historian is now the "old" rule, to the lawyer is the "erroneous" rule. A long line of precedents that has been overruled is not, to the lawyer, the former law as it would be to the historian, but incorrect law, discarded law, or not law at all.[2] What separates the lawyer's view of the past from the historian's is the reality for the lawyer of that potential. Because the lawyer thinks of the new rule as a principle that has always potentially been valid, it had always been the correct interpretation waiting to be promulgated.

Most of the techniques of arguing ancient constitutionalism outlined here are the techniques of forensic history in general—the marshaling of facts supporting only one side of a litigation, for example. There was, by contrast, one aspect of ancient-constitution forensic history not prevalent in most forensic history, a characteristic that ancient-constitution history shared with whig history: the division of the past between heroes and villains. "[W]e find nothing in our Common *Histories* of these Times, but the *Brave Feats* performed by the *English* for their Fundamental Rights and Liberties," Robert Brady complained of ancient constitutionalism. "Nothing in Sir *Edward Coke*[,] Mr. *Selden,* Mr. *P[r]yn[ne],* and all late Writers when they *chop* upon these Times, and mention any thing relating to them, but the *Magnanimity* of the *English* in Appearing for their *Birth-rights,* and the great *Privileges* they had formerly injoyed."[3]

Brady understated the complaint. Forensic practitioners of ancient constitutional jurisprudence not only saw the past of Saxon or English freedom in heroic terms but were apt to judge the existence and extent of liberty by their taught perceptions of historical times without bothering with empirical data. Why should "a modern lawyer" be interested whether feudalism was introduced by the Saxons or the Normans, a barrister, James Ibbetson, asked in 1777. He had an answer typical of eighteenth-century ancient constitutionalists.

> If we attribute to the Normans the introduction of the Beneficium or feud, with its necessary consequences, as well as its oppressive deductions; we must regard it as an innovation upon the common law, the arbitrary imposition of a tyrant inimical to the liberties of the suspected subjects of his acquired territory.
>
> If we derive the feudal constitution from the Saxons, it assumes a milder form; we connect it with a government that tended to promote the liberty of the subject, and to preserve it from infringement; with the names of Alfred and of Edward, and with the laws that have made those names venerable.[4]

Put another way: to find that an institution had Norman origins was to reveal it as an engine of arbitrary power. To find an institution had Saxon origins was to discover that it had been developed under liberty to serve a free people.

The tactic also worked the other way. A supporter of the constitution of arbitrary power could strengthen the case for government authority by attributing institutions to the Normans. That was why Ibbetson was critical of writers who he thought supported the authority of arbitrary power, especially when they pushed the origins of institutions and laws no further back in time than the Norman era. "The Dean, in attempting to debase the rights of the people," Ibbetson wrote of Josiah Tucker, "has exaggerated the oppressions of the feudal aristocracy. He has endeavoured to demonstrate that the military tenants were the only freemen of the realm, and that the charters of the Boroughs originated at the late period from the indulgent avarice of the Norman monarchs."[5] Joseph Towers also criticized Tucker, accusing him of slanting history to fit his definition of law, in other words, of writing forensic history.

> The zeal with which the Dean of Glocester [Tucker] is animated . . . to oppose the principles of the assertors of the common rights of mankind, leads him to give an account of the condition and manners of our ancestors in the greatest degree humiliating and degrading. He feels no desire to maintain the honour of his country: but, to support his own political reveries, would represent the majority of the people of England as the descendants of the lowest and meanest slaves.[6]

Facts, or what historians regard as acceptable evidence, were less important than the perceived protections of the ancient constitution and the needs of the current constitution. The ancestors of contemporary Britons could not have been slaves because, if they had been slaves, they could not have left a legacy of freedom. And they had to have bequeathed freedom if freedom was the constitutional inheritance of contemporary Britons.

A second technique of ancient-constitution history was selectiveness. Brady complained of this tactic, referring to one of Petyt's arguments, for example, as "grounded upon some parts of three several Records in the Fifteenth of King *John,* which he hath again picked out to serve his purpose, and impose upon his Readers."[7] Interestingly, the technique was used by both sides of the constitutional debate, and so, too, both sides voiced the complaint. In 1718, for instance, a student of ancient constitutionalism charged that Matthias Earbery (who argued that Saxon and Norman kings had possessed absolute power) "only transcribes what he thinks makes for him, and leaves out whatever makes against his Opinion."[8]

Although forensic historians from Coke to sitting justices on the United States Supreme Court always have used only those bits of the past that supported their legal position, the methodology has for some reason been found singularly irritating by professional historians. "The Americans' blending of empiricism and rationalism," Gordon Wood has complained of colonial whig arguments during the revolutionary controversy, "lent a permissiveness to their use of history that makes it seem to us superficial and desultory; indeed they often appear to be simply selecting from the past examples to buttress generalizations deduced by pure reason. Since it was the constant and universal principles applicable to solving immediate problems that they were really after, there was always the danger in the delicate balance between historical experience and self-evident truth that the rational needs of the present would overpower the veracity of the past."[9] Even a scholar who published a book-length study contending that the founding fathers were historians—that is, were serious students of history, and used history to guide them in making political decisions—was disturbed on making the same discovery: "The colonists were selective in their use of whig history," Trevor Colbourn complained. "They seized and made their own, specific concepts and ideas only. They took seventeenth-century arguments against the Stuarts and directed these arguments against the eighteenth-century Parliament."[10] To be more exact, the colonial whigs took seventeenth-century *constitutional* arguments against the arbitrariness of Stuart rule and directed those *constitutional* arguments against the arbitrariness of imperial legislation.

Professor Wood prejudiced his case when referring to "their use of history." He assumed that it was history without asking if it was what he usually meant by the word "history." We, however, should ask why the veracity of the past should be a consideration in an argument that admittedly was concerned with "immediate problems," not problems of history but problems of eighteenth-century constitutional law and eighteenth-century perceptions of constitutional liberty. The American whigs, like other forensic historians, did not turn to constitutional history or to legal records with open minds. They could not and did not expect to base their case upon what the past had in fact been, for had they looked with a historian's open mind they would have found conflicting authorities and they would have had to deal with precedents hostile to their argument. Practical people facing practical problems, they took from the past what they needed or found useful.

It is quite another matter that forensic historians sometimes manipulated data or changed historical facts. Altering the record or rereading the past were techniques used by forensic historians defending parliamentary autonomy in the seventeenth century,[11] and they are still employed by American courts today. Much of the history with which the federal judiciary has found new "rights" for native Americans under the resurrected and reinterpreted Intercourse Act is pure invention.

A more frequent and certainly more lawyerlike technique employed by practitioners of ancient constitutionalism was to assume that a desired principle of law was part of the ancient constitution and to shift onto the other side the burden of proving otherwise. "The standing body of our Laws is a clear proof that the power of our Kings is limited: How come we by Municipal Laws, if we must submit to their will?" the earl of Warrington asked. "But if it shall be answer'd me that this Government was the work of some King, and that he directed the form of our Constitution: I do in the first place desire to know who that King was, and in what Age he lived." Pressing the burden further should opponents of the ancient constitution find their English Justinian, Warrington formulated a presumption of fact that the other side had the burden of disproving. As it was obvious that any king who could have formed such a constitution "was extremely Wise and Just," the presumption was "[t]hat that King did believe that it was not so just and reasonable to govern by his Will, as by those rules which the Law has prescribed, that is, that it was more reasonable that the Law should controul his Will, rather than that his Will should over-rule the Law."[12] Like any competent common lawyer, Warrington was trying to put his side of the constitutional debate into a "no-lose" position. If his burden had been imposed the case could have been won. After all, what the other side had to prove was that the English Justinian knew of the tenets of the ancient constitution and deliberately rejected them, leaving Warrington with the argument that if the king knew of the ancient constitution he admitted its existence and his rejection was illegal. And, of course, the other side also contended that their opponents had to carry the burden of proof. An example was Mathias Earbery contending that, before Norman times, English kings ruled without a representative House of Commons. He said the burden was on the ancient constitutionalists to prove differently. "I say these Men must either prove the Commons were in Parliament before *Henry Ist,* or they must grant that a House of Commons, Antiently was not essential to a Parliament, and that the House of Lords was such without them."[13]

A final technique of the forensic history of ancient constitutionalism worth noting because it was so frequently employed was to make the principles of the ancient constitution a standard of official or legal conduct. *Junius* did this with vindictiveness against Lord Mansfield, accusing the chief justice of King's Bench of violating both the substance and the spirit of the ancient constitution.

> I see, through your whole life, one uniform plan to enlarge the Power of the Crown, at the expence of the Liberty of the subject. To this object, your thoughts, words, and actions have been constantly directed. In contempt or ignorance of the Common Law of England, you have made it your study to introduce into the Court where you preside, maxims of jurisprudence unknown to Englishmen. The Roman Code, the Law of Nations, and the Opinion of Foreign Civilians, are your perpetual theme; but who ever heard you mention Magna Charta or the Bill of Rights with approbation or respect? By such treacherous acts, the noble simplicity and spirit of our Saxon Laws were first corrupted. The Norman Conquest was not complete, until Norman Lawyers had introduced their Laws, and reduced Slavery to a System.—This one leading principle directs your interpretation of the Laws.[14]

This tactic, evaluating actions by the tenets of the ancient constitution, was particularly effective against Mansfield. He was a Scot, and it was part of the popular English prejudice against Scots in the 1770s that they had never been governed by the ancient constitution and, therefore, could not be trusted to defend liberty or be expected to understand the rule of law.

As *Junius* demonstrated, a tactic of ancient-constitution practitioners was to portray deviations from the standards of liberty as deviations from the ancient constitution. Instances of "liberty" standards in the second half of the eighteenth century were the right of some freeholders to representation and the constitutional autonomy of the House of Commons, both of which were claimed to be legacies of the ancient constitution. "Parliaments, in some shape," Blackstone at least twice argued, "are of as high antiquity as the Saxon government in this island; and have subsisted, in their present form, at least five hundred years."[15] This principle of the ancient constitution was so self-evident that Richard Wooddeson, Blackstone's second successor as Vinerian law professor, dismissed as a precedent without constitutional standing the fact that Edward II had not called the Commons to Parliament and had treated the Lords "merely as counsellors."

> This, however, being in exclusion of the lords of parliament, as well as of the commons, and happening when the powers of the nobles was at the highest, can hardly be thought an intended invasion of the rights of the legislature. Whatever similar instances, if any, can be produced, may justly be looked upon as violations of right, and infringements of the constitution. I am speaking of a legislative power in our kings, independent even of the lords' concurrence, which no age ever recognized.[16]

Wooddeson may have been forced to this argument because, by the 1770s, when he wrote, the notion that the House of Commons was coeval with the ancient constitution had long been under historical criticism and its exponents were beginning to retreat. For ancient constitutionalists, however, the evidence of history was no barrier. If, on one hand, you were a law professor like Wooddeson, you could use the law of the ancient constitution to deny the facts of history: the House of Commons had to have been part of the Saxon government, or there could have been no ancient constitution; there was an ancient constitution, therefore the Commons could not have originated in Plantagenet times. If, on the other hand, you were too historically minded to deny that the Commons was of post-Saxon origin or, unlike Wooddeson, felt compelled to admit there was no historical evidence of its antiquity, there was, nevertheless, another tactic of forensic history for vesting representation with antiquity. This was to assume that the eighteenth-century British constitution could not have been a constitution of freedom if its ancestor, the English constitution of earlier times, had not also been a constitution of freedom, and to project back onto antiquity the structural apparatus of constitutional liberty then existing in the eighteenth century. Edward Wynne, writing in the 1780s, described this technique as "corresponding with the abstract reason of things."

> The true antiquity of the Representation of the Commons is a point, as I take it, entirely unfathomable. There is very little evidence at all about the matter, that goes very far back; and most of that is so ambiguous, as to furnish no clear decisive conclusion. But whatever the mode of this representation originally was, or tho' it might long continue to be different from what it has since been, it is very difficult to dispute its existence: because it corresponds with the abstract reason of things in the idea of a free Government; it results from the origin of Government as founded on consent, and that of our own in particular, not an absolute but a limited Monarchy. The Body of the People must, therefore, always have had some right to share the legislative power; it cannot be supposed this right could ever be entirely given up, but only delegated to others, entrusted to act for them.[17]

Wynne's argument is not as simpleminded as it may seem on its first reading. On the contrary, it is a sterling example of what surely was the most attractive probative feature of the ancient constitution for those arguing it forensically, its pliability. The ancient constitution could be nearly anything you wanted or needed it to be. When the Earl of Carysfort wanted it to be democratic, he just looked for the evidence and, as he expected, found it. "In the early times of our history," Carysfort pointed out, "we find the strongest evidence of the Democratic spirit of our Constitution. The Sheriffs who had the charge of the counties, the execution of justice, and the preservation of the peace, were elected by the freeholders, so were the Conservators of the Peace. . . . The consent of the people is, by our best Lawyers, considered as a term equivalent to authority of Parliament."[18]

There was little on the liberty side of constitutional law that could not be supported by ancient-constitution argumentation. After all, as Wynne pointed out, "[h]istory . . . will not only explain subsequent laws, but will supply the silence of law itself."[19] Judge Robert Atkyns, sitting in the court of Exchequer Chamber, found the silence of nonexistent evidence forensically handy when counsel cited the histories of Sir Robert Cotton and William Prynne to prove that the House of Commons did not exist before the reign of Henry III. "*But we must not be* govern'd by Historians in matters of Law," Atkyns wrote, "and therefore, notwithstanding this Observation of Sir Robert *Cotton*'s and Mr. *Prynne*'s, we must presume, that the House of Commons and Elections of Knights of the Shire, are as antient as the common Law, and have been time immemorial, because we find no written Law that does first begin any such Institution."[20] Atkyns's audacity must be marked. Even the current justices of the United States Supreme Court would be hard pressed to top him. The House of Commons had to be coeval with the common law because there was no written law creating it. He was not, of course, asking for an act of Parliament creating Parliament. That would have been unreasonable. It was not unreasonable, however, to contend that the absence of a modern law was proof of ancient law. In truth, the technique is not that unusual today. The first Intercourse Act, federal judges have deducted, must have covered Indian nations wholly within state jurisdiction such as the Passamaquoddy and the Oneida or else the act would have said they were not covered.

Gilbert Stuart, the Scots advocate, used a similar technique to defend the same point of constitutional law that Atkyns defended, when citing an ancient tract that Coke and other writers had used to prove "the high antiquity of the *commons*."

> It is to be acknowledged, however, that Mr. Selden has demonstrated that this tract could not possibly be of the age of the Confessor, from its employing terms which were not in use till long after. But this does not wholly derogate from its force as to the point in question. For, allowing it to have been written in the reign of Edward III. the period which, with great probability, some writers have assigned it, it yet proves that the sense of that period was full and strong with regard to the antiquity of the constitution, as consisting of king, lords and *commons;* a circumstance which must have great weight in opposition to those, who would make us believe, that our constitution, as so formed, was unknown till the times of Henry III. and Edward I.[21]

Acknowledged forgeries of the past that had been concocted to document the ancient constitution are good evidence in the present for proving the ancient constitution because they are evidence either of what the forgers believed or of what they wanted the courts of their day to believe. This argument would not have been made after 1850, but when written in 1775 it was familiar practice, certainly to a lawyer like Stuart writing forensic history. He not only said but he intended to say that acknowledged forgeries of the past, even though concocted to document the ancient constitution, are good evidence for proving content and principles of the ancient constitution because they are evidence either of what the forgers believed or of what they wanted the courts of their day to believe.

Forensic Techniques of Timeless Constitutionalism

The ancient constitution must not be thought mainly a model of liberty that existed in the golden age of antiquity when a warrior people cherished freedom and knew how to preserve it. The forensic value of the ancient constitution was not in its past perfection but in its present timelessness. The ancient constitution was a model, true enough, but it was also a means of constitutional renaissance, resuscitation, and redemption, made all the more relevant because it was not a constitution that had existed only in the distant past, but one that still existed, now, in the present.

Strikingly, in addition to its pliability, the most potent forensic attribute of ancient constitutionalism was its timelessness. It was a concept that entailed most of the anachronisms for which ancient-constitution polemics have been criticized by recent historiographers. Richard Goodenough, discussing the American rebellion in the year of the Declaration of Independence, summed up the constitutionality of a doctrine for which Americans were fighting, the doctrine of consent, by insisting, "[I]t is prior to all written Records; it is antecedent to all Statutes; it is co-eval with, and essential to the very Existence, of this Constitution."[22] If the historical thesis strikes us as unlearned, we would do well to first recall its purpose: it provided a debating point that could be assumed, sometimes without being proved.

That was the simplest technique—to assume a proposition so obvious it did not need to be proven. Another, almost as simple, was to assume a proposition so obvious that, just by seeing it stated, every right-thinking friend of constitutional liberty would know that it needed no further proof. During the Wilkes election controversy a pamphleteer asked when the House of Commons had obtained jurisdiction to decide qualifications of members, and answered:

> That they gained it at the same time, and by the same means that they gained their right of impeaching the greatest personages in the land; at the same time, and by the same means, that they acquired the right they exercise with regard to money bills, and other undoubted privileges. In short, their jurisdiction in this respect, which is confirmed by immemorial usage, is as ancient as the *Common Law,* and must be so deemed, for no written law can be produced which shews the commencement of the institution: It is coeval with the constitution, and without such a jurisdiction the House of Commons, as has been shewn, could not exist as an independent body.[23]

When ancient-constitution conclusions had to be proved, the "proof" was established by being obvious, by being desired, or by being fitted into the generally accepted principles of eighteenth-century British constitutionalism.

Six years before Goodenough's pamphlet, John Missing had lectured no less a legal expert than Lord Mansfield, the chief justice of the King's Bench, on the rights of Britons to petition the throne by observing, "[T]he Common Law is more ancient, than that [*sic*] any Histories, Law-Books or Records can assist us to trace it; but though Histories, Law-Books and Records fail us, there is a Mode, my Lord, of discovering its Origin, and if this should lead us very far back into Antiquity, yet by a due Use of Common Sense, we shall run no Hazard . . .; for, my Lord, if we ever so little exert our rational Faculties, we shall see, this Part of it at least, to be the Law of Nature, which is, the Law of God." After all, it was obvious to Missing and should have been to Mansfield that "[t]he Right to complain when injured, is the Right of Human Nature, it is the main End of Peoples submitting to Government; it is the Origin of all Human Laws, and all

Courts of Justice are established only to hear and redress Grievances; so that your Lordship sees this is no NOVEL Institution, it is as old as human Nature itself, and the immediate Law of God."[24]

The timelessness of the ancient constitution was a matter of common sense as much as it was of knowing the contours of current liberty, for some things did not change, such as the fact that people had always lived under law and government. That was why many premises of the ancient constitution were self-evident. After all, as William Dugdale had noted the previous century, "the *Common Law* is, out of question, no less antient than the beginning of differences betwixt man and man, after the first Peopling of this Land; *it being no other than pure and tryed Reason; . . . or the absolute perfection of Reason,* as Sir *Edward Coke* affirmeth, adding, *that the ground thereof is beyond the memory or Register of any beginning.*"[25] Not just twentieth-century historians but eighteenth-century opponents of ancient constitutionalism were on notice not to ask for historical certainty. The ancient constitution was shaped by subjective not objective proof.

The timelessness of the ancient constitution was developed more in response to polemical needs than anything else. Timelessness made it possible for an advocate of certain principles or institutions, a supporter of the House of Commons for example, to place those principles or institutions in the context of continual constitutionality without being too precise about origins or by implying that origins might be irrelevant. Algernon Sidney applied this technique when noting that Filmer

> is not ashamed to cite *Bracton,* who, of all our antient Law-writers, is most opposite to his Maxims. He lived, says he, in Henry the third's time, since Parliaments were instituted: as if there had bin a time when *England* had wanted them; or that the establishment of our Liberty had bin made by the *Normans,* who, if we will believe our Author, came in by force of Arms, and oppressed us. But we have already proved the Essence of Parliaments to be as antient as our Nation, and that there was no time, in which there were not such Councils or Assemblies of the People as had the power of the whole, and made or unmade such Laws as best pleased themselves. We have indeed a French word from a People that came from *France,* but the Power was always in our selves; and the Norman kings were obliged to swear they would govern according to the Laws that had bin made by those Assemblies. It imports little, whether *Bracton* lived before or after they came amongst us.[26]

Timelessness was also a tactic allowing an advocate to place certain principles in a context of constitutional continuity no matter if they had been overturned or had become inoperative. Even long-standing constitutional custom could not supersede the timeless validity of a fundamental doctrine of the ancient constitution. Consider the grounds on which, at the very late date of 1783, the crown's right to create peers at discretion was questioned. In the reign of Henry VII, it was charged, "a power was *usurped* by the Crown of conferring titles of dignity at pleasure; which *incroachment,* not being opposed by the *Commons,* has been continued to this day, contrary to the ancient law and constitution of the kingdom."[27] We should consider the meaning of the word *incroachment.* The practice, it was said, was an "incroachment" against the timeless constitution even as late as 1783. The fact that three hundred years had passed since the "usurpation" had first been introduced did not matter. The usurpation had not become law either because the crown had no prescriptive rights against the ancient constitution, or because time did not run against immutable principles no matter what occurred.

For purposes of argument, to gain polemical advantage, one needed only to postulate a constitution of timeless continuity. John Cartwright was still practicing such a technique as late as the 1820s. "Keep in mind," he argued, "that our object is, to ascertain how it was, or must have been, according to the Constitution at its *origin.* It is only by ascending to that point, we can know what it *now is;* because, whatever it originally was it continues to be; no change ever having been made, notwithstanding the numerous changes which have occurred in the *practice* of governing."[28] Of course practice changed, but practices or innovations to which you objected became subversions of the ancient constitution as it still existed *in fact* as well as in theory. So it could be argued that, in the 1640s, a faction of the House of Commons "took the whole *Government* into their own Hands, and created themselves a *Commonwealth,* thus totally subverting the *Constitution.*"[29] The Commons had abolished the Lords, but the Commonwealth created by the abolition was not only unconstitutional but was not a precedent. It was a constitutional aberration. Even when there were changes in constitutional government that could not be denied—substantial departures from past constitutional practice such as the loss by the clergy of self-taxation or the loss by the House of Lords of jurisdiction over judicial appeals—they could often be dismissed as matters of mere form, changes in detail, not fundamental alterations. "If you ask whether these things are not an Altering or Breach of the *Constitution,*" Charles Leslie explained. "I think not. For while the *Fountain Constitution* stands Secure, any various Runnings of the *Rivulets* are no Breach of the *Constitution.*"[30] What mattered was the essence and the general principles of the constitution. It was that essence and a few "first principles" that were timeless, not particular rules or changing customs. With that timelessness, the ancient constitution was always available as a standard when arguments were made for correcting the rivulets of erroneous details.

In the early years of the reign of George III there was a reaction among some constitutionalists to the emergence of the cabinet and to the role that ministers had begun to play in the formulation of government policy. Saying that the office of "minister" was "entirely unknown to our Constitution," one pamphleteer argued for its abolition. "To demonstrate the Inconsistency of this Office, with the Principles of the Constitution, it will be sufficient to shew the Nature of it, and trace it to it's Original in other Governments, from which it appears to have been 'very improperly borrowed,' among us."[31] We must not be puzzled as to what the author meant by "constitution" and "constitutional." He was using good late eighteenth-century constitutional words when he said that an office filled by an appointee of the king and recognized by parliamentary legislation was not known to the constitution. Of course, his constitution was not the constitution of Lord Mansfield or that of the current attorney general. We might say that the constitution he cited was not so much the ancient constitution as the timeless constitution, but that would be a distinction without a forensic difference, as the appeal was still to what today's historians call a mythical constitution. What is important about the concept of timelessness is the forensic technique that timelessness kindled. Arguing for constitutional change by appealing to antiquity, it utilized the idea of timeless first principles that existed independently of changes in specific details, even changes in substance. In fact, the concept of timeless first principles gave shape to the two most prominent techniques of forensic history in the seventeenth and eighteenth centuries—the regenerative ancient constitution and the ancient constitution continually being "restored to its first principles."

There was a way of speaking and of arguing that dominated public discussion about the British constitution in the eighteenth century. It used words and phrases such as "restore," "return to," "original purity of the constitution," and "the first principles."[32] These expressions provided a reference for arguing constitutional law that came directly out of ancient-constitution thinking. That thinking in turn was the product of the eighteenth-century notion that the history of the ancient constitution was a tale of continual degradation and renewal. The Saxon constitution, Allan Ramsay pointed out, had flourished for six hundred years, "till it was overwhelmed, and destroyed, by William [the Conqueror] . . . and lay buried under a load of tyranny, for one hundred and forty seven years. When again it arose like a phenix from its own ashes, in the reign of Henry the third."[33] Or, as Viscount Bolingbroke suggested, discussing the same period of post-Norman regeneration, William may have been arbitrary, but, even under the worse tyranny, the law of the ancient constitution, no matter how weakened and battered, always rebounded as the law of liberty. The Normans

> introduced many illegal Practices, and some foreign Principles of Policy, contrary to the Spirit, and Letter too, of the *antient Constitution;* and . . . *these* [Norman] *Kings* and the *Lords abused their Power over the Freemen, by Extortion and Oppression, as Lords over Tenants*. But it will remain true that neither *Kings,* nor *Lords,* nor both together, *could prevail over Them, or gain their Consent to give their Right, or the Law, up to the King's Beck. But still the* Law *remain'd Arbiter both of* King *and* People, *and the* Parliament *supreme Expounder and Judge both of it*

> *and Them.* Tho' the Branches were lopped, and the Tree lost its Beauty for a Time, yet the Root remain'd untouch'd, was set in a good Soil, and had taken strong Hold in it; so that Care and Culture, and Time were indeed required, and our Ancestors were forced to water it, if I may use such an Expression, with their Blood; but with this Care, and Culture, and Time, and Blood, it shot again with greater Strength than ever, that We might sit quiet and happy under the Shade of it; for if the same Form was not exactly restored in every Part, a Tree of the same Kind, and as beautiful, and as luxuriant as the former, grew up from the same Root.[34]

The rebirth in post-Norman times had been complete. The ancient constitution had been regenerated to new strength, but otherwise unchanged in every material way. And as late as 1771, "though much impaired, maimed, and disfigured, it hath stood the admiration of many ages; and still remains the most noble, and ancient monument of Gothick antiquity."[35]

Ramsay and Bolingbroke were not just writing history. They were practicing the most utilized polemical device of eighteenth-century law and politics. "[T]he model of the British constitution," a reviewer explained in the year that the American Stamp Act was promulgated, "has again and again preserved its existence, when the morals and principles of the people were sunk to the lowest degree of vice, ignorance, and slavery, both civil and religious. This model prevailed against the impetuous Tudors, as well as the despotic Stuarts; and by the excellent checks it contains (whatever may be the fate of families or factions) it must survive all its enemies."[36]

Again, it should be noted that the purpose of the model can be easily misunderstood. It has the appearance of serving the conservative or the reactionary, but in truth it lent itself to almost any constitutional theory except, as a general rule, the justification of government power. It is therefore not accurate to think of eighteenth-century constitutionalists as possessing political "attitudes" that were "rather [more] reactionary than conservative."[37] If thought is given to the question, it should be evident that the concept of a self-restoring, self-healing, regenerative constitution could be more useful to radical reformers than to political or constitutional conservatives defending the status quo.

Due to the turn that ancient constitutionalism gave to eighteenth-century political controversy, in debates between the British administration and its opponents it was the government's side that was most likely to eschew arguments of the past and rely instead upon abstract constitutional reasoning or upon principles of expediency.[38] An example occurred during the debate in the House of Commons over repeal of the Stamp Act. As reported in a contemporary "history," the ministry defended Parliament's constitutional authority to tax the North American colonies but admitted that the tax was politically inexpedient.

> The constitution of this country, said they, has been always fluctuating, always gaining or losing: even the representation of the Commons was not till the reign of Henry the seventh reduced to any fixed system. What does it avail then to recur to ancient records, when the constitution is no longer the same; when no body can ascertain its state at the times, which are quoted, and when there are even in the great charter things, which are no more constitutional? Such misplaced industry is as idle as all that mass of learning and dissertation collected from natural lawyers, such as Locke, Selden, Puffendorff and other speculative men under whose arguments and refinements the subject has been almost buried. Beyond the era of Edward the first, or king John, the Mode of taxation is involved through the uncertainty of history in doubt and obscurity. Some of the writs upon record were conformable, some contrary, to law. . . . Can any just conclusion be drawn from such discordant, such opposite precedents?[39]

The argument was by no means unusual for that time; in fact it was well known and quite familiar to members of the House of Commons. It was directed against the forensic technique often employed by ancient constitutionalists or legal reformers calling for "restoring the constitution to first principles." "There are many sorts of abuses and grievances crept into the administration of government, which politicians tell us, are no way to be corrected, but by going back to the first principles on which our system is erected," a critic of the tactic explained writing in *St. James Chronicle* during 1766. "But where are these to be found? Perhaps in some mouldy records which are no longer legible, and if they were, would still be subject to be misinterpreted and wrested to the worst purposes by mercenary lawyers, who are ever ready to make their advantage of antiquated and ambiguous expressions. *Magna Charta* itself could not stand before the sort of law delivered by the judges of Charles I. in the case of *ship money,* or the decisions of Jeffers in the two following reigns."[40] "Speculative Politicians," William Vincent complained to Richard Watson in 1780, "talk lightly and fluently of *reverting to first principles,* as if it required no more trouble than to rectify a piece of clock-work that was out of order. History, on the contrary, informs us, that this cannot be effected but by civil war, and that the event, in general, is not reformation but TYRANNY."[41]

In the same Commons debate, speakers on the other side of the Stamp Act question—the pro-American side led by William Pitt and Lord Camden—apparently not only argued the relevancy of the past but also recalled how the timeless constitution regenerated itself by "recovering" legal rights.

> We acknowledge, said they, that the constitution has been always in a fluctuating state, and that the earlier periods of our history are not without obscurity. But does it hence follow that we are to form do [no] analogical reasonings upon them? Because we know not the whole, must we make no use of what we know? Had our ancestors argued in this manner, and built their arguments

> upon the actual state of the constitution, they would have crouched beneath the rod of tyranny, when it happened to be shook over them, and would never have made a single effort to recover their just rights. . . . Let the actual situation of affairs be ever so bad, we must not look up to our forefathers for precedents, because the struggles between privilege and prerogative prevented them from being regular and uniform. What then! are there no general maxims, no principles congenial to the constitution to guide our researches in this region, which you represent as obscure and perplexed? What is become of that unalienable right of a British subject, which secures him from being taxed, or judged but by the common consent of his peers? This is the first, the vital principle of our liberty.[42]

It was to provide a forensic technique for making that "effort to recover" that the timeless, regenerative, ancient constitution served its most notable eighteenth-century function. What may seem paradoxical inconsistencies to the uninformed were tools of the trade for the forensic historian of ancient constitutionalism. Innovations were argued on grounds of preserving the ancient constitution. "It is nowadays commonplace that no constitution can be static," Mark A. Thomson, the constitutional historian, explained in 1938. "But if this is obvious now, it has not always been so. Constitutional disputes have often taken the form of a controversy as to what a particular constitution already was, when the real issue was whether or not it should be altered. In England, particularly, reform has again and again been represented by its partisans not as innovation but as maintenance or restoration."[43] Robert Ashton wrote from the confining perspective of twentieth-century constitutional premises when he suggested that "The idea of an ancient and immemorial constitution . . . was designed to lend the respectability of antiquity to constitutional practices and attitudes which had far more innovations in them than their proponents cared to admit."[44]

Joseph Galloway is a good example of a would-be reformer hoping to hide the extent of innovation. He employed the strategy when contending that Pennsylvania judges, like their common-law counterparts in England, should have tenure *quam diu se benegesserint*. English judges had enjoyed that tenure since the Glorious Revolution. The Bill of Rights, however, had not been extended to the colonies where judges sat *durante bene placito*. Galloway knew that the British government would not grant colonial judges tenure at good behavior, that that tenure had been an innovation when introduced to England in 1689 and would be an innovation if introduced into Pennsylvania. Appreciating that drastic changes in the constitution were always suspect and encountered resistance for that reason alone, Galloway followed the path of least constitutional resistance. He made his case for the innovation of tenure at good behavior by transmuting it into the restoration of a lost but still extant constitutional right.

> Here it is worthy your Information, *first,* that the rights and liberties claimed and declared by the Bill of Rights, that second Magna Carta, and the Act of Settlement created no innovation of the ancient constitution. The Parliament had no design to change but only to restore the ancient laws and customs of the realm, which were the true and indubitable rights and liberties of the people of *England.* This appears as well from the Bill of Rights and the resolves which preceded the Act of Settlement as from the act itself. From whence it follows that this right of the people to have their judges indifferent men and independent of the crown is not of a late date but part of the ancient constitution of your government and inseparably inherent in the persons of every freeborn *Englishman;* and that the granting commissions to the judges *during pleasure* was then esteemed by the Parliament and truly *was* an arbitrary and illegal violation of the people's ancient liberties.[45]

Galloway was doing much more than saying that the "ancient constitution" ran in the American colonies or that a right vested in "freeborn Englishmen" by the ancient constitution was "inherent" in freeborn Americans, even though they had never enjoyed that right. The ancient constitution had a validity and a force that not only superseded time and centuries of practice but also superseded space and applied as equally to the new world as to the old. He was also adapting to the colonies the most familiar, effective, and stunning of the forensic techniques of ancient constitutionalism. It is a technique, incidentally, still popular among United States Supreme Court justices, a use of "history" that in its twentieth-century American context was described "as a precedent-breaking device,"[46] based on a "Marxist-type perversion of the relation between truth and utility" that assumes "history can be written to serve the interests of libertarian idealism,"[47] or can be manipulated to supply "an apparent rationale for politically inspired activism that can be indulged in the name of constitutional continuity."[48]

In the eighteenth century the operative verb for this forensic tactic was *restore.* Ancient constitutionalists were "Restoring the Constitution"[49] or, better still, restoring "the genuine constitution"[50] or "our true Constitution."[51] The purpose of parliamentary reform, for example, was described as "the restoration of the people to their fundamental rights."[52] A critic of ancient constitutionalism summed up the vocabulary when complaining "of those who speak of the 'principles of the constitution,' of bringing back the constitution to its 'first principles,' of restoring it to its 'original purity,' or [']primitive model.'"[53]

The process of "restoration" was generally presented as an inherent progression in British constitutionalism, something of an ongoing constitutional duty. Even some French revolutionaries learned to play the game of returning to first principles. "In a free government," Jean Paul Marat wrote to the voters of Britain, "when care is not taken from time to time to bring back the constitution to its first principles, in proportion as the epoch of its origin becomes remote, the people lose sight of their rights, they soon forget them in part, and afterwards retain no notion of them." Although a French citizen, he was urging the British to vote for anti-ministerial candidates in the next parliamentary election, by calling them to the defense of "first principles."[54]

That a fiery French radical could so easily use it, shows why the back-to-first-principles technique of ancient-constitution forensic argument could be employed by people from all sides of the political spectrum during the eighteenth century. James Burgh, who was an extreme democrat, though not of the Tom Paine type, urged his fellow Britons not to "be discouraged from using the proper means for restoring the constitution."[55] When he was denied the seat in the Commons to which the freeholders of Middlesex had elected him, John Wilkes followed an eighteenth-century political ritual by demanding the "restoration of the constitution."[56] When, by contrast, Parliament in 1701 had enacted legislation excluding certain "placemen" from membership, William Pudsey had hailed the legislation as going "a great way towards the restoring our Constitution to it's primitive Virtue and Sincerity."[57] Later, in 1744, the issue of placemen was again in agitation, and a bill "for double taxing" incomes on pensions and "places" was before the House of Commons. "[I]n order to preserve a free government," Edward Southwell told the House, quoting Machiavelli, "it often becomes necessary to bring it back to its first principles; which is a maxim the friends of liberty will always take care to observe, and, we may expect, that it will be as constantly opposed by ministers, who always have been, and always will be, grasping at arbitrary power."[58] The administration, opposing the bill, tried to reverse the argument about arbitrary power by claiming that double taxing was not a practice known to liberty; it was "the practice of arbitrary governments, or of princes that were aiming at arbitrary power."[59] Southwell did not back down. Double taxation was arbitrary, he admitted, but a little arbitrariness could be tolerated for the greater good of restoring the Saxon constitution to its ancient purity.

> Upon this principle, Sir, let us examine the motion now before us, in order to see whether it is not returning a step back to our ancient constitution; and, I am sure, no man, who has read the histories of this nation, will say, that our ancestors the Saxons ever thought of inviting men to serve the public by great salaries or pensions: on the contrary, we know, that all those offices that are of true Saxon originals, such as sheriffs, parish offices, and most of our offices in cities and boroughs, are attended with an expence [to the office holder], instead of being of any advantage to the officer. At least, if they now make any advantage of them, it is by some innovation unknown to our ancestors, and such a one as they would never have allowed to be introduced.[60]

Southwell and other opponents of corruption by pensions and places used the ancient constitution hoping to "restore" balance to the British government. That is, they hoped to "restore" more representative, responsible government by strengthening the independence of the House of Commons. It is interesting to compare that purpose to Carter Braxton's use of the same technique for an opposite end: to "restore" government to constitutional responsibility by keeping it independent of democratic caprice. Advising Virginians in 1776 on how to frame their new government, and fearful that the colonies were likely to vest all authority in their elective legislatures, Braxton wanted Americans to "restore" the virtues of the ancient constitution of balances and limitations rather than to rationalize a new scheme based on notions of equality or the sovereignty of the common people. The crown, Braxton admitted, had driven Americans to rebellion not only by its policies but by using the corruption of pensions and places to undermine the restraints on its prerogatives, which the constitution had vested in the two other branches of parliament. As a result, Virginians were "prone to condemn the whole" British constitution even though only "a part"—corruption—"is objectionable." It was wiser and safer to turn to the tried and the tested than to risk experimentation. "However necessary it may be to shake off the authority of arbitrary British dictators," he argued, "we ought nevertheless to adopt and perfect that system, which England has suffered to be so grossly abused, and the experience of ages has taught us to venerate. This, like almost every thing else, is perhaps liable to objections; and probably the difficulty of adapting a limited monarchy will be largely insisted on. Admit this objection to have weight, and that we cannot in every instance assimulate a government to that, yet no good reason can be assigned, why the same *principle* or spirit may not in a great measure be preserved."[61] The best government, then, was government responsible to the constitution itself, not one responsible to fickle public opinion. "[C]ertainly," Braxton insisted, "it would in the present case be more wise to consider, whether if the constitution was brought back to its original state, and its present imperfections remedied, it would not afford more happiness than any other."[62]

Braxton was combating what he called "popular governments." By contrast, the last significant use of the ancient constitution in eighteenth-century Great Britain was by people who wanted to "restore" popular influence to the House of Commons by "restoring" annual or, at least, triennial elections. When John Sawbridge introduced into the House of Commons the 1776 version of "his annual motion" to "restore" yearly elections, he was praised by the *London Magazine* for his zeal in "bringing government back to the original institutions by which it gained permanency and strength."[63] That argument was an instance of ancient-constitution advocacy at its best. Annual elections would have introduced a radical change to eighteenth-century British government—unless, of course, you viewed the question not from the perspective of the eighteenth century but from the perspective of the ancient constitution.

A generation after Sawbridge had died, Granville Sharp continued the fight for annual elections by invoking the ancient constitution in what, by the 1790s, had become a classic, perhaps dated argument:

> *[A] more equal representation of the Commons in annual Parliaments* (*i.e.*, ELECTED "every year once, and more often if need be") *is not only an* ANCIENT, *but even an* INDISPENSIABLE, *right of the people.* That this ancient constitution is *indispensable*

> the many fatal effects of deviating from it have rendered sufficiently obvious; and therefore no remedy can be more efficacious, and constitutionally natural, than a *revival* of that *primitive and fundamental right,* according to the rule of Law, that, *"as often as any thing is doubtful or* CORRUPTED, *we should* RECUR *to first Principles."*[64]

When people protested *"that the whole constitution must be new-modelled"* if there were to be annual elections, Sharp replied that it was not a remodeling but a restoring that he was after. "[W]e are far from desiring that *'the constitution may be new-modelled;'* we only pray, that the unjust *usurpations,* (made without the consent of the people), *the corruptions, and other such abuses,* may be taken away and reformed: and then the ancient constitution of *annual* elections, and *'more often if need be,'* will recover its full vigour without any other alteration."[65] Of course, Allan Ramsay added, it was not an innovation to "weed, from our constitution, all modern heterogeneous matter, that hath poisoned its principles, and established a tyranny upon the ruins of our ancient laws, and liberties."[66]

The technique was both familiar to readers of political tracts and easy to apply. Innovation could always be softened by being clothed in the dress of ancient constitutionalism. The strategy was to avoid the suggestion of altering this institution or introducing that doctrine. The forensic tactic, rather, was "preservation" of the purpose and the spirit of the ancient constitution. Consider the ease with which it was employed by the Society for Constitutional Information, an organization of reformers primarily interested in "restoring" popular elections for members of the House of Commons. "Let the ingenuous and uncorrupted part of our countrymen," the Society urged Britons in the early 1780s, "decide which are the real friends of the constitution, and which the introducers of innovation; those who would preserve it in its original vigour, or those who, with a seeming reverence for the forms, would annihilate the spirit."[67]

In the polemics of a constitutional debate, a forensic vocabulary was employed. The constitutional values were values familiar to us, true enough—"rights," "popular," "freedom," and the like. But the operative words were eighteenth-century, ancient-constitution words, "restore," "original purity," and "preserve." They were not the words of the nineteenth-century constitution of command: "reform," "change," or "decree." "May what you have already gained," Thomas Day told the Society for Constitutional Information at one of its county meetings for 1780, "be only a prelude to that complete redress, which can alone restore the power and freedom of this nation, by restoring the Constitution to its original purity."[68] Why not expect your readers to believe it? After all, the British knew that both the English and the Scottish constitutions had been "restored" less than a century earlier. "[I]t is our peculiar Happiness in this Reign," Samuel Johnson then said of William III, "that we live under a Prince who had no other Business here, but to restore the Constitution; which, as his Declaration speaks, was wholly overturned in former Reigns."[69]

CHAPTER SIX

The Forensic History of Gothicism and Saxonism

There is no need to ask further whether people in the late eighteenth century believed in the reality of the timeless law of the ancient constitution. It is enough to note that some students of liberty seemed to say that every restraint on power existing in 1785 had always existed,[1] but it should also be noted that supporters of prerogativism occasionally used changeless constitutionalism in much the same way for opposite purposes. It was during the very last year of that century that John Reeves was arguing that, although the House of Commons had, over the years of its existence, increased in "energy" and influence, "it has not altered the *quality of its* station; *that* remains precisely the same." "[T]he principles of Government," Reeves insisted, "like those of Nature, are not to be changed by a change in unessential modifications . . . the constitutional relation and dependence of the House of Commons upon the Crown was precisely the same in the days of Henry VIII[,] of Queen Elizabeth, and in our own times."[2] Reeves, who was clearly writing law, not history, put the timelessness of forensic history to work in a way it usually was not used, to promote prerogativism.

The question for this chapter is not the belief of forensic historians but how eighteenth-century forensic historians used the tools of ancient constitutionalism. Robert Brady notwithstanding, the probative menhirs of ancient constitutionalism in the eighteenth century remained what they had been in the seventeenth. They included Gothicism, Saxonism, Normanism, feudalism, the prescriptiveness of representative government, and the uses of Magna Carta.

The uses of Magna Carta during the eighteenth century were the uses of constitutionalism. Although constitutional and legal perceptions of Magna Carta changed from generation to generation, there was one image fairly constant throughout the eighteenth century. Magna Carta was thought of, not as a set of specific rules or generalities about governance, but in terms of fundamental, immutable law. For contemporaries of Robert Walpole and Edmund Burke, Magna Carta resembled an organic instrument not unlike what the American constitutions would come to be regarded in the next century, except that instead of allocating power, the primary function of Magna Carta (as reinterpreted in the eighteenth century) was to enhance individual liberty and restrain governmental discretion.

We know more about what Magna Carta was supposed to be in the eighteenth century than how it was supposed to operate. Unfortunately, most students of constitutional law who discussed it wrote platitudes, without giving heed to the legal mechanics of either enforcement or procedural administration. "The great Bulwark of Liberty and Property, is *Magna Charta;* the Charter of *English* Liberties," Giles Jacob, the law writer contended, thinking more of ancient-constitutional polemics than of King John and the barons. "[B]y this Law, the Freedom of our Ancestors, glorious in the History of their Times, was inviolably preserved; and by this Statute, 'tis hop'd we shall be always free from Slavery and Servitude."[3] Other eighteenth-century students of the constitution called Magna Carta "the chrystal fountain from whence our laws and liberties flow,"[4] "the basis of our liberties and constitution,"[5] and the "fundamental plan"[6] or "foundation of English liberty."[7] In England John Wilkes referred to Magna Carta as "the great preserver of the lives, freedom, and property of Englishmen,"[8] "that glorious inheritance, that distinguishing characteristic of Englishmen,"[9] and in New England a Boston newspaper boasted that it "secures the property and person of the meanest beggar."[10]

This sloganeering reflected almost no positive law. It was, at best, a broad constitutionalism intended to ward off the resurgence of arbitrary power by propagating "first principles" of liberty. It must not be thought that this aspect of eighteenth-century ancient constitutionalism was a repudiation of Robert Brady for that would be according Brady and scientific history more influence than they enjoyed. Brady was too royalist to be more than a minor consideration in constitutional affairs, contending, for example, that Magna Carta had been a "grant" or "concession" of royal grace and pleasure, and, at most, was "only a *Relaxation* of the *Feudal* Military Law, and was contrived, and Granted chiefly for the ease of Military Men . . . [who] caused it to be drawn up, [and] never intended it should be of much advantage to ordinary Free-men, or Free-holders."[11]

Although extreme, Brady's theory of law should not be passed over lightly. It is a concise summary of the constitutional doctrine that eighteenth-century students of Magna Carta thought they were combatting. Surely Jean Louis De Lolme had it or some similar legal notion in mind when, in the 1770s, he took pains to insist that King John's charter aided the general mass of the people, not just the aristocracy.[12] There was no need for De Lolme to cite specific articles, offer historical evidence, or discuss "original intent." Just to mention the "Great Charter" seems to have been enough to remind readers of what they already knew—that Magna Carta was a virtual constitution of individual rights.

> [W]hat extent, what caution, do we see in the provisions made by the Great Charter! All the objects for which men naturally wish to live in a state of society were settled in its various articles. The judicial authority was regulated. The person and property of the individual were secured. The safety of the merchant and stranger was provided for. The higher class of citizens gave up a number of oppressive privileges which they had long accustomed themselves to look upon as their undoubted rights. Nay, the implements of tillage of the *bondman,* or slave, were also secured to him: and for the first time, perhaps, in the annals of the world, a civil war was terminated by making stipulations in favour of those unfortunate men to whom the avarice and lust of dominion, inherent in human nature, continued, over the greatest part of the earth, to deny the common rights of mankind.[13]

Whether wishful thinking or factual nonsense, analysis of this sort led some critics to wonder if eighteenth-century encomiasts of Magna Carta ever read the document.[14] Yet by the second half of the eighteenth century Magna Carta could be accurately described as an instrument containing "the common rights of mankind," even if none of those rights had ever occurred to the barons who confronted King John. There was little reason actually to read the document; what was important about Magna Carta in the eighteenth century was not what it said but what it had come to mean. Had King John died on the way to Runnymede and Magna Carta never been issued, eighteenth-century constitutionalists would have "quoted" in its stead some other official or suppositive declaration of restraints on Norman government power, the coronation oath of Henry I perhaps. Magna Carta was, after all, but a medieval codicil reaffirming the ancient constitution. "For it is agreed by all our historians," Sir William Blackstone insisted, "that the great charter of king John was for the most part compiled from the antient customs of the realm, or the laws of king Edward the confessor; by which they usually mean the old common law, which was established under our Saxon princes, before the rigors of feodal tenure and other hardships were imported from the continent by the kings of the norman line."[15] That is, Charles Francis Sheridan agreed, even though he was attacking Blackstone's constitutional jurisprudence, "Magna Charta however distant the date of it, was even then only declaratory of the Principal Grounds of fundamental laws and liberties long antecedent to itself, and consequently still longer antecedent to the very existence of Parliaments."[16]

The jurisprudence of Magna Carta in the eighteenth century, therefore, was a rejection of the constitutionalism of arbitrary power. The rights that it enunciated "were not the grants and concessions of our Princes," a pamphlet that the American colonists attributed to Lord Chancellor Somers insisted, "but recognitions of what we have reserv'd unto ourselves in the original institution of our government, and of what had always appertain'd unto us by common law, and immemorial custom."[17] Magna Carta, in other words, was a restatement of the ancient constitution, "a Renewal of the *Original Contract.*"[18] It was "declarative of ancient rights" according to a late eighteenth-century political catechism,[19] *"declaratory* of the *principal* Grounds, of the *fundamental* Laws and Liberties of *England,"* according to a New England newspaper,[20] or, in the words of Algernon Sidney, "only an abridgment of our ancient laws and customs."[21]

Reduced to its essentials, the legal theory was pure ancient constitutionalism. "The contents of Magna Carta," an Irish publication noted in 1769, "is the undoubted inheritance of England, being *their antient and approved laws;* so antient, that they seem to be of the same standing with the nation. . . . [T]hey passed through all the British, Roman, Danish, Saxon, and Norman times, with little or no alteration in the main."[22] What this statement intended, of course, was not to teach a lesson in history, but to propagate a principle of constitutional law. "The rights of *Magna Charta* depend not on the Will of the Prince, or the Will of the Legislature," Connecticut lawmakers were told by a former rector of Yale College, "but they are the inherent natural Rights of *Englishmen:* secured and confirmed they may be by the Legislature, but not derived from nor dependent on their *Will.*"[23] These words were published in 1744. They stated the precise legal principle upon which Americans would fight their revolution 32 years later. In truth, it seems to have been universal American constitutional theory—much more so, certainly, than in Britain—that the fundamental law of Magna Carta limited the legislature as much as it limited the crown. For example, a Boston printer imprisoned without jury trial by the colonial House of Representatives argued: "The Rights of *Magna Charta* depend not on the Will of the Prince or the Will of the Legislature; but they are the *inherent* natural Rights of *Englishmen:* secured and confirmed they may be by the Legislature, but not derived *from* nor dependent *on* their Will."[24]

To agree that Gothicism was not the intellectual force in the eighteenth century that it had been in the seventeenth,[25] does not mean that it was not as forensically potent. "My notion of *Whig,* I mean a real *Whig,*" the editor of a pro-American, antimonarchist London newspaper explained six months after the battle of Lexington, "is, that he is one who is exactly for keeping up the strictness of the true old Gothic constitution."[26] The appeal was to the original ancient constitution: to that original ancient constitution of Germanic liberty, which, during the Dark Ages, had been the rule of government across the European continent, ranging from Hungary in the east to Sweden in the north.[27] "The Rough draught of this happy

Constitution," Jared Eliot told Connecticut's lawmakers, summing up the eighteenth-century understanding of the Gothic constitution, "was brought into *Britain* by the *Saxons* & *Angles,* into *France* by the *Franks,* into *Spain* & *Italy* by the *Goths, Vandals* and other *Northern Nations:* And it has been Refining, Polishing, Reforming and acquiring Strength for many Generations. While other Nations, who were equally Blessed with this Form of Government, by their supine Negligence . . . have suffer'd these Priviledges to be lost. Indeed, There is still subsisting the *Dyets* in *Germany,* the *Cortes* in *Spain* and the *Parliaments* in *France,* which are but faint Shadows of that once glorious Substance they have lost & we by God's Mercy still Enjoy."[28] What should be noted is that the importance of the "history" told by eighteenth-century commentators like Eliot did not lie in the story—not even in the story of how liberty had once operated and how liberty had been protected. The importance, rather, lay in the antiquity of the prescriptive right that eighteenth-century Britons possessed in that "happy" Gothic constitution with its "glorious Substance," especially glorious by eighteenth-century constitutional values because that substance was liberty.

Gothic constitutionalism was liberty because, translated into positive law, it was limited government of independent people,[29] protected by popular institutions such as trial by jury[30] as well as by the tripartite balance of monarchy, aristocracy, and democracy.[31] Perhaps the chief element that the eighteenth century added to the seventeenth century's version of the Gothic constitution was an emphasis on the elected kingship in the decades following the coronation of William and Mary. Gothic kings, it was said, had been elected to office for good behavior. Should they prove "unfit" for liberty "they were easily, and without much ceremony, set aside from reigning, and another of their family placed upon the throne in their stead."[32]

Although the prescriptive antiquity of Gothic constitutionalism was used to argue for limitations upon eighteenth-century British government, including the American claim to the right of taxation by consent,[33] its chief forensic uses were to enhance the people's rights to be represented and to be ruled by the principles of liberty. The fact that "[a]ll matters of importance were settled by the Ancient Germans, in the Common Council of the Nation,"[34] meant that the right to be represented in Parliament continued inviolate in the eighteenth century, if "that right was exercised and preserved under the Saxon and Norman Kings; even to our own days,"[35] which, of course, it had been. In fact, it has been said that "[t]he term 'Gothic' came into extensive use in the seventeenth century as an epithet employed by the Parliamentary leaders to defend the prerogatives of Parliament against the pretensions of the King to absolute right to govern England,"[36] a forensic-history use *par excellence.*

"Gothic" was also a trope for "free," reflecting the "liberty" purpose of Gothicism in eighteenth-century law.[37] "Our Civil Constitution," the Durham assize of 1764 was reminded in what was by then the classic, taught explanation, "was from the first founded on the liberty of the

People; which was an essential form of government, that universally prevailed among the northern nations."[38]

Gothicism had what might loosely be termed a "negative" and a "positive" side. The negative was a theoretical negative on power. Just about any proposed government action of an arbitrary nature could be opposed on grounds that it departed from Gothic freedom. The "positive" side summoned constitutionalists to vigilance. When the Gothic constitution was argued, it was usually with the implied reminder of how all the Gothic nations except Great Britain had lost their ancient liberty. Viscount Bolingbroke was particularly fond of the theme. "Let us justify this Conduct," he wrote of living by the spirit of liberty, "by persisting in it, and continue to ourselves the peculiar Honour of maintaining the Freedom of our *Gothick Institution of Government,* when so many other Nations, who enjoyed the same, have lost theirs."[39] In the colony of Pennsylvania James Logan said much the same to the provincial legislature. *"Britain,"* Logan memorialized Pennsylvania's House of Representatives in 1724, "is now almost the only remaining Kingdom that enjoys the ancient perfect State of Liberty, with which other Countries were formerly blessed, till politick Arts, and Contrivances of Men truly ambitious and designing, subverted those Liberties, and betrayed the unhappy Subjects into the Power of one Person, whose absolute Will became the only Rule of his Government, and his Pleasure the only Standard of all their Laws."[40] Gothicism, consequently, provided an historical perspective always useful to the opposition, seldom to administration, and was employed by those opposed to power, not often by those wanting power exercised.

We may pass by without consideration the forensic uses made in the eighteenth century of the ancient British constitution of pre-Roman and pre-Saxon times. There are two reasons. First, the uses were the same as the uses of Gothicism. That the Celtic people of Britannia had possessed rights of consenting to laws either in person or by representation[41] and of having trial by jury,[42] may have been of antiquarian interest, but because no one pretended to know much about the substance of these rights or how they had been exercised, they contributed little to constitutional debate. Second, the Saxons, as direct heirs of the Goths, were much more important than the British Celts because writers who linked eighteenth-century liberty to Gothic liberty claimed that they could establish the continuity necessary to prove prescriptive right. Lack of continuity relegated the ancient British Celtics to minor interest. They proved little more than the universality of a usage, not significant in establishing constitutional rights. "If we look back to the Times of the Saxons," the Earl of Abingdon explained, "whence we must date the Origin of our Constitution (for although there were many *British* Rights or Customs engrafted upon it, and which do still remain, and although the Britons themselves were free; yet the Form of the Constitution is certainly of Gothic Institution, and brought by the Saxons over into England,) we shall find that the Constitution was . . . of a *mixed* Nature; and its Principles that of Liberty."[43]

Abingdon was writing of the Saxon constitution and of the current eighteenth-century British constitution, for, forensically speaking, they were one and the same. If scholars would study "Anglo-Saxon government as it was at first settled and administered in this island," Bishop Samuel Squire contended, they would be able "to trace out the original stamina of our present most happy constitution."[44] To say in 1771 that "this excellent form of government was established in our island above 1300 years ago" and that "we are indebted to them [the Saxons] for all that is beneficial to society in our present civil and political system" was to make a strong statement about prescriptive rights under the constitution of 1771, as well as a much weaker statement about the Saxons.[45] For as James Tyrrell had said three quarters of a century earlier, "it is certain that the Freemen of *England* have always from beyond all times of memory enjoyed the same Fundamental Rights and Privileges (I mean in substance) that they do at this day."[46] By stressing substance he meant, of course, that first principles were the same then as now. He did not mean that every form of action, mesne process, procedural practice, or adjective rule was the same.

Except for theorists favoring law-as-command, and scholars doubting the historical accuracy of Saxon freedom,[47] there was remarkable general consensus about those first principles. They included the elected monarchy, attributed to the Saxons long before the Glorious Revolution,[48] and several democratic characteristics of governance, for among the Saxons "the people bore a considerate part in the government,"[49] including representation of the freemen,[50] annual elections,[51] and, of course, the right to trial by jury.[52]

Two lessons stood out in this forensic history: that Saxon government had been mixed, limited government,[53] and that, during its transferral from Germany to Britannia, Saxon government had lost none of the elements of Saxon liberty.[54] If anything, it was more free, "founded" as Virginia's Richard Bland claimed, "upon Principles of the most perfect Liberty."[55] It was so perfect in fact, that James Ibbetson, in a book arguing that the Saxons, not the Normans, brought feudalism to England, ended in a manner uncharacteristically floral for a legal treatise. "When we survey the Saxon constitution, that rude and irregular mass of Gothic architecture," he exclaimed, "we are sometimes presented with a proportion so exquisite, a beauty so enchanting, that we no longer despise it as the obsolete establishment of a barbarian tribe, but revere it as the foundation of the Liberty of Britain."[56] It was so perfect, indeed, so much the ideal of liberty, that if it had not existed in the Saxon past it would have had to have been concocted to serve the British and American present. "Though I would not be thought to talk like a constitutional enthusiast," Allan Ramsay insisted, "yet I am of opinion, that, if ever God Almighty did concern himself about forming a government for mankind to live happily under, it was that which was established in England by our Saxon forefathers; under which they continued to live free, and happy, for six hundred years, before the Norman conquest; when, for a time, it was totally lost or little regarded."[57] God need not have been concerned. The Norman Conquest did not permanently change the ancient constitution.

CHAPTER SEVEN

The Forensic History of the Norman Conquest

When encountering seventeenth- and eighteenth-century arguments about the Norman Conquest it is wise to be cautious. One can easily be led astray by misunderstanding the role of law. It is sometimes claimed, for example, that the debate over the Norman Conquest was a "controversy over the origin of the English Constitution."[1] True enough, but a better way of putting it is that the controversy was over the *nature* of the constitution, with origins but one of many issues in contention. There are two other problems. First, the role of history can be easily overemphasized. "In England," it has been said, "few subjects have been studied for longer than the Norman Conquest, and few have been . . . more bent and twisted in the process by misinterpretation caused by unhistorical considerations and emotions."[2] Again somewhat true, but the better view is that the considerations and emotions were constitutional. They were only incidentally "unhistorical." Second, there is the problem of oversimplifying the complexities of the issues at stake. It is not quite accurate, for instance, to say that the question for scholars of Conquest history to answer was whether "*William* the *first,* was King by *Conquest* or *Compact.*"[3] Those who claimed that William the Conqueror had not been a conqueror in the meaning of law explained his right to the English throne not only by right of contract but also by right of inheritance, by right of election, and by right of bequest (or gift).

The best that can be done in this study is to summarize, and the premises of the Norman Conquest controversy can most easily be summarized by considering the forensic history of Edward Cook's *Argumentum Anti-Normannicum.* It was, J. G A. Pocock suggests, "a minor Whig Tract," that has been "entertainingly discussed" by David C. Douglas.[4] Actually, Douglas treats the work in a fashion only a professional academic would find entertaining. *Argumentum* was part of what Douglas considered a "baleful tradition" of English history writing, a book of little significance except for exposing "the tendency of a large body of pseudo-historical literature." "Few historical treatises of the late seventeenth century," he added, "admit such easy criticism as the *Argumentum,*" but sadly, "the prejudices which animated its author" are characteristic of many other studies of the late seventeenth century "devoted to the same topic."[5]

The better view is that *Argumentum* was a common lawyer's brief. After all, it was entitled *An Argument Proving,* not a "history proving." Moreover, it probably deserves to be remembered as a rather courageous brief, for it was published in 1682, and by claiming that the ancient constitution had not been altered by the Conquest, it could have made Restoration England uncomfortable for Cook.

Cook, a barrister of the Middle Temple, began his treatise just as he would have begun a brief, by framing the issues or "questions" he intended to answer. There were four: "I. *Whether* William, *Duke* of Normandy, (who *was afterwards* William *the First) got the* IMPERIAL CROWN *of* England *by the Sword, and made* an ABSOLUTE CONQUEST *of the Nation at his first Entrance*?; II. *Whether this first* William *did* ABOLISH *all the* ENGLISH LAWS, *and changed the whole Frame and Constitution of the Government*?; III. *Whether it be true, That the* ENGLISH *had neither Estates nor Fortunes left, but all was divided between the* KING *and his* Normans?; IV. *Whether it be not* a *grand Error to affirm, That there were no* ENGLISH *Men* in *the* COMMON COUNCIL *of the whole* Kingdom?"[6] These questions were legal questions and were important, not because Cook was interested in the history of the Norman Conquest, but because Charles II was on the throne and the Duke of York was heir presumptive.

We need not spend time on Cook's evidence. It is spread over 110 pages of "history" that clearly was forensic history, proving that William the Conqueror had never been a conqueror—that is, not a conqueror in the meaning of law. His readers, Cook concluded, should "rest satisfied in these great and powerful Authorities, which I have here presented to publick view, and serious consideration: and I think these have sufficiently made out and proved, That,

> 1. *William the first,* vulgarly called the *Conqueror,* did *not* get the *Imperial Crown of England* by the *Sword,* nor made an *absolute Conquest* of the Nation at his *first entrance.*
>
> 2. Nor that he *abolished* all the *English Laws,* or changed the *whole Frame* and Constitution of the *Saxon Government.* But
>
> 3. That the *English* had still *Estates* and *Fortunes* continued to them; and that it was a *great mistake,* in any way to affirm, That the *king* and his *Normans* divided and *shared* them all among them. As likewise,

> 4. In the fourth place, It has been a grand Error to ascertain, That there was no *English men* in the *Common Council* of the whole Kingdom, in the reign of *William* the *Conqueror*.[7]

It is worthwhile to consider one of the aspects of *Argumentum Anti-Normannicum* that Professor Douglas thought amusing. His reaction to the frontispiece to the book (see frontpeice of this book) underlines some of the different perspectives dividing the twentieth-century academic prepared to judge arguments about the past only in terms of the accepted, taught canons of scientific scholarship, and the seventeenth-century forensic historian who believed himself engaged in a serious constitutional struggle. Douglas wrote: "The spirit of the treatise was expressed in an allegorical frontispiece which depicted a highly complacent Britannia presenting to a dejected William a sceptre with one hand and the Laws of St. Edward with the other, while William in return gave thanks to his 'Sacred Queen' for the dominion she had conditionally bestowed upon him."[8] For Cook, by contrast, the picture was so serious he published "An Explanation of the Frontispiece." William, Cook pointed out, had defeated Harold the Saxon.

> The *Rest* of the ENGLISH (if they had not look'd upon his coming, as a Design to *conquer* the *Nation,* and not to assert *his pretended legal Title* against HAROLD,) were then able to have driven him back to his *own Country* . . . but DUKE WILLIAM and the ENGLISH soon came to an Agreement, and the latter entered into *solemn Compact* to make him *king.*
>
> Thereupon BRITANNIA holds forth to him the Scepter with *one* Hand, And
> With the *other* shews him the *excellent* and most famous *Laws* of St. EDWARD.
> As also, at the same Time, a *Noble Prelat[e]* tenders him the *Coronation Oath.*[9]

In contrast to those who, in the twentieth century, have found Cook entertaining, Robert Brady in the seventeenth century was concerned enough to write an answer to *Argumentum.*[10] Again there is no need to detail the debate. Some of Brady's observations on Cook's first question should sum up the drift. "This *Question,*" Brady contended, "is not truly stated, for it ought not to be put, whether at his first Entrance or Invasion he [Duke William] obtained the Crown by the Sword, *but whether in process of time, and by degrees,* he *did not by force and artifice, make an absolute Conquest of the Nation*?" Proof was a matter of conjecture and inference. Just what William had said and promised or what oaths he took were immaterial. "We seldom, or never read of any one who designed to Conquer a Nation or People, that told them before hand, that he would *deprive* them of their *Estates* or *Fortunes, give* them new *Laws,* or *abridge* their *Liberties,* especially if he had any pretence of a Title, as Duke *William* then had to *England.*" Even Cook's "proof from the Conquerors taking an Oath signifies nothing," Brady argued, "unless he can also *prove* that he *kept* it."[11]

Like Douglas, Brady faulted Cook's history. Unlike Douglas, he faulted it not for its methodology but for its constitutional law. To prove a different constitution Brady answered forensic history with forensic argument. His conclusion can be summed up by quoting a paraphrasing of it by his chief critic, William Atwood. *"William the Conqueror brought in a New Law, and imposed it upon the People,"* Atwood summarized. *"The greatest part of the Antient Law, as it was brought hither by the Normans, was exacted and observed* by, and upon, *only the Normans:* For the *English,* they had no *Property* or *Rights* left: And so were all *Outlaws."*[12] In other words, William of Normandy not only had conquered the English but had conquered constitutional Saxonism and the ancient constitution as well.

The Eighteenth-Century Conquest

Christopher Hill has suggested that with the election of William and Mary, "The Conquest theory had ceased to be a threat and became a joke."[13] If so, a surprising number of constitutionalists and lawyers were not let in on the fun. Forensic historians, including distinguished jurists like Sir Matthew Hale and Sir Martin Wright, continued to argue that William's military conquest had not been a constitutional conquest.[14] Indeed, members of the House of Lords thought the conquest theory serious enough in 1693 to resolve, "That the assertion of king William's and queen Mary's being king and queen by conquest was highly injurious to their majesties, and inconsistent with the principles, on which this Government is founded, and tending to subversion of the rights of the people."[15] Certainly Bishop Gilbert Burnet did not think the matter a joke. The resolution was directed against his book, *A Pastoral Letter Writ by the Right Reverend Father in God Gilbert, Lord Bishop of Sarum, to the Clergy of his Diocess, Concerning the Oaths of Allegiance and Supremacy of K. William and Q. Mary*. The Commons joined the Lords in ordering that the book, and another entitled *King William and Queen Mary Conquerors* "be burnt by the Hand of the common Hangman."[16]

That Parliament was so intent that William III not be styled a conqueror indicates more was at stake than merely history writing or dealing with jokes. Less dramatic but just as serious were all the seventeenth- and eighteenth-century constitutional scholars who devoted volumes and uncounted pages to proving that William the Conqueror had not been a conqueror. As explained above, the reason for the fuss was the law of conquest. "[I]f the King's Title and Government was as a *Conqueror,"* Nathaniel Bacon had explained in the 1640s, "then was his Will the onely Law, and can administer no cause of complaint of wrong and oppression."[17]

There was little dispute about the law of conquest. True, there were a few commentators on law who denied that conquest affected the rights of the people,[18] and there were others who argued that a conqueror succeeded only to the place and power of the deposed monarch,[19] but the prevalent view was that a conqueror acquired absolute power and that absolute power descended down through the successors of a conqueror. Hobbes could be quoted on that law but Hale is much better authority. "[I]t seems to be admitted as a kind of Law among all Nations," Hale explained, "That in case of a Solemn War between Supream Princes, the Conqueror acquires a Right of Dominion, as well as a Property over the Things and Persons that are fully conquered."[20]

A conqueror conquered everything—the deposed monarch, the people, the land, and even the ancient constitution. A conqueror's authority obtained legitimacy from raw power, it did not depend on original contract, custom, prescription, or consent. That is why the question of William I's entry to the throne was so important to Cook and Brady. If the Normans had conquered England in the meaning of law, the Saxon original contract would have been canceled and the ancient constitution obliterated.[21] Whatever the Saxon constitution may have been it was entirely "swallow'd up at the *Conquest,*" Lord Hervey wrote, disposing of the ancient constitution with one historical and legal conclusion.[22] "Admit a *Conquest,*" William Atwood warned, "and the Inheritance which every one claims in the Laws will be maintainable only as a *naked Right,* and *naked Rights* are thin and metaphysical Notions, which few are Masters or Judges of."[23] The whig divine, Samuel Johnson, agreed. "*Conquering* and *Enslaving* the Nation," he wrote, "are equivalent Words."[24]

Atwood tells us why seventeenth- and eighteenth-century constitutionalists got so upset when William the Conqueror was called a conqueror. A legal conquest would have drained both the common law and English civil rights of their prescriptive authority and their prescriptive shield. It may be that the argument was based on a projection of the "worst case," but that was the case on which most eighteenth-century constitutional arguments were based in Great Britain and in the American colonies. "The friends, therefore, to absolute power," the Irish law professor, Francis Stoughton Sullivan, cautioned, "sensible that the original constitution is against them, choose to look no farther back than the Conquest. Then, say they, the Saxon government and laws were extinguished, the English by Conquest lost their rights, . . . and the Conqueror and his son William acted as despotic monarchs."[25]

For constitutionalists who were lawyers, such as Sullivan, there did not have to be an actual and immediate danger to be motivated to take up pen and raise the alarm against anyone saying that William the Conqueror had been a conqueror. Under the unwritten British constitution, the potential alone had to be prevented by denying its possibility. In his famous book on the English constitution, De Lolme attributed "the constitution to a Norman rather than a Saxon origin." His 1807 editor was so upset by this slip that he appendaged a footnote, hoping to qualify the implication of William I's absolutism by pointing that "instead of *subverting* the Saxon Constitution," William, even though he "introduced many of the laws of Normandy," also "seems to have retained a considerable proportion of those which had been established in England."[26]

Twenty-first-century historians who do not credit the persuasion of ideas may be puzzled by the fears of constitutionalists such as De Lolme's editor. Even when today's scholars respect the conquest theory they seek its authority in the wrong places. "Mr. Pocock . . . thinks that I exaggerate the extent to which the theory of absolutism based on conquest was used by the Royalists," Christropher Hill has written. "He may be right: it is indeed difficult to find more than scattered pieces of written evidence for it. But why did the parliamentarians find it necessary so regularly and consistently to attack a view which nobody held? . . . . I suspect that the conquest theory must have been prevalent at a rather low level of argument, perhaps in the sort of sermons that did not get into print."[27] A good point, except why look at sermons? When discussing matters of law such as the resistance theory, the authority of the original contract, or the conquest theory, why do historians not think to look at *legal* treatises? Not just in the seventeenth century but even during the age of the American Revolution, warnings of how despotic the Normans had been were to be found in all sorts of legal treatises, including studies of jurisprudence.[28]

There were, to be sure, many constitutionalists who insisted that the Norman Conquest had been a legal conquest,[29] but only some of these used the Conquest to contend for absolute power[30]—perhaps not even those saying that absolute power vested in parliament rather than the monarchy. What troubled constitutionalists like De Lolme's editor was the legal potential that, even if not an immediate likelihood, was safer resisted than ignored. "[S]hould we allow our Laws to have an uncertain Original," John Fortescue-Aland warned, "I fear that some People would of themselves fix their Original from *William* the First, and if that should be taken for granted, I don't know what ill use, the Champions of Absolute Monarchy may be inclined to make, of such a Concession; that our Laws began in a Conqueror's Time, and consequently were given by a Conqueror."[31] After all, what was presented to be an undeniable fact, William's conquest over the ancient constitution, had been cited during the Interregnum to legitimize the arbitrary power exercised by the Long Parliament and by Oliver Cromwell.[32]

Rather than dispute the law of conquest,[33] seventeenth- and eighteenth-century constitutionalists disputed the history of the Conquest. It was forensic history at its best—arguing the law of conquest against the facts of the Norman Conquest to prove the Conquest had not been a conquest within the meaning of law. Just about every explanation genius could think of was thrown into the constitutional controversy—all undoubtedly bad or suppositive history, but argued as points of law with at best a secondary regard to historical proof. Once more it is not possible to survey the debate; all that can be offered is a sample of some of the forensic points raised.

Undoubtedly the most frequently argued fact was whether William had conquered the Kingdom of England or had conquered only Harold the Saxon[34] in a personal trial by battle won over an usurper.[35] Partly legal and partly factual was the argument that the word *conquer* had had a different legal meaning in the eleventh century than it had for the lawyers serving the House of Stuart.[36] William, it was contended, had not acted as an eighteenth-century conqueror might have acted either by subjecting the land and law to his will[37] or by "destroying the Liberty which was the vital Principle of the Constitution."[38] One reason why William had not been the tyrant Brady pictured him to be was that the "conquest" had readily been acquiesced in, or so it was claimed. The argument was not one of historical fact but of constitutional law. To say that the Anglo-Saxons had acquiesced in the "conquest" was, as a matter of law, the same as saying that William had obtained "the crown by a free choice and submission of the Peers and body of the people,"[39] taking "the Ordinary Coronation Oath of all lawfull [Saxon] Kings."[40] In other words, he had become king "by a kind of mutual Agreement, and express compact"[41] or he had become king "by Election."[42]

The strongest argument for William not being a conqueror—in point of constitutional law, not history—was that William took the English throne by claim of right,[43] either as the heir of Edward the Confessor or from Edward's grant.[44] The implications of either fact changed the legal nature of the Conquest in every respect. For if William took the throne as Edward's heir, he became king under the revered laws of St. Edward.[45] The Conqueror would not have conquered the ancient constitution, after all. He became king instead, under the law of the ancient constitution, and his heirs succeeded to his right because of that law.[46]

There was a variation on the Conquest-was-not-a-conquest argument encountered with increasing frequency in the eighteenth-century literature after the better history of Brady and his followers made it difficult to deny that William had come to the throne by the sword. It was the assertion that the ancient constitution had proven too strong for the Normans. There had been a legal conquest, it would seem, but then the conquerors had been conquered in turn by the law of the conquered. The ancient constitution had been simply too cherished by the Anglo-Saxon people or too suitable for English life to have been laid aside for long. *"[A]bsolute Monarchy,"* Viscount Bolingbroke confidently asserted, "could never be established in *Britain;* no, not even by *Conquest.* The Rights of the People were soon re-asserted; the Laws of the *Confessor* were restored; and the third Prince of this Race, *Henry* the 1st, covenanted in a solemn Speech to his People for their Assistance against his Brother *Robert* and the *Normans,* by promising that *sacred Charter,* which was in other Reigns so often and so solemnly confirmed, by engaging to maintain his Subjects in *their ancient Liberties,* to *follow their Advice,* and to rule Them in Peace with *Prudence* and *Mildness."*[47]

It was a remarkable turnabout, so remarkable that only lawyers and constitutionalists could have believed the story. One of the fruits of conquest had been snatched from the Conqueror or his successors by the resilience and superior merits of the ancient constitution. "The People," John Campbell surmised in 1774, "shewed not only an attachment to, but also a passionate Love for their Laws, by continually demanding them, they were often promised, and in some Measure were at last, indeed, gradually and partially restored. At this very Day they are the Basis of the most valuable Parts of our Constitution."[48] Put another way, because Anglo-Saxons were so devoted to the rights and liberties of the ancient constitution, one of the Norman kings—William I, Henry I, or perhaps Henry II—adapted the conquered laws of the conquered English to the governance of both the conquered and the conquerors. By this theory, the continuous thread of Gothic liberty was preserved,[49] making Magna Carta a superfluous, though still treasured promulgation.

The Evidence of Conquest

The concept of a law irrepressible by power because popularly cherished was a marvelously manipulative forensic theory of the dynamics of legality and the strength of the rule of law. Even Blackstone succumbed to the enticement of its simplicity when he agreed that the most extortionate of all Norman innovations, feudalism, had received the consent of Parliament. The introduction "of the feodal tenures into England, by king William," he pointed out, "does not seem to have been effected immediately after the conquest, nor by the mere arbitrary will and power of the conqueror; but to have been consented to by the great council of the nation long after his title was established."[50]

Blackstone was disposing of the most troublesome historical fact standing between eighteenth-century liberty and its prescriptive derivation from the ancient constitution. Feudalism—the law of feudal tenures, incidents of tenure, and feudal status—was the chief piece of evidence used by those arguing that the Norman Conquest had been a legal conquest. Theorists and historians who, like Brady, insisted that feudalism was a Norman import, did so, James Tyrrell bemourned, because "they, being greater friends to the Arbitrary Power of Kings, than to the Laws and Liberties of their Country, lay down the Hypothesis of a Conquest, thereby to confer on the Prince an absolute power to break our Laws, and seize upon our Liberties and Properties at his Pleasure."[51] All that was arbitrary and oppressive in eighteenth-century English law could be attributed to feudalism, William Jones claimed in 1782:

> What caused the absurd, . . . odious distinction between *free* and *base* holdings [of real property], and thus excluded copyholds of any value? The feudal principle. What introduced an order of men, called villains, transferable, like cattle, and with the land which they stocked? The feudal principle. What excludes [from the franchise] the holders of beneficial leases? The feudal principle. What made personalty, in those times, of little or no estimation? The feudal principle. What raised the silly notion, that the property, not the person of the subject was to be represented? The feudal principle. What

> prevented the large provision in the act of *Henry* IV. by which *all freeholders* were declared electors, from being extended to *all* holders of *property*, however denominated, however inconsiderable? The same infernal principle, which then subdued and stifled the genuine equalifying spirit of our constitution.

There was a constitutional solution to the arbitrary legacy of feudalism, Jones announced, and it belonged to forensic history. "[I]f we find that this demon was himself in the process of time subdued, . . . we shall not hesitate to pronounce, that, by the *spirit* of our constitution, all *Englishmen*, having property of any kind or quantity, are entitled to votes in chusing parliamentary delegates."[52] For about two hundred years, that had been the task of forensic historians: to prove that feudalism had not been a Norman imposition: not a product of the Conquest, imposed by the Conqueror's will and pleasure.

The forensic historical task was to deny the historically undeniable, to prove that the Conqueror who was not a conqueror had not imposed as law what he had certainly imposed as fact. The arguments were often made in the alternative. If one was not accepted, try another. Some proposals did not attract much support, as, for example, the solution offered by the English barrister James Ibbetson and the Scots advocate John Dalrymple, that feudalism was Gothic law, first brought to England by the Saxons, and made internecine to liberty by Norman abuse.[53] Another solution, equally strained, was the suggestion that even though it was a Norman import, feudalism had not been introduced into England by the Conqueror but by William II,[54] or, if brought in by the Conqueror, it had been a secondary development, not part of the spoils of conquest.[55]

A slightly better forensic argument, advanced by Vinerian Professor Richard Wooddeson and by Judge Martin Wright of King's Bench, was that the Anglo-Saxons had been "totally Strangers to the *Feudal* Law, and were ignorant of the Extent and Consequences of it."[56] As a result, when "that national synod or parliament, which was convened for this important purpose," adopted feudalism, the English had been unaware of just what they were being asked to do. "From the use of a few feudal expressions, probably little understood by these legislators, inferences were drawn [by later Norman lawyers] tending to aggrandize each feudal superior, and in particular to advance the prerogatives of the crown."[57] Not until somewhat later did the Anglo-Saxons discover they were committed to much more than a program of military service. In terms of law, feudalism was the result of Norman fraud, not Norman conquest.[58]

The best forensic argument depended more on law than history. It limited feudalism as narrowly as possible—to those areas of law having the least to do with civil rights. There were three origins for eighteenth-century English law, Wooddeson explained. They were Saxon, feudal, and Roman. "The frame of our whole constitution, the trial by jury, and many received doctrines respecting crimes and punishments, may be considered as of

Anglo-Saxon original: much of the law concerning landed estates depends on feudal principles; and in contracts affecting personal property, even our legal judicatures (as distinguished from those of equity) have been long acquainted with the use of the Roman institutions."[59] Farfetched, true enough, but it solved the feudal dilemma by limiting the feudal origins to estates in land and leaving constitutional law bathed in the liberty of Saxonism.

The ultimate defense against the precedent of feudalism was the doctrine of consent. If the Anglo-Saxons had been asked to consent to feudalism and if they had done so, then it had not been an imposed policy, and would not be evidence proving that the Norman Conquest had been a conquest in the meaning of law. Here forensic history came to the aid of law. Both Blackstone and Wooddeson have been quoted saying that the "national synod or parliament" had been "convened" to give consent—even though a century earlier Brady had "proved" that parliament had not existed in Norman times. "Tenures," Judge Wright agreed, "however grievous or odious they became in their Consequences, were not imposed, but nationally and freely consented to."[60]

One way of implying the free consent of the people was by establishing the reception by the gradual, deliberate growth of an institution through custom. The technique was especially popular among common lawyers in the late eighteenth century after Blackstone used it to argue for popular acceptance of the common law. Judge Wright employed it to prove that feudalism had not been imposed by the Normans. "Feudal Policy," he argued, "did not at once prevail in the several Parts of *Europe,* by a conquering power, or in a legislative uniform Manner, but that it obtaining as a mere Policy, and as such, gradually spreading itself over the Western Parts of the World, was variously received, every Nation so modelling it, as to preserve its Aim, and at the same Time to make it conform as far as possible with the Notions of Government and Conditions of Property entertained and established in each Country, Antecedent to its Reception of such Policy."[61] In fact, it was the free acceptance of feudalism by the Anglo-Saxons that provided them the leverage needed to force Henry I's novation of the original contract resuscitating the ancient constitution. The explanation was as marvelously illustrative of the common-law mind as it was ahistorical.

> Our Ancestors again, who were not direct *Beneficiaries,* but had barely consented to a *Fiction* of *Tenure* as the meer *Substratum* of a new military Policy, must needs look upon such Fruits or Consequences of *Tenure,* as arbitrary Conclusions from Principles that had not, as to them, any Foundation in Reason or Fact, and as in Truth they were most grievous Impositions; and yet grievous as they were, they fell short of the Exactions advanced upon *Tenures* in the Time of *William* II. our Ancestors therefore harassed and wearied with the Extravagancies of this Reign, earnestly desire to get rid of them, and having upon the Death of this King a favourable Opportunity, as they thought, from the Pretensions of *Henry* I. to obtain the utmost of their Hopes; they demand and

> are promised the Restitution of King *Edward's* Laws, and upon this Condition crown him: The King, when crowned, instantly by his *Charter* abolished all the evil Customs with which the Kingdom was oppressed, defeated the great Grievances of Tenure *relating to Relief, Wardship* and *Marriage,* and then restored the Laws of *King* Edward in all Respects, saving *Tenures,* which he retained as Amendments made by his Father, with the Assent of his Barons.[62]

A variation of these facts was to say that the laws of Edward the Confessor were "indeed confirm'd by *William* the Conqueror, at the earnest Suit of the *English;* but qualify'd with the Addition of many (*Norman*) Feudal Services and Tenures."[63] By arguing such facts, feudalism, an institution that could be used by royal absolutists or by scientific historians to prove the constitutionality of arbitrary power and that the Conquest had been a conquest in the meaning of law, became instead, in a reversal of a type familiar to "history" written by common lawyers, a basis for the law of freedom, by helping to restore the ancient constitution. Charles Yorke may have given the argument its crowning touch when he claimed that feudal "principles are the principles of freedom, of justice, and safety. The *English* constitution is formed upon them."[64]

Again, the point is not that the law was less harsh or less a departure from the law of Saxon times, but that although rules, applications, and tenures might change, "law" remained the same. Even if it were granted that there had been as great alterations in laws as was "pretended" by writers of royalist forensic history, Nathaniel Bacon concluded, "it makes nothing to the point of Conquest, so long as the new Laws are made by advice of Common-council, and for the common good; and so long as they are established to be Rules for Government."[65]

It may have been pure invention, but it was very satisfying for the inventors in their battle against arbitrary power. Not only were Norman parliaments taken for granted, but when constitutionalists looked for evidence whether either William I or Henry I acted without consulting "Parliament," they found, of course, that neither ever did. *"Parliaments* were never interrupted, nor the Right of *any Estate* taken away, however the Exercise of it might be disturb'd," Bolingbroke boasted.[66] The evidence was easily deducted from the fact that if the law of the ancient constitution remained the law despite the Conquest, the Saxon freemen remained freemen and as freemen insisted on law by consent. And so it was "true that neither *Kings,* nor *Lords,* nor both together, *could prevail over Them, or gain their Consent* to *give their Right, or the Law, up to the King's Beck. But still the* Law *remain'd Arbiter both of* King *and* People, *and the* Parliament *supreme Expounder and Judge both of it and Them."*[67] It was in this sense, William Pitt, the Earl of Chatham, told the House of Lords in 1775, that the timeless law of the ancient, fixed constitution remained, requiring a legislature of consent that neither armed force nor the submission of the people could eradicate. It remained through Norman times and Tudor times to serve the nation again in Stuart times. "It was this doctrine that was the great guide and spirit of the framers of the bill of rights at the period of the glorious revolution."[68]

The Unrevolutionary Revolution

The forensic-history question dominating seventeenth-century constitutional debate had been whether the Norman Conquest was really a conquest. The question for constitutional debate during the first half of the eighteenth century was whether the Glorious Revolution had been really a revolution—not whether William of Orange had been a conqueror.[69] The issue, John Brand wrote in 1796, was "how far the Revolution was a change of the pre-established form of Government and of the Laws?"[70] The twenty-first-century answer is that the government was changed forever, but the eighteenth century was fond of quoting William III's message to the House of Commons, "I came hither to restore the ancient constitution."[71] The claim then was that much less had changed than met the eye. What the twenty-first century sees as a new constitution, the eighteenth century saw as the ancient constitution again restored.[72]

It may be that we can no longer understand what the eighteenth century meant by a revolution preserving the ancient constitution or ever again agree with the Earl of Chatham that the framers of the Bill of Rights were codifying sections of the ancient constitution. Twenty-first-century scholars resent being fooled, and there is a notion currently rife that the drafters of the Bill of Rights tried to fool us. "The authors of the Declaration of Rights described all these rights as 'ancient' and 'undoubted,'" Lois G. Schwoerer recently complained, and then she proceeded to show that most of the rights claimed in the Declaration were neither "ancient" nor "undoubted" but "had for decades been at the centre of *contention* between the king and the parliamentary opposition."

> Now, there is nothing surprising about such an assertion. Throughout the seventeenth century, constitutional change was regularly clothed in conservative dress. What is surprising is the willingness of historians to accept this language at face value. No one would want to deny the power of the concept of the Ancient Constitution. No one would want to contest the idea that seventeenth-century politicians and lawyers regarded the Constitution as precedential and prescriptive, based upon immemorial custom, the principles of common law. But it may be that too much emphasis has been given to the Ancient Constitution and not enough to the willingness, even of lawyers, to change the Constitution and the law.[73]

There is a question to ask about this argument, but we should be careful that the question does not become the answer. The answer may seem obvious today, but in 1689 the question was whether the constitution and the law were, in fact, changed by promulgating new prohibitions or declaring new rights if those prohibitions and rights were to preserve the old constitutional theory. If the function of the ancient constitution had been to restrain arbitrary power of the crown, and if the events of the 1640s and 1680s had demonstrated that standing armies were a new ingredient of arbitrary power, cannot the seventeenth century say that a prohibition on standing armies is a reaffirmation of an ancient and undoubted right?

Members of the Convention Parliament had been careful to avoid the impression of embarking on a new constitutional beginning, or making a break with the past. There was a "public and authorized theory of what had occurred in 1688–89,"[74] which repudiated both natural law and the social contract, basing the authority of the kingship of William and Mary on the old law, including the ancient constitution and the original contract.[75] In contemplation of law, therefore, in what would become forensic history, not scientific history, "the object of the Bill of Rights was to reassert those parts of the Laws and Constitution which had been violated in act, or of which doubts were entertained." In legal theory "all change of the legal Constitution was sedulously avoided, even such as might appear evident ameliorations, and which recent experience seemed to call for."[76] It may have been the making of a "myth," but it was also "law" making, and it made good law as evidenced by the grand juries in England, which all through the century after the Glorious Revolution were charged that the law they were to apply was the law of the ancient constitution.[77]

The purpose of the "myth" makers was not to rewrite historical "nonsense" as it has been called,[78] or to disguise the fact that they were declaring to be law what they wanted to be law but knew had not been law. It was, in part, to create authority against a new theory of constitutional law threatening to supplant the validity of prescriptive, precedential custom. Arbitrary power or law as the command of the sovereign could more easily replace the older, safer definition of law if history taught that the Glorious Revolution had "made a new settlement of the whole Constitution," which was what David Hume said and which in turn was called "*a libel on the* Revolution."[79] It should not be surprising, therefore, that during the eighteenth century, proadministration, but not opposition publications, spread the themes: (1) that the Revolution was "the *Foundation* of our Civil and Religious Liberties;"[80] (2) that from the banishment of James II should be dated "the Birth of *real Liberty* in this Kingdom, and the *Establishment* at least, if not the Commencement, of every valuable Privilege we now enjoy;"[81] and (3) that before the Revolution "there was no such thing as Liberty."[82]

American whigs encountered this new theory of constitutionalism at the very outset of the prerevolutionary controversy, when Lord Chancellor Northington dismissed their claim that the customary constitution freed them from parliamentary taxation by declaring, "I seek for the liberty and constitution of this kingdom no farther back than the Revolution."[83] He may even have asserted a much more drastic point of law if we can believe one eyewitness who reported that Northington said, "He took the constitution no higher up than the Revolution as this country never had one before."[84] The lord chancellor was telling the colonists that their constitution no longer was a constitution of immutable prescriptive rights traceable to the ancient constitution. If his law was valid, their constitution was now whatever a majority of the two Houses of Parliament said it was. "The constitution of England, as it now stands, was fixed at the Revolution, in 1688," a loyalist argued after the Battle of Lexington. "What is it to us, what the constitution of England was two or three hundred or a thousand years ago? That constitution, as fixed at the revolution, as it *now* stands, is what we are interested in."[85] American whigs had already answered his question by rebelling on behalf of the authority of the ancient constitution.

For British constitutional theorists who thought of law in the same way that colonial whigs did, the Glorious Revolution had not been a revolution, but a preservation,[86] which should not be called a "revolution," but an "abdication,"[87] as it changed no law with the exception of mandating a Protestant succession.[88] In one of the most celebrated common-law adjudications of the age of the American Revolution, Camden, C.J., ruled on the legality of general search warrants issued by authority of a secretary of state in cases of seditious libel. As there were no supporting legislation and no precedents prior to the Revolution, the government argued that the warrants were valid by a usage which had been tolerated since "the era of liberty" had begun in 1688. "If the practice began then," Camden ruled,

> it began too late to be law now. If it was more ancient, the Revolution is not to answer for it; and I could have wished, that upon this occasion the Revolution had not been considered as the only basis of our liberty. The Revolution restored this constitution to its first principles. It did no more. It did not enlarge the liberty of the subject; but gave it a better security. It neither widened nor contracted the foundation, but repaired, and perhaps added a buttress or two to the fabric; and if any minister of state has since deviated from the principles at that time recognized, all that I can say is, that, so far from being sanctioned, they are condemned by the Revolution.[89]

Camden was joining what was then a sustained constitutional argument. Three decades earlier, the administration of Robert Walpole had begun to enforce and to propagate the constitution of the future by denigrating the constitution of prescriptive rights. "Thus (according to our *Ancient* Constitution) the *People* of *England* . . . were *absolute Slaves* to the King, the Barons, or the Church," the administration's press contended. "They were *Slaves* by *Law established;* they knew no *Liberty,* they knew no *Property;* no, not so much as in their *Persons,* which were not their own, but their several *Lords.*"[90] Brady's history had, at last, become semiofficial government history, but the Walpoleans wanted matters both ways. They embraced Brady the historian and rejected Brady the constitutionalist. They believed or pretended to believed that they could abandon the authority of prescription without succumbing to arbitrary power. It was the lawfulness of custom, the precedential liberty of the ancient constitution, that came under direct attack, not liberty as preserved or first established by the Glorious Revolution.

> What have *Facts* to do with *Principle*? . . . Is it not then the most ridiculous Thing in Nature, that a Man should gravely assert, *whoever affirms our Ancestors were Slaves,* affirms at the same time, that we, their Sons, have no *Right* to be free? Or that a *Fact* about the *Ancient Constitution,* should destroy *the Reason* of the *present Constitution*? And yet all this, absurd as it is, Mr. *D'Anvers* [Viscount Bolingbroke] asserts when he affirms "that they who say *our ancestors were Slaves,* strike at the *fundamental Principles* of our Government." Whereas our Government is the same, and *the Principles* of it the same, whatever is true or false concerning the ancient Constitution. If our Forefathers were *Free* or *Slaves,* the Revolution stands on *the same Foundation,* and *its Principles* are the same; for *Principles* cannot be more or less true, by *any Facts* in the World: They are eternal and unchangeable, being founded in *the Nature* and *Reason* of Things.[91]

The government then, would have secured rights, liberty, and the rule of law by reason and natural law, not immemorial custom. By natural law, it could be argued, "If Liberty were but a Year old, the *English* wou'd have just as good a Right to claim and to preserve it, as if it had been handed down to them from many Ages."[92] The government newspaper was quoting Lord Lyttelton's *Persian Letters,* where, on the same page as that quotation, Lyttelton also asked, "Is a long Prescription necessary to give Force to the Natural Rights of Mankind?"[93]

The opposition to Walpole would put no more faith in natural law than would American whigs 40 years later. If liberty were but a year old, the opposition press replied, there might be a good title to claiming it, "yet such is the natural Temper of Mankind, that They are generally more tenacious of their *antient Birthright* than of any *modern Acquisitions;* and as *long Possession* gives a Title in LAW, or at least enforces it, even in cases of *private Property,* so the *Publick Rights of Mankind* acquire Strength by *long Prescription;* and if to This we add *particular Compacts with our Governors,* they become our *legal* as well as our *natural Rights.*"[94] Rights might have origins in time, but because of the prescriptive authority of immemorial custom, they would rest on much more secure constitutional ground, if the origin were, in law, a reaffirmation and not a beginning.

> At the Time of the *Revolution,* our *Constitution* received a considerable Strength by *that Act,* which is call'd the *Declaration of Rights.* . . . I don't reckon that we obtain'd any Thing *new* by it; any Thing, that was not our just Right before;

> nor does it provide such *Remedies for us, or such Penalties* for the Offenders against it, as might have contrived; yet it is an Advantage to have That expres[s]ly declared and acknowledged to be *our Right,* which had once been brought, how unjustly soever, into Dispute.[95]

Of course, Professor Schwoerer is correct. This is bad history and there is no reason to deny it. But why should we forget that it was once good law? Bad history had been a small price to pay for the security of believing that fundamental law was immutable. It is Britain's loss that it no longer matters to common lawyers whether the Declaration of Rights promulgated rights unknown to the ancient constitution.

There is a question that students of ancient-constitution jurisprudence might ask students of ancient-constitution historiography: if Sir Edward Coke and other lawyers who practiced ancient-constitution jurisprudence are judged by the standards of the historical method, why are Brady and those who wrote and argued as he did in the seventeenth and eighteenth centuries judged only in terms of historiography, never constitutionalism? The question could be asked of those historians who recently have celebrated the triumph of Brady's history, praising Brady the historian while ignoring Brady the advocate for constitutional absolutism. "When Englishmen commemorated the seven hundredth anniversary of the Parliament in 1965," it was noted with apparent satisfaction, "there were no dissents from Brady's scholarship."[96] Why would there have been dissents? By 1965 the British government possessed all the arbitrary power that Brady could have hoped for. Brady's history can be universally embraced because Brady's law has made history constitutionally irrelevant.

CHAPTER EIGHT

The Forensic History of Reform

In the final decades of the eighteenth century, with the close of the American Revolution, the cause of parliamentary reform became the cause of ancient constitutionalism. It was a development that has charmed historians with its apparent inconsistency. "Paeans in praise of the ancient constitution suited those who wished to preserve the *status quo,*" Christopher Hill suggested,[1] but in fact that was not what happened. Parliamentary reformers connected what Colin Bonwick calls their "radical ideology" to "the putative Anglo-Saxon or ancient constitution"[2] to attack, not preserve the status quo.

There was no need for innovations. With exemplary forensic scholarship the reformers of the 1780s discovered that everything they sought to introduce had once been staple to the ancient constitution: a more equal representation, annual elections, extension of the franchise, representation of people rather than property, ending borough representation (especially rotten boroughs), and elimination of "corruption" through patronage.[3] *"Resolved,"* the London Livery voted in 1782, after listing complaints including parliamentary abuses that drove Americans to rebellion, "that these grievances can never be removed until the right of the people to their constitutional share in the English government shall be re-established, by a fair and equal representation in parliament, and a *frequent election* of their representatives, according to ANCIENT USAGE."[4]

The argument was phrased not in the radical language of reform but in the forensic language of "restoration" and the ancient-constitution language of regeneration. There was no better means, a typical example of the argument insisted, "for supporting the constitution, besides restoring it to its true spirit and efficiency by shortening parliaments, by making representation adequate, by incapacitating placemen and pensioners, &c."[5] What they sought to "restore" was "our antient Constitution of *frequent, new Parliaments,*"[6] and they would have done so by reestablishing representation "in exact conformity to the primaeval principles of the Constitution of this country."[7] "*[A]nnual parliaments,*" it was claimed, "are the *ancient constitution* of this kingdom, and the *birthright of Englishmen,*"[8] a birthright "according to the ancient and sacred Laws of the Land."[9] What the reformers wanted people to demand, consequently, "is your own undoubted right; not the destruction of the Constitution, or even a new-modelling of it, but only its restoration."[10]

Most of these arguments were forensic history, pure and simple. Surely many of the writers knew they could not prove that what they were claiming to have been the ancient constituition had in fact ever existed. A petition from the county of York in 1785 asserted that as they were *"sensible of the* ORIGINAL EXCELLENCE *of the constitution,"* the petitioners *"wish to have it maintained upon the* GENUINE PRINCIPLES *on which it was founded."* Arthur Young was sure they were just repeating old slogans. "If that meeting had been asked, what those genuine principles were," he wrote a decade later, "not a man of them could have answered the question."[11]

Young was right. The petitioners should have known better or at least should have been more cautious claiming historical antecedents for the reforms they championed. By the second half of the eighteenth century there was a large well-documented historical literature proving that the ancient constitution had not known such things as equal representation,[12] annual elections,[13] or even a representation of the commons.[14] "Let these *Advocates for Antiquity* shew us the Law for *Annual new Parliaments chosen by the People,*" Walpole's *London Journal* challenged Bolingbroke and the opposition.[15] "To bring the Government of *England* back to *its first Principles,* is to bring the People back to *absolute Slavery:* The *Primitive Purity* of our Constitution was, that the People had no Share in the Government, but were the *Villains,* Vassals, or Bondsmen of the Lords. . . . This was our Ancient Constitution; *This* the fair *Model* by which we are to reform; and *This* the *Primitive Purity* of our old *Gothick Founders.*"[16]

To be sure there were many ancient constitutionalists unconvinced by even the most convincing proof, and who, on the best forensic grounds, refused to accept the evidence of canonial history. There was, after all, the certainty of the prehistorical Goths to infer what must have existed, among the historical Anglo-Saxons, even if undocumented. The Scots advocate Gilbert Stuart provides a typical though simplistic example of the genre. "If the commons were so considerable in Germany," he contended, "they must also have constituted a part of the Anglo-Saxon parliament."[17] Another stratagem was to put the burden of proof on those asserting an established historical fact, such as that the House of Commons had not been part of the ancient constitution, and to conclude that the case for the Commons dating only from the reign of Henry III was "far from being a clear irrefragable fact."[18] After all, if you drew your own conclusions from the lack of direct evidence, you could make it as difficult for the other side to disprove the antiquity of annual elections as it was for you to prove it. "There are several ways of proving there was a New Election every Year," Samuel Johnson in the seventeenth century had written about the right of annual elections. "They tell me there are Writs extant for New Elections for Fourscore Years Successively, where there are but about Six wanting. What if they had been all lost, imbezelled or made away? What then, is our Constitution lost, when Bundles of Writs are lost?"[19] A century later Granville Sharp looked for the same evidence and came to the same conclusion by making the same argument. He searched for proof of annual elections in the fourteenth century and satisfied himself that he had found writs of election for every year between the 34th to the 50th of Edward III with three exceptions. "And yet this affords no absolute proof that Parliaments were not holden *in those very years* for which the Writs are wanting; because the bundles of Writs for the said years may have been lost or mislaid."[20]

Constitutional reformers like Johnson and Sharp knew that documented evidence was unessential, if not irrelevant. They could clinch forensic arguments as easily without probative data as they could with incontrovertible records.

> Our ancient historians, 'tis true, make not the least mention, give us not the least hint of any such-like Senate in England, as that which formerly subsisted amongst our fore-fathers in Germany. . . . But let not their omission mislead our research. . . . On the contrary, as we most manifestly trace the old German constitution thro' all the other branches of their civil government, so I am well persuaded, that if we find not the remains of their ancient Senate likewise in this kingdom, it must be owing rather to the defective and imperfect account left behind of those matters, than to a total inobservation or abolition of the constitution itself.[21]

The absence of evidence could be proof not only that an institution of today had existed in the ancient constitution but that it had worked satisfactorily. "[I]f any person should object, that such *very frequent Elections* must be attended with insuperable difficulties and inconveniences," Granville Sharp reasoned, "we may quote the experience of all ancient times, as affording ample and sufficient proofs to the contrary, 'there being not above two or three cases of elections questioned or complained of, from Henry III. to 22 Edw. IV.' (that is more than two hundred years,) 'for ought that appears by the Retornes or Parliament-Rolls.'"[22]

Some of the parliamentary reformers demanding "return" to the ancient constitution did not bother to argue this history. There was no need once you asserted the existence of the ancient constitution. That constitution was immutable as well as timeless, and hence was its own authority. Not just the repository for those principles to which the law should be "returned," it was the actual law itself. From this perspective of constitutionalism, the right of annual elections that had once been the heart and soul of the ancient constitution was still the law because neither the Triennial Act nor the Septennial Act nor any other parliamentary legislation could alter the rights of the ancient constitution.

> [A]s the *suspension* of it [the right to annual elections] has never been promoted by the requisition or instruction of the people at large, their right to it remains intire. The presumption and treachery of their representatives, in consenting to the *triennial* and *septennial* acts, cannot injure their just title to it; because, in both these instances, the representatives presumed to act contrary to an established rule of parliament, by adopting a *new device,* (which even affected a fundamental law of the kingdom,) . . . .[23]

Even people who did no more than favor triennial over annual elections "would *betray the* constitution of the kingdom."[24] One explanation, voted by a constitutional society in Nottingham, was that "Annual Parliaments are the old constitutional usage of Parliament, the true law of the land, and the best security which can be furnished for the virtuous conduct of Parliament, and for its Independence on every power whatsoever unless that of the People alone."[25]

Another way to put the principle was that, although the law of the current constitution might not be sovereign over Parliament, the law of the ancient constitution was. "When you have chosen your representatives," British electors were urged in 1771, "instruct them, and oblige them on oath . . . to endeavour . . . to obtain an act for annual parliaments, according to your old constitution; by a repeal of the . . . act of Queen Ann, called the Qualification Act, by which rich men in land are only qualified to be chosen. This mode of choosing representatives was never thought of, or so much as surmised, in your constitution."[26]

It would be well not to jump to conclusions. The constitutional law of the parliamentary reformers of the 1780s was not the old constitutional law that the Americans had just defended in their revolution. Nor are we discussing another example of the forensic history of the regenerative constitution. The radicals of the late eighteenth century were truly radical. Just as they were not defending Christopher Hill's status quo, so they were not calling for what they said they were calling for, a return to the ancient constitution. The parliamentary reformers, rather, were repudiating the jurisprudence of ancient constitutionalism.

From the perspective of twenty-first-century jurisprudence, the eighteenth-century parliamentary reformers appear hopelessly inconsistent. They seem to have rejected the two opposites of eighteenth-century constitutional law: the future of parliamentary sovereignty and the past of prescriptive, precedential authority. The radicals' rhetoric that the ancient constitution was "the constitution" implied that parliamentary statutes not conforming to the precedents of ancient constitutionalism were unconstitutional. That was not what was meant. "Septennial Parliaments," the freeholders of Coventry complained of the Septennial Act of 1716, "are an Innovation upon, and injurious to our Constitution."[27] The contention was not that the Act was void in the American sense of "unconstitutional," but that it had been an act of "power" rather than an act of "right" in the eighteenth-century meaning of "constitutional."[28] The best way to think about the argument is not as a rejection of parliamentary sovereignty but as a technique for questioning parliamentary wisdom.

The parliamentary reformers of the 1780s may not have been doing what they seemed to be doing, but they certainly were doing what they did not seem to be doing, rejecting the old definition of law—the authority of immemorial and prescriptive custom. Twentieth-century scholars were sometimes fooled by these eighteenth-century arguments,[29] but the parliamentary reformers understood what they were about. When they called for a "return" of representation of people rather than of property, and looked back to the rules governing elections "before feudal tyranny eclipsed the constitution,"[30] they knew that the franchise had once been based on tenure and that the property requirement for either voting or for eligibility to elective office had been introduced and altered by legislation.[31] What is important for us is not that this forensic strategy permitted them to claim they were not remodelling the constitution. That the use of history always makes radicalism appear conservative has been discussed above. The lesson, rather, is that they were using history and the ancient constitution to repudiate the prescriptive authority of "history," that is the prescriptive authority of custom and time.

When John Cartwright in 1778 pledged that if elected to the House of Commons he would resign "the moment that a majority of my Constituents shall command me to do so," he claimed that he would be acting "according to those antient and sacred laws of the land, which when the Parliament violated they exceeded their authority, and stabbed the very vitals of the Constitution."[32] When Granville Sharp demanded annual elections, he denied he wanted the constitution *"new-modelled."* "[W]e only pray," he explained, "that the unjust *usurpations* . . . may be taken away and reformed: and then the ancient constitution of *annual* elections . . . will recover its full vigour without any other alteration."[33] Both Cartwright and Sharp knew they were ignoring centuries of customary law and prescriptive rights. They seem to have been doing something else besides. They were undermining the authority to that law and of those rights.

Consider two arguments that on first reading may appear in agreement, but on closer inspection should prove to be espousals of opposing eighteenth-century definitions of British constitutional law. The first is Edmund Burke's statement of eighteenth-century prescriptive jurisprudence.

> On what grounds do we go to restore our constitution to what it has been at one given period, or to reform and reconstruct it upon principles more conformable to a sound theory of government? A prescriptive government, such as ours, never was the work of any legislator, never was made upon any foregone theory. It seems to me a preposterous way of reasoning, and a perfect confusion of ideas, to take the theories which learned and speculative men have made from that government, and then, supposing it made on those theories, which were made from it to accuse the government of not corresponding with them.[34]

Burke was opposing reformation of parliamentary representation. One of the "learned and speculative men" about whom he warned was the Earl of Carysfort, who used forensic history to prove that the British people had an "ancient" constitutional right to equal representation.

> [I]t seems clear, that in the first idea of Parliament (the Great Council of the nation) the whole people were included. Laws were enacted by the King, with the Archbishops, Bishops, Earls, Barons, Knights, Citizens, Burgesses, and other Freemen. The people are, to this day, said to be represented in Parliament. The Commons is a general description, including all ranks. So that, whatever blemishes and imperfections may now appear in the Constitution, the cause is to be sought rather in the lapse of time, and the gradual revolution and change of circumstances, than in any fundamental defect.

In ancient times "the Government of this country was in its origin a pure Democracy," Carysfort concluded. "We must now enquire how far the spirit of our Constitution has been impaired by time, and in what points it is materially different from that which has been considered by our ancestors as the best inheritance they could transmit to their posterity."[35]

Just as Burke rejected the rational theorizing of Carysfort, so Carysfort rejected Burke's prescriptive constitution "whose sole authority is that it has existed time out of mind."[36] In Carysfort's constitutional theory the role of time was reversed from what it was in ancient constitutionalism. No longer the source of constitutional authority, the element of time was blamed for constitutional erosion; it was the cause of constitutional "blemishes and imperfections." Carysfort's ancient constitution was the opposite of the ancient constitution of Sir Edward Coke and Sir Matthew Hale. A rejection of history and a rejection of customary law, it used history as a disguise to soften the innovation of law by will and pleasure. The Levellers had used the same technique of ancient constitutionalism for the same purpose in the seventeenth century,[37] and Thomas Jefferson would use it in the United States when attempting to destroy the authority of prescriptive common law.[38] The Levellers, the parliamentary reformers, and Jefferson did not look to the ancient constitution for guidance, precedent, analogy, or authority. Like Justice William Brennan and Attorney General Edwin Meese in the

1980s, they turned to the past to conceal how much more their proposals owed to political choice and speculation than to legal methodology.[39]

Contemporaries of the eighteenth-century parliamentary reformers understood their manipulation of history better than have many of the twentieth-century historians who are both pleased and puzzled by their apparent use of history. "I know not what the petitioners mean by the original excellency of the constitution," Baron Basset complained when opposing a scheme for more "equal" representation,

> and I am sometimes tempted to think they have no meaning at all; it sounds well certainly, because under the name of friends, they conceal their rooted enmity of our glorious constitution. . . . If the petitioners want to introduce the feudal system, as the original constitution, let them say so: if they wish to have the Saxon witten gemot, let them declare it; and may I hope, at the same time, that they will give us an accurate description of the constitution of that assembly, on which the best and ablest antiquaries have been so much divided, and which probably is reserved for their profound learning and erudition to explain.[40]

For Basset, as for Burke, the eighteenth-century parliamentary reformers were seeking to impose their personal wisdom and partial preconceptions in place of the restraining safety of custom, contract, precedent, analogy, and prescription as authority for constitutional law. "[T]hey wish us to . . . prefer their speculations," Burke warned, "to the happy experience of this country of a growing liberty and a growing prosperity for five hundred years." It was not just a definition of constitutionalism that was at stake. It was the rule of law itself.[41]

Forensic History of Magna Carta

Striking ironies dominate the concluding history of ancient constitutionalism. One irony has been obscured from view by a persistent misunderstanding about the American Revolution. There has been a notion, still repeated by some historians, that colonial whigs had been forced to abandon claims to specific English and common-law rights. Discovering that the British constitution did not support their case, they turned to nonconstitutional generalities, to claims of natural law, the rights of mankind, or "the broad and undefined Magna Carta."[42] Nothing could be more wrong. The colonial whig case was based on the British constitution. It started with a constitutional grievance in 1765 against the Stamp Act and ended with the Declaration of Independence, which was a listing of constitutional grievances, without citing a single natural-law grievance.[43] What is true is that the Americans put great stock in Magna Carta. They referred to it more than any other English constitutional document, more often, certainly, than they mentioned their own charters or the ancient constitution.

How Americans used Magna Carta to argue their rights should not surprise us. They did not argue some "simplistic version" of a "fixed and static" Magna Carta as has sometimes been said,[44] but as it had been argued in England and Great Britain since at least Lord Coke's time, as declaratory of fundamental common law or of the principles of the ancient constitution.[45]

When Benjamin Franklin in 1766 gave evidence to the House of Commons during the debate about whether to repeal the Stamp Act, he was asked if the Pennsylvania charter did not contain "an express reservation of the right of parliament to lay taxes there." Admitting there was such a provision, Franklin pointed out that "by the same charter" the people of Pennsylvania "are intitled to all the privileges and liberties of Englishmen; they find in the great charter, and the petition and declaration of rights, that one of the privileges of English subjects is, that they are not to be taxed but by their common consent." Were there "any words in the [Pennsylvania] charter that justify that construction?" Franklin was asked. "The common rights of Englishmen," he replied, "as declared in Magna Carta, and the, petition of right, all justify it."[46]

It is a bit ironic that the uses Franklin and other American whigs made of Magna Carta have been dismissed as *sui generis* liberties when in fact they were exactly the same as the uses made of Magna Carta in the mother country at exactly the same time—that is, as an ideal of constitutionalism, in the taught, time-honored, common-law practice of ancient constitutionalism.[47] Indeed, the uses of Magna Carta during the Stamp Act crisis were but echoes of the uses of Magna Carta just two years earlier in Great Britain during the cider excise controversy. In both parts of the empire the same vocabulary and the same slogans were used: the language of liberty and the slogans of Magna Carta. In the colonies the cry against the Stamp Act would be "Liberty, Property, and no Stamps." Two years earlier in Great Britain the cry had been "liberty and property and no excise."[48]

The point is not that the British arguments of 1763 were the same that Americans would make from 1765 to 1776. After all, the constitutional issues were different.[49] In North America the complaint was that the colonists would be taxed "without consent." In Great Britain the complaint was that excisemen were authorized to enter private houses, to compound assessments at their discretion, and to adjudicate liability without trial by jury. Our lesson rather, is that the vocabulary was the same because on both sides of the Atlantic Magna Carta was a synonym for liberty and liberty was a synonym for constitutionalism. The lord mayor, aldermen, and commons of London described the excise as "[a]n attack upon the liberty of the subject," the method of enforcement as "inconsistent with those principles of liberty which have hitherto distinguished this nation from arbitrary governments,"[50] and the method of trial as "inconsistent with the principles of liberty, and the happy constitution of your majesty's government."[51] Each extension of the excise was "an encroachment upon the liberty of the subject"[52] and "most dangerous to the liberty of the subject,"[53] because it was "a mode of taxation altogether inconsistent with the nature of Freedom, and which must be forever odious to a people who are duly impressed with the glorious idea of liberty."[54]

> The laws of *excise* have, by *freeborn Englishmen,* been always looked upon as most grievous to the subject. They have been ever considered as *unconstitutional*—as an abridgment of *English* Liberty—as the most oppressive method of collecting taxes—as an infringement of *Magna Charta*—and as inventions of cruelty, founded on the principles of the most *arbitrary* and tyrannical governments in *Europe.*[55]

As with the Stamp Act, the excise issues argued by British critics were constitutional issues and "liberty" issues, not economic ones. The excise was condemned as "a mode of taxation inconsistent with the nature of Freedom, and which must be forever odious to the people who are duly impressed with the glorious idea of Liberty."[56] The amount of the tax was not the grievance, "but whether we shall any longer, according to *Magna Carta,* enjoy the *rights* and *privileges* of *Englishmen,* the uninterrupted possession of freedom of our Houses? This is the question, this is the grievance that affects us all as *Englishmen*! . . . Surely there is a great difference between opposing *all taxes,* and a particular method of collecting them."[57]

Forensic History of the New Jurisprudence

It was not a matter of Americans imitating the British. Ancient constitutionalism and Magna Carta belonged to the colonies as much as to the mother country, more than Magna Carta did to the Scots or Welsh. There was a fundamental difference in the uses made of the ancient constitution, however. Americans were the constitutional traditionalists in the late eighteenth-century English-speaking world. It was not in revolutionary America but in aristocratic Great Britain that the security of the prescriptive liberty of ancient-constitution jurisprudence was put in jeopardy by the newer jurisprudence of the coercive law of sovereign command. But that is not the irony. The irony is that the parliamentary reformers of the 1780s were intent on curtailing the increasing arbitrary power of Parliament when they argued the ancient constitution to prove the people's right to a broader, annual representation.[58] What their program of resorting to "first principles" would lead to was not the "restoration" of the seventeenth- and early eighteenth-century definition of liberty, but to parliamentary reform so beguiling that ancient constitutionism was abandoned almost without debate. Arbitrary government by a closed oligarchy was avoided, only to be replaced by the arbitrary government of a popularly elected political party. The cherished right to "security," the core eighteenth-century British foundation of liberty,[59] would be laid aside. It would not be done consciously or deliberately, but as a result of a change in legal attitudes. The centuries-old fundamental of English constitutionalism—fear of arbitrary power—somehow dissipated. The reasons are unclear—possibly the old bugbear of royal arbitrariness was no longer tenable—and, unlike the Americans, the British, who enjoyed some parliamentary representation, did not shift their ancient fear of arbitrary power from the power of the king onto the power of Parliament. The authority of prescriptive right lost its jurisprudential centrality.[60] The ancient constitution was never allowed to go full circle. Having surrounded royal arbitrariness with the barrier of the rule of law, it would not be extended to restrain the arbitrariness of parliamentary sovereignty.

The transformation was well marked by leaders in the United States. David Hume's *History of England* with its "elegant Lies against the Republicans and gaudy daubings of the Courtiers," John Adams lamented, "has been the Bane of G[reat] B[ritain]. It has destroyed many of the best Effects of the Revolution of 1688."[61] Thomas Jefferson agreed. "This single book has done more to sap the free principles of the English constitution than the largest standing army of which their patriots have been so jealous. . . . Hume has consecrated . . . all the arbitrary proceedings of the English kings, as true evidences of the constitution, and glided over it's whig principles as the unfounded pretensions of factious demagogues."[62]

It should no longer be necessary to point out that Adams and Jefferson were not discussing history but were agreeing on a point of constitutional law. What deserves attention is that they were lamenting the passing of the British constitution and of what they had called British liberty. It may be that neither Adams nor Jefferson thought they were discussing American law, but in a real sense they were. To mourn the end of customary, precedential, prescriptive liberty in the mother country was to celebrate the salvation of ancient constitutionalism in the new republic.

It cannot be said that liberty had cut its moorings on the Saxon shore and drifted across the Atlantic to a republican home. What can be said is that the jurisprudents of Britain had cut their Cokean moorings by conferring a new definition on law and a new liberty upon themselves. The ancient constitution was scrapped, but customary constitutionalism had at least one more important role to play in the nineteenth century. Where the ancient constitution had been a legal fiction securing liberty, customary constitutionalism became, in the age of parliamentary sovereignty, a fictive apparatus accommodating economic and social change without political and legal upheaval. The new financial groupings and the rising commercial classes were free to function in novel ways in what had the appearance of a traditionalist, customary legal system. Changes in power, in structure, and in governance occurred without sweeping away the symbolic security of constitutional anachronisms. The ghost of the fiction of the ancient constitution commanded the allegiance of traditional interests for what was truly a new order.[63] Nineteenth-century British constitutionalism retained the trappings of an age-old Gothic exterior while building an industrial, efficient, noncustomary state of coercive power. It was the British constitution without English constitutionalism as constitutionalism had been understood at least as far back as the *Institutes* of Coke, if not back to Fortescue or even Bracton and beyond.

For Americans after 1764 the ancient constitution worked in an opposite way than it did for the British. It revealed arbitrariness; it did not disguise it. When Parliament exercised what was perceived as unprecedented arbitrary power over the internal governance of the colonies, the constitutional consciousness of Americans suffered a collective shock. A single statute altering the charter of Massachusetts Bay stripped off the veneer covering the security of prescriptive law that had been the guarantee of liberty for as long as there had been an English people and, in theory, before—when the English had been Saxons and even Goths. Americans learned again the lesson they had been taught many times by their ancestors: constitutional form without constitutional substance was not constitutionalism but arbitrariness.[64]

Something was going on in the 1770s that our historians of republicanism, countryism, and commonwealthmenism have not told us. The Americans fought to keep the ancient constitution. The British abandoned it without an argument. That was not the significant difference between the separating people, however. The important distinction was that the Americans knew what was occurring. The British did not or, at least, pretended not to know. As late as 1799 the chief justice of the Isle of Ely, without blushing we may suspect, told the Ely grand jury: "Old rights have been secured to the people, and new privileges have been granted to them, yet the original form of government remains unimpaired."[65]

John Lord Campbell, who was born during the American Revolution and lived to be lord chief justice and lord chancellor in the age of Austinian law, was typical of nineteenth-century British jurists for whom the passing of the immemorial, prescriptive, precedential, customary constitution had not changed the substance of liberty. "Nor do I see," he wrote, "how our constitutional rights would be at all endangered by acknowledging the undoubted fact, that representation was unknown in this country till the end of the reign of Henry III., and that the Commons did not till long after sit in a separate chamber as an independent branch of the legislature."[66] We may wonder if Campbell any longer understood what his predecessors, Lord Coke or Lord Hale, had meant by "the law of the land," or if he understood what the words "due process" meant to his American contemporaries who drafted and ratified the Fourteenth Amendment.

CHAPTER NINE

The Forensic History of Liberty

We are not quite done with the historiography of the ancient constitution. There are two lingering questions that should be addressed, even though they may never be answered to the satisfaction of most scholars. The first is whether twentieth-century historians of the ancient constitution really believed that history was so controlling of people in the seventeenth and eighteenth centuries that it not only provided the context of argument but dictated the outcome of events. The second is whether the lawyers and other practitioners of ancient constitutionalism cared whether the facts that they argued from the past were historical or provable and, indeed, whether it is likely they gave the matter much thought.

Strong claims have been made in recent years for the authority of history in the seventeenth century. The most obvious is that history shaped thought. "The ideology of the Ancient Constitution," one argument maintains, "can be accounted for by means of a purely structural explanation: all English law was common law, common law was custom, custom rested on the presumption of immemoriality; property, social structure, and government existed as defined by the law and were therefore presumed to be immemorial."[1] One of the most striking manifestations of this theory about history in the seventeenth century, or—put another way—about this seventeenth-century way of looking at the past, is how it depictes common lawyers. It assumed that they were isolated from other intellectual studies both in England and the European continent and even implied that they were relatively ignorant of noncommon-law matters. Consider how strongly the argument has been stated: "The unitary legal system in England, the prestige of the law and the lawyers, the intimate relationship between views of law and legal history and political realities combined to keep Englishmen wilfully ignorant of the past of their own society."[2] Even more amazing have been explanations why common lawyers remained opposed to civil law long after better *scholarship* led French lawyers to abandon ancient constitutionalism. It had nothing to do with the writ system, constitutional government, or opposition to arbitrary power. It was because the English were "curiously" reluctant "to consider historical perspective or context." "Their tendency was rather to move directly from the most abstract principles of natural law to the most technical practices of English courts without any reference to contacts or parallels with continental jurisprudence."[3] Liberty apparently had nothing to do with it.

Less obvious are twentieth-century assertions of how the practice of history was capable of shaping legal events in the seventeenth century. If only the opponents of Coke, Selden, and the ancient constitution had been able to invest "the civil law, the martial law, or the . . . feudal law with histories of their own," it has been surmised, then they and not the common lawyers might have determined the course of constitutional development. The reason, apparently, is that had these other laws possessed histories of their own they, rather than the common law, might "have shaped the governance of England."[4] The fact of the matter is that the opponents of Coke and Selden could have come up with these histories, but what would have been the point? They were not arguing for civil law or martial law, but prerogative law, and prerogative law had just as much "history" as common law or ancient-constitution law. It was not their histories that were in controversy but their jurisprudence. Both sides argued "history" not so much when the past seemed relevant but when the past seemed arguable—when they thought the past-as-precedent could be argued to carry the point of law for which they were contending. That is why the advocates for law by royal command found their "history" in the Tudor century and "the constitutionalists were forced into" what has been called "a kind of historical obscurantism—compelled to attribute their liberties to more and more remote and mythical periods in the effort to prove them independent of the will of the king."[5] But were the two sides exploring history, or, because already committed to a theory of government, did they turn to the epochs that supported their theory by precedents, analogies, and appeals to custom? Was it "two different views of history"[6] or two different views of constitutionalism that were at stake? Perhaps what the material of this study comes down to is whether, as is often assumed, "[t]he past was looked to . . . to solve the problems of the present,"[7] or whether, as has been suggested here, the past was looked to for selective incidents which were cited not as historical evidence but as constitutional authority in the form of legal precedents or legal analogies to argue issues of current law, politics, or religion.

There is no need to defend forensic history. There is not even a need for historians to understand it, although they might save themselves much puzzlement if they made the effort. One factor that apparently has caused some of the puzzlement may be that too much credit is given to Sir Edward Coke,[8] and, as Christopher Hill pointed out, regrettably he was not an intellectual. Like so many other practitioners of forensic history he was merely a lawyer.[9] But then it may be a mistake to look to the intellectual, just as it is a mistake to look for history that considers every side of every issue. As Hans Pawlisch pointed out, "the creation of a common law 'frame of mind' to explain the use of a mythical Anglo-Saxon past in structuring the course of English history needs to be throughly revised, because it implies that lawyers . . . did not understand what they read."[10] They not only understood what they read but understood that forensic history in the seventeenth and eighteenth centuries was not merely an intellectual pursuit. It was a pragmatic, professional, and above all constitutional pursuit, with a pragmatic, professional, and above all constitutional purpose. It relieved the lawyer, judge, or legislator of the burden of resolving gravid legal issues aided only by the limited insight of one mind and one age.[11]

One could stress the pragmatic and point out that the legal issues being resolved were English legal and constitutional issues. What were required were English solutions, that is, English legal judgments, and legal or constitutional judgments are not the same as moral judgments or even political judgments. How better to arrive at those judgments, it might be argued, than by English experience, even if that experience is selected by a picking and choosing of supporting evidence. Even if the evidence compiled of the past is not a historian's "true" picture of the past, it may be a legally relevant picture of what, for the issue at bar, is the legally relevant part of the English experience.

There was another purpose to forensic history, a constitutional purpose that in the twentieth century has come to be called "the search for neutral principles." That we, today, acknowledge that no principles can be applied neutrally does not mean that the common lawyers of the seventeenth and eighteenth centuries had received that insight. The common lawyer's use of forensic history was part of the legal imagination of those centuries and was essential to what people in those centuries thought was the rule of law. Even selective, polemical forensic history can have the appearance, no matter that it does not have the reality, of freeing constitutional and judicial decision from the caprice of being based on the policy of the day rather than on impersonal, objective principle. And it does so by elucidating standards of law (or the rule of law) much like the common law's "artificial reasoning" that was at the heart of Coke's legal philosophy. Forensic history brought to the process of decision making both a canon of relevance and a measure of "rightness," by steering decision from the dictates of mere power.

Right would prevail over naked power or mere reason if the law were autonomous from will and pleasure, and law was autonomous to the extent that seventeenth-century people—and, most likely, eighteenth-century people as well—had trust in the neutrality of law's methodology for formulating decisions. Aside from the procedure of the common-law writ system and the tradition of a relatively independent judiciary, there was little in English or British law to blunt the will and pleasure of arbitrary decision except the mechanics of balance in the tripartite British constitution and the entrenchment of rights in the prescription of a neutral past. Rights to physical property were secured by being answerable only to certain forms of action, extending over the years from the possessory assizes to the more recent writ of *ejectment*. Liberty was secured by analogizing it to property—saying that people "owned" liberty—and arguing the ancient constitution not just as a constitution of liberty but as a source of "first principles" that had always been neutral and would continue to be neutral because they were timeless and their origins were divorced from any discoverable politics.

Acceptance was the most important element of constitutional neutrality. The English in the seventeenth century and the British and Americans in the eighteenth century, to a high percentage, accepted as a fundamental given of liberty that the abstraction of "law" could be trusted where personal decision could not. Common lawyers made concerted efforts to persuade people of the law's equal protection. Sir Edward Coke, for example, had not been solving contemporary problems "by the recovery of an ancient heritage," as has sometimes been suggested,[12] when telling the English that their material property in their goods and their intangible property in liberty and country were secured by the neutrality of the ancient patrimony that was their shared inheritance. The right to be secured both in their ownership of private possessions and their property in liberty belonged to all English citizens equally because they owned that right and every other civil right individually. That was the lesson Coke sought to teach. It was, he explained, partly a matter of instruction, a matter of people learning that what they had—rights as well as chattels—they owned because they also owned the right to live under the common law and could depend on the "learned & faithfull Councellors" of the law.

> There is no Subject of this Realme, but being truely instructed by good and playne euidence of his auncient and vndoubted patrimony & byrth-right, (though hee hath for some time by ignorance, false perswasion, or vaine feare, bene deceiued or dispossessed) but will consult with learned and faythful Councellors for the recouerie of the same: The autient & excellent Lawes of England are the birth-right and the most antient and best inheritance that the subjects of this realme haue, for by them he inioyeth not onely his inheritance and goods in peace & quietnes[s], but his life and his most deare Countrey in safety.

"I know," Coke added, "that at this day al[l] Kingdomes and States are gouerned by Lawes, & that the particular & approued custome of euery natio[n], is the most vsuall binding & assured Law."[13]

We may wonder how much of this Coke believed. We cannot doubt that he believed English laws "excellent," the best in the world, but did he really believe they were immemorially "auncient"? The guess of the historiographers of ancient constitutionalism has been that Coke believed he was writing history and that he intended to write history, not law. There are outstanding scholars of the history of English law[14] as well as outstanding scholars of English intellectual history who say that Coke believed that he wrote provable, scientific history. It must be surmised that this is a guess because there is no indication they asked themselves if Coke intended to write history more than to write law or whether he cared if his "history" was canonally provable as long as it supported the constitutional proposition that he was then advancing. The conclusion that he was serious about his history seems always to be assumed. Yet there is a legitimate question whether not just Coke but any of the forensic historians discussed in this study gave much thought to whether the history they wrote provided a historically accurate as well as a constitutionally useful picture of the past. The question is not whether the forensic historians of the seventeenth century were interested in correct, canonical, provable history. As Corinne Weston has reminded us, lawyers such as William Petyt were keen students of history, a fact proven by an inventory of Petyt's personal library.[15] The threshold questions we should be asking, rather, are whether accurate history was one of their primary considerations when arguing constitutional law, and whether forensic historians should be judged by the canons of scientific historians.

The questions can be limited to lawyers, as it has been the lawyers, not nonlawyer forensic historians of the seventeenth and eighteenth centuries, whom the better historians of our day have accused of not knowing what they were about. And if we are concentrating on lawyers, there is yet another way—in regard to lawyers—to put the question we have been asking. It may be thought that that question is whether the lawyers, who certainly knew that they were practicing forensic history, also thought that their history of the ancient constitution was history by the historical method. That, however, is not the question we need answered. The significant question is, "Did lawyers care?" Had Coke or Selden, Hale or Atkyns, been told of Quentin Skinner's "truism" that "the most accepted ideology is by no means always the one based on the most acceptable evidence,"[16] would they have cared?

Perhaps the question should not be answered with regard to Coke alone. It is now generally acknowledged that the caricature of his theory had been misstated,[17] that he and other lawyers knew that law—even common law and English constitutional law—changed and evolved over time.[18] Of course it is possible that Coke believed everything he wrote about British, German, Saxon, Norman, and English history. It is also possible that he did not really care whether there had or had not been a historically provable ancient constitution. It is hard to disagree with Donald R. Kelley's conclusion that

"Coke was not interested in 'history' at all."[19] Although we cannot say that Coke wanted English citizens to believe that there had been, in actual fact, an ancient constitution, we can be certain why he wanted them to accept at least the fiction of ancient constitutionalism. The jurisprudence of ancient constitutionalism—whether the ancient constitution was fact or fiction—was the jurisprudence of limited, mixed government, the jurisprudence of what Coke understood to be liberty.

As for the practitioners of ancient constitutionalism in the two centuries after Coke and Selden, we can be no more certain, but it is safer to venture a guess. For those lawyers of the seventeenth and eighteenth centuries the questions may not be whether they thought they were writing scientific history or whether they cared if their history was according to the historical method. There is a more revealing question: aside from being able to claim that their argument about constitutional law was more persuasive, why should they have cared?

Although it is not permissible to suggest that the historiographers of the ancient constitution could have been mistaken, it may be permissible to point out that there are questions that they appear to have overlooked. For it does seem that they forgot to ask what lawyers are, and they forgot to consider what lawyers do. It is an irrevocable error to miss the fact that lawyers are advocates and assume they are something else. The general assumption seems to have been that when they are not writing amateur history they do work akin to that of political theorists.[20] Lawyers are not political theorists and political theory is not law, at least not seventeenth- or eighteenth-century common or constitutional law.

We can forget custom, even though custom had more to do than did history with how the ancient constitution was argued in the seventeenth and eighteenth centuries. We may concentrate on history and ask again the question asked and answered before, whether ancient-constitution advocacy was history. If historiographers are correct that there is such a thing as "true" history, than there is also something quite its opposite, history that is "true only in a brief."[21] The same could be said for most "history" appearing in judicial opinions.

In *Commonwealth v. Chapman* in 1847, Chief Justice Lemuel Shaw observed that from the time of the first settlement of Salem and Boston to the Declaration of Independence, the people living in the colony of Massachusetts Bay "were governed and protected by the laws of England, so far as those laws were applicable to their state and condition."[22] The next lawyer appearing before Shaw's court for whom *Chapman* was squarely and favorably on point might know that colonial Massachusetts law was only partly English law, that it contained many rules from English local custom and included some rules adapted from the law merchant. That lawyer would not be advised to write a "correct history." Better for the purpose of winning the case at bar to copy the words of Chief Justice Shaw or just to cite *Commonwealth v. Chapman*.[23]

To return to the question being asked: if Shaw thought the history he was stating useful for the law that he wished to promulgate, did he have much reason to be troubled by the fact that there were exceptions to the general historical proposition on which he was relying for authority? Mr. Justice Joseph Story had stated a similar historical conclusion some years before. "The common law of England," he wrote in a United States Supreme Court decision, "is not to be taken in all respects to be that of America. Our ancestors brought with them its general principles, and claimed it as their birthright; but they brought with them and adopted only that portion which was applicable to their situation."[24] Story was pronouncing a rule of jurisprudence useful to federal judges willing to exercise judicial discretion—the purpose he had in mind. He was inviting judges to pick and choose among English common-law precedents and decisions, adopting doctrines that would advance commercial growth, and rejecting rules like the law of waste that might retard it. It is possible—barely possible—that Story believed that the principle he promulgated was based on sound history provable by the canons of the historical method. It is more likely that the historical soundness of the rule had little bearing on why he adopted it. The rule was desirable as law, and for that reason alone the forensic value of holding that the early settlers had brought to America only that part of the common law "which was applicable to their situation" made the claim also good "history," at least for purposes of supporting the rule.

Today's judges writing decisions in, let us suppose, a native American land case, do not say to their law clerks, "What rule does history support?" Rather, the judges tell them, "We're going to adopt such-and-such rule. Find me some history to support it." It will not matter to those judges or their colleagues on the court what quality of historical evidence the clerks find. If the question at bar concerns the validity of a Plains Indians treaty, an authoritative pronouncement by Francis Paul Prucha will be all to the good. Suppose the only "history" that supports the desired result is a quotation out of a book commissioned by the plaintiff Indian nation, a book that tells only the Indians' side of events from the Indians' prejudices, published locally in Pierre, South Dakota, and not known or respected by any scholar of native American history. None of those considerations, making that book "bad" history to academic historians, would be controlling. What would be material is that there is a published statement to be quoted and the judges have no reason not to quote it. They use it, after all, not as a piece of historical evidence but as authority.

Today's judge in the native American land case is no different than Sir Edward Coke, William Prynne, or Robert Atkyns. Undoubtedly they all wanted their history to be canonically accurate history because the only reason that they had turned to history was to persuade others to adopt or support their political or constitutional arguments, and they wanted to be persuasive. But with questions of law there are other means of persuasion than the scholarship of another discipline. When a case was being argued, if it took forensic history to win, then forensic history would do. Bad history can produce good law as readily as can scientific history. Justice Hugo Black based the "incorporation doctrine" of the Fourteenth Amendment on what he possibly thought was a careful reading of the past. It was not careful at all according to Leonard W. Levy. It was, rather, selectively forensic. "Black did not merely misread history nor wishfully attribute to it a factual content that it did not possess; he mangled and manipulated it by artfully selecting facts from one side only, by generalizing from grossly inadequate 'proof,' by ignoring confusion and even contradictions in the minds of some of his key historical protagonists, and by assuming that silence on the part of their opponents signified acquiescence."[25] Had Levy talked to Black and had he convinced him that forensic history is not history, we may imagine Black would have been mildly interested. "What is important," he might have replied, "is that it is now indisputable law that the states of the union must adhere to the principles of the Bill of Rights in the same way that the federal government must." By the same token, if J. G. A. Pocock were able to communicate with Sir Edward Coke, we may suppose that Coke might express surprise that history has come to doubt the perfection of Saxon law and might offer some complicated explanation, having more to do with constitutional law than with history, about what he thought ancient constitutionalism should stand for. It is, however, unlikely that his answer would be much different in meaning than if he said, "So what? The ancient constitution may have been bad history but Charles I and James II both learned that it was effective law."

Justice Black's "incorporation doctrine" was based on what he claimed was the "original intention" of the framers of the Fourteenth Amendment. There are parallels linking ancient constitutionalism in the seventeenth and eighteenth centuries with today's doctrine of "original intent." Robert Brady's 1684 political complaint that the theory of "*Ancient Rights* and *Privileges*" taught people "to prescribe against the Government for many Things they *miscal*[*l*] Fundamental Rights"[26] was not that much different from the historian of 1988 calling for canonical history to "bury" the doctrine of original intent, "that badly battered theory of Constitutional interpretation."[27] Both ancient constitutionalism and original intentism came under criticism in their own days for reasons that were not likely to persuade their practitioners.

Critics of original intentism, like recent critics of ancient constitutionalism, confuse forensic history with academic history and concentrate on irrelevancies such as the unreliability of the record.[28] Also like critics of ancient constitutionalism, they seem to have slight regard for the jurisprudence that protected liberty through customary restraints or for the rule of law.[29]

The principle of the rule of law is the striking connection between the ancient constitution and the doctrine of original intent. Both ancient constitutionalism and original intentism may be "bad" history, but both, if used with the discipline of the common-law method, can be restraints on the will and pleasure of arbitrary decision, whether royal, legislative, or (especially in the case of original intent) judicial. "Original intent, sensibly defined, provides a limited Constitution that properly applies to new situations," Robert Palmer pointed out in 1987. "Original intent analysis, however, will not yield a constitutional law that is equivalent to that now practiced, nor will it yield a constitutional law that is demonstrably superior in handling social needs or maximizing individual liberties. . . . The only sure consequence of original intent analysis is that it would require less judicial discretion and consequently more frequent resort to the people in the amendment process."[30] Commenting on Palmer's conclusion, Frederick Schauer pointed out issues usually not considered by those scholars of scientific history who are ever ready to disparage not just the doctrine of original intent but the practice of ancient constitutionalism.

> For those who fear the risks of expansive judicial interpretation of open-ended constitutional provisions, obedience to the commands of history provides a way of narrowing, albeit not completely, the options open to the conscientious judge. Here history is used to control not exclusively or even primarily because an historical view of intent is special, but because it is a pragmatic device for cabining the discretion of judges . . . . Reference to historical intent as a method for limiting judicial discretion might still be thought to be more legitimate or perhaps more constraining than some of these other techniques, but it is the constraint and not the legitimacy that under this view justifies taking original intent as command.[31]

The same jurisprudential end was served by the correct use of ancient constitutionalism. When advocates and legislators in the eighteenth century made an attempt to tie decision and policy to the accepted, taught, time-honored tenets of the ancient constitution, they were saying that judgment should be guided and that law, not discretion, should rule. To use the ancient constitution in argument or in judgment could persuade an individual that impartial justice had been done or persuade a generation that a principled decision had been reached.

We need not be convinced. The historians will continue to carry the day, for historiography is their preserve and lawyers are always fair game. And yet, is history so narrow that there is no other measure than the norms of professional historiography? Something worth remembering happened in the England where those uneducated lawyers clung tenaciously to ancient constitutionalism during the seventeenth and eighteenth centuries; something setting that country and its constitutional tradition of rule by law apart from the continent of Europe. It is not irrelevant to keep in mind that the triumph of history among continental lawyers, a fact so often held up to prove the comparative intellectual barrenness of the common-law mind,[32] coincided with the defeat of constitutionalism in nation after nation on the continent. It is a wonder for historians to consider that those common lawyers were the only lawyers of Europe to keep viable the ancient constitution, if not as a source of liberty, at least as a restraining force on arbitrary government. A question remains: Why were these narrow-minded, ahistorical English common lawyers among the very few lawyers in Europe who, during the seventeenth and eighteenth centuries, had any idea what it was like to live under the rule of law and the jurisprudence of liberty?

NOTES

Introductory Note

1. For an introduction to forensic history generally, see "Law and History."

2. Kelly, "Clio and the Court," p. 121.

3. Warren, "Introduction," p. 1.

4. Wolfe *v.* Shelley, 76 *Eng. Rep.* 206 *(K.B.* 1579*).*

5. Maitland, "Why History is Not Written," p. 491.

6. Gough, *Fundamental Law,* pp. 6–7.

7. Pocock, *Politics,* p. 229.

8. Pocock, "Robert Brady," p. 190. Also, see Hulsebosch, "Ancient Constitution," p. 445.

9. Pocock, *Politics,* p. 209. Also, see Bailyn, *Ideological Origins,* p. 33; Levack, *Civil Lawyers,* p. 146; Fussner, *Historical Revolution,* p. 318.

10. Twysden, *Certaine Considerations,* p. 23.

11. Siegel, "Aristotelian Basis of Law," p. 57.

12. Hill, *Intellectual Origins,* p. 178.

13. Douglas, *English Scholars,* p. 153.

14. Adair, *Fame,* p. 91; Douglas, *English Scholars,* p. 148; Hill, "Norman Yoke," p. 91 ("propagandist").

15. Earl, "Procrustean Feudalism," p. 33. For other references to "myth," see Pocock, *Ancient Constitution Retrospect,* p. 264 (also, see pp. 124–25); Pocock, *Politics,* p. 245, Dickinson, *Liberty and Property,* p. 141; Fussner, *Historical Revolution,* pp. 28, 31–32; Kramnick, "Augustan Politics," p. 38.

16. Wilsher, "Power Follows Property," p. 8; Kelley, "Rejoinder," p. 145; Laslett, "Book Review," p. 143. Recently, even lawyers who should know better have called the ancient constitution, or forensic history invoking the Saxon past, a myth.

Richards, "Interpretation and Historiography," pp. 500, 503–4; Grey, " Unwritten Constitution," pp. 852, 870.

17. Elton, "Butterfield," pp. 734–35. Also, see Kelley, "English Law and Renaissance," p. 25; Laslett, "Book Review," p. 143; Sommerville, "History and Theory," p. 250.

18. Douglas, *English Scholars,* p. 150.

19. Styles, "Politics and Research," p. 62.

20. Schuyler, *Empire,* p. 3.

21. Hulme, "Charles and Constitution," p. 114.

22. Butterfield, *George III and People,* p. 347. Law professors also fault lawyers and judges for bad history, although, of course, they need to cite authority for the rule, and for authority any historian will do. See, e.g., McGowan, "Ethos in Law and History," pp. 886–87.

23. Kelley, "Rejoinder," p. 143.

24. Douglas, *English Scholars,* pp. 149–54; Douglas, *Conquest and Historians,* p. 5; McDonald, *Novus,* p. 11.

25. Kirtland, "Sobering Reflections," p. 691.

1: Forensic History

1. Proclamation of Brigadier General Francis M'Lean, 15 June 1779, and Proclamation of Brigadier General Solomon Lovell, 29 July 1779, as printed in [Calef,] *Siege of Penobscot,* pp. 26–27, 32.

2. "The Resolutions as Recalled by Patrick Henry," reprinted in Morgan, *Prologue,* p. 48.

3. *Pennsylvania Gazette,* 15 May 1776, p. 2, col. 1. Similarly, on the British constitution: "How different from, and how much superior to, our present form of government, was the Saxon, or old constitution of England." *Maryland Gazette,* 2 May 1776, p. 2, col. 2.

4. "Demophilus," *English Constitution,* p. 17.

5. *Critical Review* 20 (1765): 475.

6. Abingdon, *Dedication to the People,* p. xlii (footnote); Abingdon, *Thoughts on Burke's Letter.*

7. John Wilkes once said: "I hold Magna Carta to be in full force in America as in Europe." Royle and Walvin, *English Radicals,* p. 24. For an American contention that the ancient constitution ran in the colonies, see "The British American, No. V," Williamsburg, 30 June 1774, *American Archives* 1: 495–98. Earlier, Lord Coke had held that English rights were not part of colonial law. Hulsebosch, "Ancient Constitution."

8. A procedure by which a private action allowed a person to accuse another of a crime, the practical purpose of which was to avoid the possibly that, following conviction, the accused's property was forfeited to the crown. On conviction by appeal, the accuser could recover damages because there was no forfeiture. By the eighteenth century appeal of felony was out of date because of the method of proof: trial by battle.

9. Speech of John Dunning, Commons Debates, 4 May 1774, *Parliamentary Debates* 4: 385. Similarly, see speech of John Dunning, Commons Debates, 29 April 1774, ibid., p. 323.

10. Speech of Alexander Wedderburn, Commons Debates, 4 May 1774, *Parliamentary Debates* 4: 386.

11. Speech of Edmund Burke, Commons Debates, 4 May 1774, *Parliamentary Debates* 4: 386.

12. Speech of Edmund Burke, Commons Debates, 29 April 1774, *Parliamentary Debates* 4: 324.

13. Otis, *Rights,* p. 441.

14. Lowth, *Durham Assize Sermon,* pp. 7–8.

15. Bailyn, *Ideological Origins,* p. 80 (quoting Otis).

16. Blackstone, *Commentaries* 2: 52.

17. Cartwright, *Constitution Produced,* p. 207.

18. *London Journal,* no. 696, 28 October 1732, p. 1, col. 2.

19. "In Legitimate Stirps."

20. Address of a Meeting of Freeholders of Hanover County to John Syme and Patrick Henry, 20 July 1774, *Revolutionary Virginia* 1: 140.

21. Bland, *An Inquiry,* reprinted in *Revolutionary Virginia* 1: 30–31.

22. *Craftsman,* no. 470, 5 July 1735, quoted in Kramnick, *Bolingbroke's Circle,* p. 179.

23. *Craftsman* 12, no. 405, 6 April 1734, p. 182.

24. *Craftsman* 12, no. 394, 19 January 1733–4, pp. 94–95.

25. *Craftsman* 14, no. 467, 14 June 1735, p. 20.

26. Nor was it, as has been claimed, "an historical myth . . . by which they [e.g., the seventeenth-century opponents of the Stuart kingship] sought to justify their actions, both to themselves and to others." Greenberg, "Confessor's Laws," p. 611.

27. Pocock, *Virtue, Commerce, History,* p. 94.

28. Pocock, "Origins of Study," p. 233.

29. Willman, "Blackstone and Caroline Law," p. 42.

30. Kelley, "English law and Rennaissance," p. 25.

31. Pocock, *Myth of Locke,* p. 3.

32. Burgess, *Ancient Constitution,* pp. 19, 87, 226–27. Also, see Resnick, "Locke and Ancient Constitution," p. 99; Fine, "Rule of Law and Marxism," p. 202.

33. Pocock, "Origins of Study," p. 237.

34. Pocock, "Political Thought," p. 290. Similarly the debate over the origin of Parliament has recently been described as "a perennial battleground for political factions seeking charter myths to legitimate their contemporary positions." Wilsher, "Power Follows Property," p. 9. Also, see Douglas, *English Scholars,* p. 120; Hill, "Norman Yoke," p. 63; Weston, "Legal Sovereignty," p. 412; Styles, "Politics and Research," p. 61.

35. "Parliament," *Scots Magazine* 38 (1775): 15.

36. For a short discussion, see *Abridged Edition,* pp. xvii–xx; for a more detailed discussion, see *Authority to Legislate,* pp. 17–33.

37. Fortescue, *De Laudibus,* pp. 45–47.

38. Styles, "Politics and Research," p. 55.

39. *Authority of Rights,* pp. 47–59.

40. Ferguson, "Fortescue," p. 189.

2: The Advocacy of Lawyers

1. For example, Burgess, *Ancient Constitution,* pp. 17–18, 90; Thompson, "Significant Silences," pp. 282–83; Miller, "Potential for Absolutism," p. 197; Resnick, "Locke and Ancient Constitution," p. 112.

2. Pocock, *Ancient Constitution,* p. 36.

3. Laslett, "Book Review," p. 143. Also, see Pocock, *Politics,* p. 213; Earl, "Procrustean Feudalism," p. 36; Styles, "Politics and Research," pp. 49–72; Dickinson, *Liberty and Property,* p. 63.

4. "[A] number of practising English lawyers in the period (such as Lord Ellesmere) were perfectly capable of contemplating historical change in the English law, and in a way the real puzzle is why men like Edward Coke did not do so." Tuck, *Natural Rights Theories,* p. 83. Also, see Pocock, *Ancient Constitution Retrospect,* pp. 273–74.

5. Willman, "Blackstone and Caroline Law," p. 44. Also, see p. 42.

6. Sharpe, *Sir Robert Cotton,* pp. 23, 224–25; Schoeck, "Elizabethan Society," p. 421.

7. Yale, "Hobbes and Hale," p. 128. Also, see Kelley, "English Law and Renaissance," pp. 65, 24ff.

8. [Leslie,] *Constitution, Laws and Government;* Anon., *Dectector Detected,* p. 7; [Campbell,] *Liberty and Right,* p. 25; St. Amand, *Historical Essay,* preface (n.p.); Anon., *View of Internal Policy,* pp. 11–13; [Ferguson,] *Remarks on a Pamphlet,* p. 40.

9. [Ramsay,] *Historical Essay,* pp. 12–13.

10. Paley, *Principles of Philosophy,* pp. 465–66; Halifax, *Charles II,* p. 68.

11. As John Toland wrote in 1717. Kenyon, *Revolution Principles,* pp. 197–98. Toland was not a lawyer. For lawyers, both common and Scots, see Plowden, *Rights of Englishmen,* p. 129; Millar, *Observations Concerning Ranks,* pp. 228–50; Canning, *Letter to Hillsborough,* pp. 24–25; Speech of Lord Mansfield, Lords Debates, 3 February 1766, in Holliday, *Life of Mansfield,* pp. 242–43.

12. Fortescue-Aland, "Preface," pp. xxviii–xxix. Also, see [Grange,] *Late Excise,* p. 7. For a recent discussion, see Lucas, "Burke's Doctrine of Prescription," p. 56.

13. [Bolingbroke,] *Dissertation,* pp. 147–48.

14. [Reeves,] *Thoughts, Second Letter,* pp. 65–66.

15. "[E]ven Coke . . . was far from being the blind idiot that some historians of ideas have tried to make him. In the end, his immemorial law boils down to general principles and maxims, while he knew that the positive law itself was capable of change and development." Elton, "Review Essay," p. 97.

16. Fielding, *Increase of Robbers,* p. v.

17. Hale, *History of Common Law,* p. 40. For Hale's Argonaut jurisprudence, see Berman, "Origins of Jurisprudence," pp. 1713–14. John Selden also wrote of the ancient constitution as an often repaired ship retaining its shape while refitted with new materials. Christianson, "Young Selden," p. 298. For Hale and history, see Yale, "Hobbes and Hale," p. 127; Klein, "Ancient Constitution," p. 43. The analogy of changing law to an everchanging ship was also employed to explain Roman law. Kantorowicz, *King's Two Bodies,* p. 295.

18. St. Amand, *Historical Essay,* preface.

19. Fortescue Aland, "Preface," pp. xiii–xiv.

20. King, *Essay,* p. 33.

21. "Book Review," *Critical Review* 22 (1766): 363 (quoting Edward King).

22. Wynne, *Eunomus* 3: 327. Also, see Tucker, *Letter to Burke,* pp. 31–32; Anon., *Letter to Doctor Tucker,* p. 3; Lowth, *Durham Assize Sermon,* p. 8.

23. Wooddeson, *Jurisprudence,* p. 143.

24. Wooddeson, *Laws of England* 1: 28.

25. Wooddeson, *Jurisprudence,* p. 70.

26. Squire, *Foundation,* pp. 81–82.

27. *London Journal,* no. 696, 28 October 1732, p. 1, col. 1. Also, see Rutherforth, *Natural Law* 2: 110; Thompson,"Fundamental Law," p. 1112.

28. "The Federalist No. 5," in *Federalist,* p. 24.

29. Stuart, *Historical Dissertation of Constitution,* p. 290.

30. Reeves, *Thoughts, Second Letter,* pp. 8–9.

31. Gregor, "Preface" to Fortescue, p. iv. "If Men would apply Themselves more than They generally do to the reading of antient [Roman] History, They would justly be alarm'd at our present Circumstances." *Craftsman* 12, no. 413, 1 June 1734, p. 229. Also, see Herring, *Regicide Sermon,* p. 23.

32. Lee, *Speech Intended,* p. 13.

33. [Rymer,] *Prospect of Government,* p. 66. One hundred years later a survey starting with 1264 concluded: "I have proved, that the constitution, through a series of years, has been arriving at that perfection which it attained at the revolution." [Basset,] *Equal Representation,* p. 12.

34. Adair, *Fame,* p. 97. Also, see Commager, *Jefferson,* pp. 127, 144–45, 150; Commager, "Enlightenment," p. 27.

35. For example, Madison's use of history discussed in Adair, *Fame,* pp. 134ff.

36. "History was the main field of interest. If law is associated with history—and the colonists so regarded it—history emerges as the largest single category" of what was read by eighteenth-century Americans. Colbourn, *Lamp of Experience,* p. 20.

37. Colbourn, *Lamp of Experience,* p. 25.

38. Colbourn, *Lamp of Experience,* p. 84. Somewhat similarly see p. 25.

39. "By 'law-office' history, I mean the selection of data favorable to the position being advanced without regard or concern for contradictory data or proper evaluation of the relevance of the data proffered." Kelly, "Clio and the Court," p. 122n13.

40. Oaks, "Legal History," p. 451.

41. For an extended discussion, see "Forensic History."

42. *London Journal,* no. 696, 28 October 1732, p. 1, col. 1.

43. Quoted in Roche, "Convention as Case Study," p. 180.

44. Douglas, *English Scholars,* pp. 20–21; Sharpe, *Sir Robert Cotton,* pp. 104–5, 248; Smith, *Gothic Bequest,* pp. 28–30, 56–57.

45. Squire, *Foundation,* pp. 3–4.

46. Speech of Edmund Burke, Commons Debates, 8 May 1780, *Parliamentary History* 21: 603–4. Also, see Pocock, *Virtue,* pp. 301–2.

47. Clive, *Not By Fact Alone,* p. 7.

48. It should be added that this use of history has both been noted and approved by some recent historians. Greenberg, "Confessor's Laws," pp. 611–13; Tarlton, "Rulers now on Earth," p. 295; Christianson, "Young Selden," p. 277; Christianson, "Five Knights' Case," pp. 74–75. Similarly, see Seaberg, "Norman Conquest," p. 805.

49. [Hervey,] *Ancient and Modern Liberty,* pp. 4–5.

50. [Bolingbroke,] *Dissertation,* p. 102.

51. [Bolingbroke,] *Dissertation,* p. 144.

52. Fielding, *Grand Jury Charge,* p. 16.

53. *Concept of Liberty,* p. 24. For a more detailed discussion of the ownership and purchase of civil rights as well as of liberty, see *Authority of Rights,* pp. 96–131 (for purchase by blood also, see pp. 127–29).

54. Even though that premise was often stated: "Besides, says the author of the letter on General Warrants, an Act of Parliament newly made, is not so venerable

in the eyes of the world, or so secure against future alterations, as the old common law of the land, which has been from time immemorial, the inheritance of every Englishman, and is on account of its antiquity, held, as it were sacred in every man's mind." [Glover,] *Considerations,* p. 8.

55. [Molesworth,] "Preface," pp. ii–iii.

3: The Authority of the Past

1. "In the Taught Tradition," pp. 931–74.

2. Fortescue-Aland, "Preface," p. xv.

3. [Wilkes,] *Letter to Johnson,* pp. 14–15.

4. Digges, quoted in Prynne, *Seasonable Vindication,* p. 18.

5. "The Word Parliament made such a terrible sound as wou'd Intimidate a person of small Resolution and Courage, and make him forego the Argument even thro' Fear. A Stranger to the Controversy wou'd Imagine, that Parliaments were as Ancient at least, as the Flood, and that a House of Commons was preserv'd in *Noah's* Ark." Earbery, *Old Constitution,* p. i.

6. See, e.g., Prynne, *Second Part,* pp. 3–14. The appeal was frequently made in grand jury charges. See, e.g., Shelton, *Charge to Suffolk Grand Jury,* p. 17.

7. Gregor, "Preface," p. v.

8. There is, however, little merit to the suggestion that in the early seventeenth century "the antiquity of a system of positive law was proof of its conformity to the eternal Law of Reason." Styles, "Politics and Research," p. 54.

9. [Cook,] *Argumentum,* p. xviii.

10. Speech of Lord Keeper Finch, 3 November 1640, printed in Rushworth, *Historical Collections* 1: 13.

11. Browning, *Court Whigs,* p. 38.

12. Pole, *Gift of Government,* p. 4. What change actually threatened was not the character of the state but the authority of law.

13. Pocock, *Politics,* p. 82.

14. Although the rule was that legal arguments were given strength by the passage of time. "[T]here is no legal argument which hath such force in our courts of law, as those which are drawn from the words of antient writs." [Barrington,] *Observations on Statutes,* p. 78.

15. Shelton, *Charge to Suffolk Grand Jury,* p. 21.

16. "Book Review," *Critical Review* 22 (1766): 362–63.

17. Lawson, *Politica Sacra,* p. 148.

18. Hargrave, "Preface," pp. iv–v.

19. [Somers,] *Brief History,* p. 13.

20. Atkyns, *Power of Parliament,* pp. 17–18.

21. In another work, Prynne proved English fundamental laws and rights "in a *Chronologicall way*" by surveying *"the ancient Britons, Saxons, Danes, Normans, and English Kings, till our present times; plentifully, undeniably evidencing, declaring, vindicating, asserting, establishing, perpetuating these Fundamentall, Hereditary Rights, Liberties, Priviledges, Franchises, Customes, Lawes."* Prynne, *Second Part,* p. 1.

22. Prynne, *Plea for Lords,* "To the Reader," p. [11].

23. Prynne, *Plea for Lords,* p. 5.

24. Prynne, *Plea for Lords,* p. 5.

25. Prynne, *Plea for Lords,* pp. 14–15.

26. "[I]f the Laws and Customs of the Realm were, that the King himself might call two Knights, Citizens and Burgesses to Parliament, such as himself should nominate in his Writ out of every County, City and Borough, without the Freeholders, Citizens, and Burgesses election of them, by a common agreement and consent to such a Law and usage made by their Ancestors, and submitted and consented to for some ages without repeal, this Law and Custom were sufficient to make such Knights, Citizens and Burgesses lawfull Members of Parliament, obliging their posterity whiles unrepealed." Prynne, *Plea for Lords,* p. 15.

27. Prynne, *Plea for Lords,* pp. 18–19.

28. For a recent discussion of this point of law, see Lamont, *Prynne,* pp. 179–80.

29. Prynne, *Plea for Lords,* p. 19.

30. Prynne, *Plea for Lords,* p. 21.

31. Prynne, *Plea for Lords,* p. 21.

32. [Rokeby,] *Further Examination,* p. 100.

33. [Ramsay,] *Historical Essay,* p. 144.

34. Pocock, "Origins of Study," p. 237.

35. Atkyns, *Power of Parliament,* p. 17. Edmund Burke also overstated the principle when he claimed, "Our Constitution is a prescriptive constitution; it is a constitution whose sole authority is that it has existed time out of mind." Dickinson, "Debate on Sovereignty," p. 199.

36. Quoted in Pocock, *Politics,* p. 226. In the eighteenth century, unlike today, the right to government was considered to be a fundamental civil right. *Authority of Rights,* pp. 39–46.

37. Wooddeson, *Jurisprudence,* p. 46.

38. Dickinson, "Debate on Sovereignty," p. 197.

39. Wooddeson, *Jurisprudence,* pp. 35–36.

40. Adams in *Boston Gazette,* 1 February 1773, reprinted in Adams, *Works* 3: 540.

41. Adams in *Boston Gazette,* 18 January 1773, reprinted in Adams, *Works* 3: 526–28. Adams's lesson that custom made law is one that some twentieth-century scholars have indicated is not worth keeping in mind, causing them to make misleading statements. For example, it was said of the dispute during the reign of James I concerning the antiquity of the House of Commons: "The statements of the anti-royalist party contain frequent references to the antiquity of the House. And nothing can have served better than this assumption to convince men that the privileges of Parliament were not of royal grace but of inherent right." Butterfield, *Englishman and History,* p. 47. Butterfield's history is correct, but the implication misses the mark of accuracy. The evidence of antiquity was argued not to "convince" but to *prove* the constitutionality of the privilege.

42. Adams in *Boston Gazette,* 1 February 1773, reprinted in Adams, *Works* 3: 546.

43. But see Earbery, *Old Constitution,* pp. xii, 6–7. Whigs, of course, still made much of the royalists' claims of passive obedience preached in Charles II's and James II's reigns. Withers, *Whigs Vindicated,* p. 5.

44. A recent historian, writing of the "prejudice" and "[t]he chauvinism of common lawyers," has suggested that in the seventeenth century "the enemies at the gates, of course, were those twin menaces, civil and canon law," which common lawyers believed was the law of arbitrary tyranny. Kelley, "English Law and Renaissance," pp. 37–38. Whether true or not for the seventeenth century, Kelley's statement is not true for the eighteenth, when common lawyers were not concerned

with civil law but theorized that it and canon law were rendered harmless by merging into immemorial custom. "Many of our present ecclesiastical laws are undoubtedly of foreign extraction, and some are entirely of English origin. But now they all alike depend, as to their general binding authority, on the same foundations as the whole body of our English laws, immemorial custom, and express act of parliament." Wooddeson, *Jurisprudence,* pp. 155–56.

45. [Barrington,] *Revolution Principles,* p. 68.

46. Shelton, *Charge to Suffolk Grand Jury,* pp. 10–11. The Westminster grand jury was reminded that "the Patriarchal Scheme, and the Doctrines of indefeisible, unalienable Hereditary Right are of mere modern Invention. . . . So that you see, the Title of his present Majesty King GEORGE is unquestionable, and most agreeable to our Ancient Constitution and Laws." Charge of 24 April 1728, Gonson, *Charges,* p. 20.

47. Petyt, *Jus Parliamentarium,* preface.

48. Jones, *Constitutional Criterion,* pp. 2–3.

49. Jones, *Constitutional Criterion,* pp. 3–4.

50. Jones, *Constitutional Criterion,* p. 3.

51. Burgh, *Political Disquisitions* 3: 271.

52. Pocock, "Machiavelli," p. 572; Pocock, *Politics,* p. 133.

53. *Authority of Law,* pp. 29–37; "In Legitimate Stirps."

54. Eliot, *Give Cesar his Due,* p. 36n.

55. [Bolingbroke,] *Dissertation,* p. 159.

56. Locke, *Two Treatises,* Book 2, Sec. 139.

57. Browning, *Court Whigs,* p. 196.

58. [Arbuthnot,] *Freeholder's Catechism,* p. 9.

59. *Concept of Liberty,* pp. 55–67, 74–83.

60. Campbell, *Duty of Allegance,* pp. 24–25. This sermon got Campbell into trouble with the authorities, and he thought it advisable to publish a second edition, which is available in many more research libraries than is the first. In the second version of the sermon the passage quoted is altered in wording but not in meaning. Campbell, *Duty Second Edition,* pp. 41–42, 43.

61. Eliot, *Give Cesar his Due,* p. 36n.

62. It has been suggested that during the early seventeenth century, the ancient constitution was not a doctrine opposed "to the royal sovereignty or even prerogative." Pocock, *Ancient Constitution Retrospect,* p. 270. The issue may be whether it opposed arbitrary prerogativism and not prerogative power exercised by law. It should be recognized, however, that exponents of prerogativism could speak of championing the rule of law through immutable ancient liberties. The earl of Strafford in 1628 had that in mind when speaking on behalf of the Petition of Right: "We must vindicate—what? New things? No; our ancient lawful and vital liberties, by reinforcing the ancient laws made by our ancestors, by setting such a stamp on them as no licentious spirit shall dare hereafter to enter upon them." Straka, "Sixteen Eighty-Eight," pp. 149–50.

4: The Advocacy of the Past

1. Pocock, *Ancient Constitution,* p. 51.

2. See, e.g., Posner, "Blackstone," p. 584 (quoting Blackstone, *Commentaries*); Lucas, "Burke's Doctrine of Prescription," p. 56; Hulsebosch, "Ancient Constitution," p. 445.

3. Quoted in Fussner, *Historical Revolution,* p. 135.

4. Anon., *Defence of English History,* p. 11.

5. "Grand Jury Charge," Warrington, *Works,* p. 649 (also, see pp. 655, 388).

6. [Atwood,] *Antiquity and Justice,* p. 83. Also, see Anon., *Enquiry into Legal Rights,* p. 16; [Barrington,] *Revolution Principles,* p. 55; Pocock, *Ancient Constitution,* p. 16.

7. Johnson, *Notes on Pastoral,* p. 57. This was the essence of the argument made to persuade Oliver Cromwell that he should assume the familiar office of "king" rather than be Lord Protector. *Rule of Law,* pp. 52–67.

8. Johnson, *Notes on Pastoral,* p. 22.

9. Johnson, *Notes on Pastoral,* pp. 57–58. Also, see Anon., *Enquiry into Legal Rights,* pp. 3, 13, 16.

10. "The great *Security* of the Prince consists in this, That the *same Medium* which secures the Peoples *Rights,* secures his *Prerogative.*" *London Journal,* no. 722, 28 April 1733, p. 1, col. 2.

11. Speech of Thomas Hedley, Commons Debates, 28 June 1610, in *Proceedings in Parliament 1610,* 2: 173–74.

12. Abingdon, *Thoughts on Burke's Letter,* p. li. For the strongest reaction to Blackstone's new jurisprudence of arbitrary sovereignty, see [Sheridan,] *Observations on the Doctrine.*

13. *Concept of Liberty,* pp. 91–97. Among the radicals of Britain the new law of parliamentary sovereignty was resisted long after it was law and the old law still was appealed to. "*Trial by Jury,* as an element of the *Constitution,* was, consequently, *antecedent* to all *Law,* and *superior* to all *Law,* as no law can abolish it. It was even centuries anterior to Lawyers by profession." Cartwright, *Constitution Produced,* p. 138.

14. Pocock, "Machiavelli," pp. 571–72.

15. [Bolingbroke,] *Dissertation,* p. 198. Also, see Sommerville, "History and Theory," p. 254.

16. Kern, *Kingship,* p. 179. Also, see Clanchy, "Remembering Past," p. 172.

17. "Power" was Chief Justice Hale's word: "Usage and Custom generally receiv'd, do *Obtinere vim Legis.* . . . This is that which directs Discents, has settled some ancient Ceremonies and Solemnities in Conveyances, Wills and Deeds, and in many more Particulars." Hale, *History of Common Law,* p. 44.

18. Wooddeson, *Jurisprudence,* pp. 35, 47. It was not a matter of how well an institution worked, but of public approval of its force and operation.

19. Atkyns, *Enquiry into Power,* p. 6. Fortescue-Aland also meant implied consent when he wrote: "Besides, the Laws themselves gain Strength and Authority by the Antiquity of their Profession. The longer any Laws continue in Use and Practice, the stronger and more forcible is the Argument for their Goodness and Excellence." Fortescue-Aland, "Preface," p. xv.

20. [Johnson,] *Defence of Magna Charta,* pp. 3–4 (quoting Fortescue). For the contrary contention that this was historical proof, see Skinner, "History and Ideology," p. 174.

21. The contention that custom extant for several generations was, therefore, approved by generations of people, and, for that reason, was republican or "democratic" law, was effectively employed by American common lawyers during the early republic to counter Jeffersonian contentions that law should be made by the "living generation," and that custom qua law was a "monarchial" device by which law was made not by elected legislatures, but by elitist lawyers. *Controlling the Law,* pp. 51–55.

22. Prynne, *Plea for Lords,* p. 5.

23. Quoted in Pocock, *Politics,* p. 227.

24. Gray, "Reason, Authority, and Imagination," p. 31.

25. Pocock, *Politics,* p. 173.

26. Thus it was reasoned that Parliament had the authority to legislate for and to tax the colonies because, even if the right had never before been exercised, "it is essential to government, founded in justice and equity, and in the law of nature and nations." Carlyle, *Justice and Necessity,* p. 10.

27. Hurd, *Moral and Political Dialogues,* p. 224.

28. [Dowdeswell,] *Sentiments of Freeholder,* p. 8.

29. Dimwiddy, *Wyvill,* p. 2.

30. Cartwright, *Constitution Produced,* p. 164n7.

31. It is not suggested that there have not been historians who have pointed out that "history" was a weapon in the struggle over sovereignty. Weston, "Legal Sovereignty," p. 417; Thompson, "Idea of Conquest," pp. 37–38; Styles, "Politics and Research," p. 54.

32. [Bacon,] *Discourse,* "Advertisement" to "First Part" (n.p.).

33. [Bacon,] *Continuation,* p. 1. The "Mens Pens" were royalist "histories" that rejected Cokeian constitutional law, claiming that the crown created Parliament at its pleasure. Earl, "Procrustean Feudalism," p. 35.

34. [Bacon,] *Discourse,* pp. 69, 70.

35. Starkey, "Advertisement" to [Bacon,] *Discourse* (n.p.).

36. [Cook,] *Argumentum.*

37. Heylyn, *Stumbling-Block,* p. 267.

38. Skinner, "History and Ideology," p. 169.

39. Quoted in Earl, "Procrustean Feudalism," p. 38. Earl says Tyrrell was commenting on royalist history, but it is evident he was commenting on constitutional law.

40. Atkyns, *Power of Parliament,* p. 14.

41. Atkyns, *Tracts,* p. 31.

42. Rex *v.* Williams, 13 *State Trials* 1369, 1392 [1684–95].

43. Ironically, Prynne was one of the "Innovating Writers" whom Atkyns condemned. The reason is that, "disillusioned by the outcome of the civil war, [he] switched sides and became a crypto-royalist." Professor Weston suggests that Prynne cannot be discussed in the context that he is here discussed unless it is understood that he switched sides. But why? Because it bears on his sincerity? Weston, "Diverse Viewpoints," p. 248.

44. Prynne, *Seasonable Vindication,* p. 9.

45. Prynne, *Plea for Lords,* "Epistle," p. [2].

46. Prynne, *Seasonable Vindication,* pp. 3, 7.

47. Prynne, *Truth Triumphing over Falsehood,* "The Epistle to the Reader," p. [1].

48. Prynne, *Seasonable Vindication,* p. 5.

49. Prynne, *Seasonable Vindication,* p. 8 (also, see p. 7).

50. Prynne, *Second Part,* pp. 13–14.

51. Prynne, *Second Part,* p. 49.

52. Prynne, *Second Part,* p. 17.

53. Prynne, *Second Part,* pp. 64–65.

54. *Authority to Tax,* pp. 280–84.

55. Anon., *Divine Rights,* p. 60.

56. This paragraph summarizes a theme that is dealt with more extensively in *Authority of Law,* e.g., pp. 163–73.

57. Anon., *Divine Rights,* p. 81 (quoting a critic of the legal theories of Bishop Benjamin Hoadly).

58. Pocock, *Ancient Constitution Retrospect,* p. 351.

59. Smith, *Gothic Bequest,* p. 17.

60. Pocock, "Origins of Study," p. 234. See "Editor's Introduction" to Bolingbroke, *Political Writings,* p. xlii; Kramnick, *Bolingbroke's Circle,* p. 128.

61. Kramnick, "Augustan Politics," p. 37. Brady is said to have "raised out of the morass of a pseudo-historical argument the first serious study of the Norman Conquest." Styles, "Politics and Research," p. 72. Also, see Dickinson, "Debate on Sovereignty," p. 191.

62. Klein, "Ancient Constitution," p. 24.

63. Brady, *Introduction,* "Epistle" (n.p.).

64. See, e.g., [Brady,] *Great Point,* pp. 2–25.

65. Kramnick, "Augustan Politics," p. 37. Also, see Kramnick, *Bolingbroke's Circle,* pp. 128–29.

66. Weston, "Legal Sovereignty," p. 431. Also, see Weston and Greenberg, *Grand Controversy,* pp. 196–97.

67. [Brady,] *Great Point,* pp. 25–26.

68. Brady, *Complete History,* "Preface" (n.p.).

69. Pocock, *Ancient Constitution Retrospect,* p. 353.

70. Kramnick, "Editor's Introduction" to Bolingbroke, *Political Writings,* p. xlii. For similar evaluations of Brady as a monarchy absolutist, see Skinner, "History and Ideology," p. 153; Weston, "Ancient Constitution," p. 407; Weston, "Legal Sovereignty," p. 431; Gough, "James Tyrrell," pp. 585–86, 606.

71. St. Amand, *Historical Essay,* p. 89; charge of 9 October 1728, Gonson, *Charges,* p. 107. For an earlier anonymous recognition, see N. N., *Letter from Oxford,* p. 8.

72. Sullivan, "A Discourse Concerning the Laws and Government of England," in Sullivan, *Lectures on the Constitution,* p. xix(n); Hargrave, "Preface," pp. lxxxiii, lxxix.

73. [Atwood,] *Additions Answering Omissions,* pp. 37–38. For Atwood on Brady, see Weston, "Legal Sovereignty," pp. 412–13.

74. [Reeves,] *Thoughts, Second Letter,* pp. 117–18.

75. [Atwood,] *Jus Anglorum,* "Preface," p. [18].

76. Atkyns, *Power of Parliament,* p. 14.

77. [Atwood,] *Additions Answering Omissions,* p. 37.

78. [Atwood,] *Jus Anglorum,* "Preface" p. [1].

79. Moore, "Comment on Pocock," p. 174.

80. Johnson, *Reflections on the History,* p. 1; Johnson, *Answer to the History,* p. 1. Johnson was criticizing [Seller,] *History of Passive Obedience.*

81. Petyt, *Jus Parliamentarium,* "Preface".

82. Atkyns, *Power of Parliament,* p. 17.

83. Atkyns, *Power of Parliament,* p. 13.

84. Smith, *Gothic Bequest,* p. 8.

85. Kramnick, "Editor's Introduction," p. xliii. "But Nemesis awaited Brady. The Revolution robbed him of place, and, for over two hundred years, of recognition of his true stature." Smith, *Gothic Bequest,* p. 8.

86. "The ancient Constitution of *England* was as arbitrary as any on the Continent." Anon., *Ancient and Modern Constitution,* p. 7.

87. Anon., *Defence of English History,* pp. 13–14.

88. *Daily Gazetteer,* no. 6, 5 July 1735, p. 1, col. 2.

89. [Reeves,] *Thoughts, Second Letter,* p. 117.

90. Anon., *Spirit and Principles,* p. 29.

91. Ellys, *Tracts on Liberty,* p. 195.

92. [Galloway,] *Letter,* pp. 260–62; [Sinclair,] *Considerations on Proceedings,* pp. 6–7.

93. For a discussion of some of these, see Kenyon, *Revolution Principles,* p. 158, and Pocock, *Ancient Constitution Retrospect,* p. 303.

94. Neale, *Elizabeth I and Parliaments* 1: 407. Neale also described the incident as "Deviationist history castigated by authority: another curious example of the likeness of those days to ours!" Ibid., pp. 408–09.

95. Kramnick, "Augustan Politics," p. 35.

96. "This scurvy Pedigree of the Commons in Parliament, drawn up by Dr. *Brady,* was so well liked by the Loyal Clergy . . . That Mr. *Petyt* found the Tide so strong against him, as not to venture on a Reply." Johnson, *Argument Proving,* p. 4.

97. Witmer, *Property Qualifications,* p. 28.

98. Speech of the earl of Albemarle, Lords Debates, 2 December 1795, *Parliamentary History* 32: 681–83.

99. Speech of Serjeant Adair, Commons Debates, 23 November 1795, *Parliamentary History* 32: 625.

100. Speech of John Courtenay, Commons Debates, 26 November 1795, *Parliamentary History* 32: 645.

101. Proceedings of 5 December 1795, *Parliamentary History* 32: 681.

102. Brady, *Introduction,* "Epistle" (n.p.).

103. [Atwood,] *Additions Answering Omissions,* p. 41. Atwood went on to contend that representation did not receive its "Perfection" from the king, but "that *its Perfection* were such as we say it has at this day, *viz.* for Lords to come of Right in their own Persons, and that the Commons should send Representatives of their free Choice." Ibid., p. 42.

104. Weston, "Legal Sovereignty," p. 416. For another good discussion, see Thompson, "Idea of Conquest," p. 38n26.

105. [Ibbetson,] *National Assemblies,* p. 36.

106. Sullivan, *Lectures on the Constitution,* p. 16.

107. Wooddeson, *Laws of England* 1: 6.

108. Sullivan, *Lectures on the Constitution,* p. 170.

5: Forensic Techniques of Ancient Constitutionalism

1. Coke especially. See Holdsworth, "Coke," p. 306.

2. Gough, *Fundamental Law,* p. 6.

3. Brady, *Complete History,* "Preface" (n.p.).

4. [Ibbetson,] *Folclande and Boclande,* pp. 8–9.

5. [Ibbetson,] *National Assemblies,* p. 33.

6. Towers, *Vindication of Locke,* p. 55.

7. Brady, *Introduction,* p. 39.

8. Anon., *Old Constitution,* p. 52. The work criticized was Earbery, *Old Constitution.*

9. Wood, *Creation,* pp. 8–9.

10. Colbourn, *Lamp of Experience,* p. 189.

11. Sharpe, *Sir Robert Cotton,* p. 44.

12. Warrington, "A Speech against the Assertion of Arbitrary Power, and the Non-Swearers," in Warrington, *Works,* p. 389.

13. Earbery, *Old Constitution,* p. ii.

14. *Junius,* "To the Right Hon. Lord M[ansfield]," *Gentleman's Magazine* 40 (1770): 516.

15. Blackstone, *Tracts,* p. 20, and Blackstone, *Analysis of the Laws,* p. 11.

16. Wooddeson, *Laws of England* 1: 18–19.

17. Wynne, *Eunomus* 3: 61–62.

18. Carysfort, *Letter to Huntingdonshire,* p. 5.

19. Wynne, *Eunomus* 1: 60.

20. Atkyns, *Tracts,* p. 150.

21. Stuart, "Discourse," pp. vii–viii, n8.

22. [Goodenough,] *Constitutional Advocate,* p. 27.

23. [Dyson,] *Case of Middlesex,* p. 41.

24. Missing, *Letter to Mansfield on Instructions,* pp. 10–11.

25. Dugdale, *Origines Juridicales,* p. 3, col. 1.

26. Sidney, *Discourses Concerning Government,* p. 289.

27. [Seward,] *Rights of the People,* p. 37.

28. Cartwright, *Constitution Produced,* pp. 207–8.

29. [Leslie,] *Constitution, Laws and Government,* p. 8.

30. [Leslie,] *Constitution, Laws and Government,* p. 17.

31. Anon., *Political Disquisitions,* p. 3.

32. Paley, *Essay upon the Constitution,* p. 3.

33. [Ramsay,] *Historical Essay,* p. 10.

34. [Bolingbroke,] *Dissertation,* pp. 194–95.

35. [Ramsay,] *Historical Essay,* p. 10.

36. "Book Review," *Critical Review* 19 (1765): 208. Also, see Burgh, *Political Disquisitions* 1: 171.

37. "Those eighteenth-century Englishmen who were dissatisfied with their constitution and wanted to reform it typically presented their proposed reforms as involving a return to the constitution's original principles—a doctrine not characteristic of opposition thought under the first four Stuarts and involving attitudes rather fundamentalist than prescriptive, rather reactionary than conservative." Pocock, *Politics,* p. 133.

38. As was also true for the "prerogative" side in the seventeenth century. Evans, "Antiquity of Parliaments," p. 221.

39. [Macfarlane,] *History of George III,* pp. 235–36.

40. "Hanseaticus," *St. James's Chronicle,* 26 August 1766, reprinted in *Collection in Favour of Liberty* 2: 44–45.

41. [Vincent,] *Letter to Dr. Richard Watson,* p. 14.

42. [MacFarlane,] *History of George III,* p. 239.

43. Thomson, *Constitutional History,* p. 3.

44. Ashton, "Tradition and Innovation," p. 213.

45. [Galloway,] *Letter,* pp. 266–67.

46. Kelly, "Clio and the Court," p. 155.

47. Kelly, "Clio and the Court," p. 157.

48. Kelly, "Clio and the Court," p. 131.

49. Burgh, *Political Disquisitions* 3: 428–29. Of course, it was a technique that used what purported to be history to disguise reform, and was indulged in even by individuals, such as John Locke, who were not historically minded. "[T]he set[t]lement of the nation upon the sure grounds of peace and security . . . can noe way soe

well be don[e] as by restoreing our ancient government, the best possibly that ever was if taken and put togeather [*sic*] all of a peice [*sic*] in its originall constitution." Letter from John locke to Edward Clarke, 29 January/8 February 1689, *Correspondence of Locke* 3: 545 (letter 1102).

50. Cartwright, *Constitution Produced,* p. 172.

51. Cartwright, *Constitution Produced,* p. 177.

52. Day, *Two Speeches,* p. 17.

53. Paley, *Principles of Philosophy,* p. 465.

54. [Marat,] *Chains of Slavery,* p. 185; Gottschalk, *Jean Paul Marat,* pp. 6, 19.

55. Burgh, *Political Disquisitions* 3: 308.

56. Letter from John Wilkes to Fletcher Norton, 20 April 1773, *Gentleman's Magazine* 43 (1773): 201 (not directly quoting the letter).

57. Pudsey, *Constitution and Laws,* p. 51.

58. Speech of Edward Southwell, Commons Debates, 8 December 1744, *Parliamentary History* 13: 1039. That comment enjoyed other moments. E.g., "Machiavel," it was said, "asserted, that no government can be lasting which is not frequently reduced to its first principles." *Second Address;* Smith, *Gothic Bequest,* p. 85.

59. Speech of Edward Southwell, Commons Debates, 8 December 1744, *Parliamentary History* 13: 1045.

60. Speech of Edward Southwell, Commons Debates, 8 December 1744, *Parliamentary History* 13: 1039–40.

61. [Braxton,] *Address to the Convention,* pp. 11, 13.

62. [Braxton,] *Address to the Convention,* p. 11.

63. "Parliamentary history," *London Magazine* 45 (1776): 403. That same year it was contended that if the ministry restored triennial parliaments it would "heal the Breach, by restoring the Constitution." [Stewart,] *Letter to Dr. Price,* p. 18.

64. [Sharp,] *Legal Means,* pp. 3–4.

65. Sharp, *Defence,* pp. 15–16.

66. [Ramsay,] *Historical Essay,* p. 153.

67. *Second Address,* p. 14.

68. Day, *Two Speeches,* p. 11.

69. [Johnson,] *Argument Proving,* p. 3.

6: The Forensic History of Gothicism and Saxonism

1. Wynne, *Eunomus* 3: 55–56. Also, see Charge to Westminster Grand Jury, 9 October 1728, Gonson, *Charges,* pp. 102–7; Pocock, "Burke and Ancient Constitution," p. 138 (quoting Edmund Burke).

2. [Reeves,] *Thoughts, Second Letter,* pp. 67–68.

3. [Jacob,] *Laws of Liberty,* p. 1. Also, see the broad concept of Magna Carta in 1705, discussed in Gough, *Fundamental Law,* p. 166.

4. Anon., *Court of Star Chamber,* p. 12. Coke used the same metaphor, calling Magna Carta "the fountain of all the fundamental Laws of the Realm." Coke, "First Part," p. 17.

5. [Barrington,] *Observations on Statutes,* p. 3 (in this case referring to the 29th article of Magna Carta).

6. Anon., *Foundation of British Liberty,* p. 8.

7. De Lolme, *Constitution: New Edition,* p. 226.

8. Address of John Wilkes to the Gentlemen, Clergy, and Freeholders of Middlesex, 3 November 1768, in Wilkes, *English Liberty,* p. 209.

9. Speech to the Court of Commons Pleas, 6 May 1763, *Complete Collection of Wilkes,* p. 31.

10. Article of 27 June 1774, *American Archives* 1: 487.

11. Brady, *Complete History,* p. xxxiv.

12. De Lolme, *Constitution: New Edition,* pp. 26–28.

13. De Lolme, *Constitution: New Edition,* pp. 226–27.

14. Magna Carta, it was said, was "most boasted of by those who never read it. Those who have, can see that it is not at all in favour of what is fondly called the natural liberty of mankind, but only calculated for the benefit of a few landed tyrants who extorted it from their weak sovereign." Anon., *Essay on the Constitution,* p. 11.

15. Blackstone, *Great Charter,* p. vii; Blackstone, *Law Tracts* 2: xii–xiii.

16. [Sheridan,] *Observations on the Doctrine,* pp. 5–6.

17. Anon., *Judgment of Whole Kingdoms,* p. 20.

18. Colbourn, *Lamp of Experience,* p. 37 (quoting Roger Acherley).

19. [Robinson,] *Political Catechism,* pp. 34–35.

20. *Boston Gazette,* 10 May 1756, p. 1, col. 1. The *Gazette* was echoing a frequently reprinted pamphlet written around 1690. See, e.g., Care, *English Liberties Providence Edition,* p. 7.

21. Sidney, *Discourses Concerning Government,* p. 356. Magna Carta "is only an Abridgement of the ancient Laws and Customs of the Realm. Of the same Nature is the Petition of Right. . . ." *American Gazette,* p. 48. The connection with the Petition of Right was also old theory. "*Magna Charta,* instead of being superannuated, renews and recovers its pristine strength, and athletick vigor, by the *Petition of Right,* with our many other explanatory or declaratory Statutes." [Rymer,] *Prospect of Government,* p. 67.

22. Anon., *Defence of Magna Charta,* pp. 3–4. Also, see Twysden, *Certaine Considerations,* p. 58.

23. [Williams,] *Essential Rights,* p. 65.

24. [Fowle,] *Appendix to Eclipse,* pp. 20–21.

25. Kramnick, *Bolingbroke's Circle,* p. 139.

26. *The Crisis,* 8 September 1775, p. 542.

27. For further eighteenth-century uses of this "history," see Carysfort, *Letter to Huntingdonshire,* p. 4; Anon., *Reflections on Wilkes,* p. 7; Mr. Ralph, *A General View of Government in Europe,* reprinted in *Works of Algernon Sydney,* pp. 7–8; Anon., *Representative of London,* p. 6; Pudsey, *Constitution and Laws,* pp. 43–44.

28. Eliot, *Give Cesar his Due,* p. 33. For Gothicism in another election sermon, see Lockwood, *Worth and Excellence,* p. 11.

29. Pocock, *Politics,* p. 138.

30. De Lolme, *Constitution: New Edition,* pp. 127–36.

31. Frink, *Election Sermon,* p. 77n; Charge of 9 October 1728, Gonson, *Charges,* p. 76.

32. [Squire,] *Historical Essay on Ballance,* p. 37. Also, see [Barrington,] *Revolution Principles,* p. 69.

33. "Book Review," *Monthly Review* 51 (1774): 474 (reviewing Lee, *Appeal to Justice*).

34. Carysfort, *Letter to Huntingdonshire,* p. 4. Also, see Ralph, *General View,* in *Works of Algernon Sydney,* p. 28; St. Amand, *Historical Essay,* p. 15; [Rymer,] *Prospect of Government,* p. 73. For one of the most impressive uses of forensic history in this respect, see the survey of all the European kingdoms with common councils or parliaments,

leading to the conclusion that the English surely were "under the same constitution" as the Saxons and were "descendants from *Gaul.*" Petyt, *Ancient Right,* p. 84.

35. *Craftsman* 5 July 1735, quoted in Kramnick, "Augustan Politics," p. 52.

36. Kliger, *Goths,* p. 1.

37. Kliger, *Goths,* p. 3. Perhaps the chief eighteenth-century critic of the Gothic constitution was Dean Tucker, who insisted that Gothic liberty was not civil liberty but the liberty of warlords to plunder. Tucker, *Treatise,* pp. 61–62.

38. Lowth, *Durham Assize Sermon,* p. 7.

39. [Bolingbroke,] *Dissertation,* p. 102. Also, see Charge to Tower of London Grand Jury, 16 July 1728, and Charge to Westminster Grand Jury, 3 July 1729, Gonson, *Charges,* pp. 75, 129.

40. Memorial from James Logan to the House of Representatives, 2 February 1724, *Pennsylvania Archives* 2: 1638.

41. [Oldfield,] *History of the Boroughs* 1: 25.

42. Fielding, *Grand Jury Charge,* p. 4; Wright, *Grand Jury Speech,* p. 2.

43. Abingdon, *Dedication,* pp. xl–xli.

44. Squire, *Foundation,* pp. 12–13. Edward King in 1767 said that the Anglo-Saxons "*formed* the *embryo* of our constitution." Not so, John Cartwright replied. "[W]hat he calls an 'embryo', was in truth *the Constitution itself,* and nothing but the Constitution." Cartwright, *Constitution Produced,* pp. 46–47.

45. "Book Review," *Critical Review* 31 (1771): 15. Also, see *Monthly Review* 44 (1717): 469; [Hurd,] *Moral and Political Dialogues,* p. 243.

46. [Tyrrell,] *Brief Enquiry,* p. 10. For even earlier assertions of this law, see Saltern, *Of Antient Lawes,* cap. 1; Hunton, *Treatise on Monarchy* (London, 1643), quoted in Kliger, *Goths,* p. 131.

47. For what is perhaps the best criticism of Saxonism during the age of the American Revolution, contending that most Saxons were slaves to the arbitrary will of the barons and churchmen, see Tucker, *Treatise,* pp. 301–56.

48. Bacon, *Discourse,* p. 30. Some of Bacon's arguments were reprinted in Kliger, *Goths,* p. 139. The "electiveness" of the Saxon monarchy was debated at the Convention Parliament. Cherry, "Convention Parliament," pp. 394–95.

49. Wooddeson, *Laws of England* 1: 7. Also, see Cartwright, *Constitution Produced,* pp. 199, 206.

50. Bolingbroke quoted in Kramnick, "Editor's Introduction," p. xliii. Also, see James Tyrrell (1681) quoted in Kliger, *Goths,* p. 171.

51. Cartwright, *Appeal Civil and Military,* p. 216; [Ramsay,] *Historical Essay,* pp. 6–7.

52. Trumbull, *Discourse at New Haven,* p. 19; *Lloyd's Evening Post* (London), 14 July 1769, reprinted in *Massachusetts Gazette and Boston Post Boy,* 13 November 1769, p. 1, col. 1; Hawles, *Englishman's Right,* p. 4.

53. Prynne, *Seasonable Chapter Three,* pp. 1–2, 388–96; Shelton, *Charge to Suffolk Grand Jury,* p. 14.

54. Wooddeson, *Jurisprudence,* pp. 142–43; [Ramsay,] *Historical Essay,* p. 8.

55. Colbourn, *Lamp of Experience,* pp. 145–46 (quoting Richard Bland).

56. Ibbetson, *Folclande and Boclande,* p. 33.

57. [Ramsay,] *Historical Essay,* p. 32. There are good historical grounds for doubting that Ramsay was the author of this book. Butterfield, *George III and People,* p. 349n1. Contemporaries quoted it without attribution. See, e.g., *Society for Constitutional Information,* p. 30 (Huntington Library rare book #310802). Ramsay's Saxonism is discussed in Hill, "Norman Yoke," p. 86.

7: The Forensic History of the Norman Conquest

1. Thompson, "Idea of Conquest," p. 38.
2. Brown, "Norman Conquest," p. 109.
3. [Fullwood,] *Agreement Betwixt,* p. 7.
4. Pocock, *Ancient Constitution,* p. 212.
5. Douglas, *English Scholars,* pp. 150, 153. Also, see Douglas, *Conquest and Historians,* pp. 5–6, 8, 13; Evans, "Antiquity of Parliaments," pp. 208–9.
6. [Cook,] *Argumentum,* pp. ii–iii.
7. [Cook,] *Argumentum,* pp. cxii–cxiii.
8. Douglas, *English Scholars,* pp. 152–53.
9. [Cook,] *Argumentum,* "An Explanation of the Frontispiece" (n. p.).
10. Brady, *Introduction,* pp. 235–303.
11. Brady, *Introduction,* pp. 235–36, 241.
12. [Atwood,] *Answerer's Principles,* p. 5.
13. Hill, "Norman Yoke," p. 90.
14. Hale, *History of Common Law,* pp. 47–71; Wright, *Law of Tenures.* And, of course, as late as the 1820s John Cartwright was pursuing the argument. Cartwright, *Constitution Produced,* pp. 200, 208.
15. Minutes of 21 January 1692/93, *Parliamentary History* 5: 756.
16. Resolution of 21 January 1692/93, *Journals of Commons* 10: 786, col. 1. Burnet's book was published in London, 1689. Also, see [Burnet,] *Submission to Supream Authority,* "Preface." Other pamphlets that were burnt or got their authors into trouble for calling William III a "conqueror" included: [Blount,] *William and Mary Conquerors;* [Bohun,] *Non-Resistance.* But also, see Lloyd, *God's Ways,* pp. 54–60.
17. Bacon, *Discourse,* p. 99.
18. Anon., *Animadversions on Discourse,* pp. 4, 8.
19. Anon., *Obedience to Government,* p. 9; Anon., *Enquiry into Legal Rights,* pp. 19, 28–29, 30.
20. Hale, *History of Common Law,* p. 49. For Hobbes, who in the twentieth century seemed to be regarded somewhat of an authority, see Skinner, "History and Ideology," p. 168. For a discussion of the theory of the law of conquest, see Hale, *History of Common Law,* pp. 74–75; [Ramsay,] *Right of Conquest,* p. 3; Sutherland, "Conquest and Law," pp. 35–51.
21. [Tyrrell,] *Brief Enquiry,* p. 32.
22. *Craftsman* 14, no. 466, 7 June 1735, p. 3 (quoting [Hervey,] *Ancient and Modern Liberty*).
23. Pocock, "Robert Brady," p. 190n12.
24. Johnson, *Argument Proving,* p. 27.
25. Sullivan, *Treatise on the Feudal Law* (1772), quoted in *Monthly Review* 47 (1772): 45.
26. De Lolme, *Constitution: New Edition,* p. 10 footnote.
27. Hill, "Norman Yoke," p. 62n4.
28. Bever, *Discourse on Jurisprudence,* pp. 17–18.
29. [Ramsay,] *Historical Essay,* p. 50; Anon., *Whigs and Tories,* pp. 7–9; Anon., *Defence of English History,* p. 14; Earbery, *Old Constitution,* p. v.
30. See, e.g., [Collier,] *Vindiciae Juris Regii,* pp. 13–14.
31. Fortescue-Aland, "Preface," p. xv.

32. Prynne, *Seasonable Chapter Three,* p. 380. Also, see Vane, *A Healing Question propounded . . . .* (1660), in *Somers Tracts* 6: 306.

33. But see [Tyrrell,] *Brief Enquiry,* p. 33.

34. Wright, *Law of Tenures,* pp. 61–62; St. Amand, *Historical Essay,* p. 100; Hale, *History of Common Law,* pp. 83, 89–91; [Neville,] *Plato Redivivus,* p. 106; Colbourn, *Lamp of Experience,* pp. 34–35 (quoting Roger Acherley).

35. Hale, *History of Common Law,* pp. 58–59; Petyt, *Ancient Right,* Preface, p. 12; Prynne, *Seasonable Chapter Three,* p. 383.

36. Petyt, *Ancient Right,* Preface, pp. 18–19.

37. Wright, *Law of Tenures,* pp. 60–62; [Neville,] *Plato Redivivus,* pp. 106–7; Petyt, *Ancient Right,* Preface, p. 12; Bacon, *Discourse,* pp. 97–98.

38. Abingdon, *Dedication,* pp. xliii–xliv. Also, see Prynne, *Seasonable Chapter Three,* pp. 384–85.

39. Anon., *Judgment of Whole Kingdoms,* p. 55.

40. Prynne, *Seasonable Chapter Three,* p. 382. For the argument made as late as the age of the American Revolution, see Stuart, "Discourse," p. xi.

41. [Cook,] *Argumentum,* p. xx.

42. Nicolson, *English Historical Library,* p. 25; Bacon, *Discourse,* pp. 72–73.

43. *Guide to Rights,* p. 10; Charles M. Gray, "Editor's Introduction" to Hale, *History of Common Law,* pp. xxvii–xxviii (discussing arguments made by Sir Matthew Hale).

44. [Tyrrell,] *Brief Enquiry,* p. 33; [Fullwood,] *Agreement Betwixt,* pp. 6–7; Prynne, *Seasonable Chapter Three,* p. 380; Bacon, *Discourse,* p. 71; Sommerville, "History and Theory," p. 255 (discussing some early seventeenth-century arguments).

45. [Atkyns,] *Treatise of Jurisdiction,* p. 6; Churchill, *Divi Britannici,* pp. 190–91; Bacon, *Discourse,* p. 72.

46. "The laws of Edward the Confessor are principally declaratory of the ancient constitution of the Saxons. . . ." Ibbetson, *Folclande and Boclande,* p. 26. "[T]hese Laws of *Edward* the Confessor, were not only such as *Edward* the Confessor himself framed, and were enacted in his time; but the Substance of all the Laws made . . . in the Reign of other *Saxon* Kings . . . for many hundred Years before him, the whole body of *Saxon* Laws." Fortescue-Aland, "Preface," p. xxvii.

47. [Bolingbroke,] *Dissertation,* pp. 143–44 (also, see pp. 194–95). In his memorable address to the Lords, William Pym made a similar argument about the "vigour and force" of Saxon law "overliving" "the Conquest." *Proceedings Against Manwaring,* p. 10.

48. Campbell, *Political Survey* 2: 361.

49. Kramnick, "Augustan Politics," p. 35.

50. Blackstone, *Commentaries* 2: 48. Chief Justice Hale claimed that William I changed no law "without common Consent *in communi Concilio Regni,* or in Parliament." Hale, *History of Common Law,* p. 70.

51. Earl, "Procrustean Feudalism," p. 38 (quoting Tyrrell). A lawyer who would in 1770 become lord chancellor charged that by the introduction of feudal law "the evidences of our constitution were perverted." [Yorke,] *Forfeitures for High Treason,* p. 68.

52. Jones, *Speech to Middlesex,* pp. 12–13.

53. Ibbetson, *Folclande and Boclande,* pp. 3–6, 9; Dalrymple, *Feudal Property,* pp. 1, 15.

54. Wright, *Law of Tenures,* pp. 46, 57.

55. Wright, *Law of Tenures,* pp. 46–63.

56. Wright, *Law of Tenures,* p. 79.

57. Wooddeson, *Jurisprudence,* pp. 146–47.

58. For a detailed discussion of the law, see Wright, *Law of Tenures,* pp. 79–83.

59. Wooddeson, *Jurisprudence,* pp. 146–47.

60. Wooddeson, *Jurisprudence,* p. 142; Wright, *Law of Tenures,* 86.

61. Wright, *Law of Tenures,* pp. 135–36.

62. Wright, *Law of Tenures,* pp. 81–82.

63. Nicolson, *English Historical Library,* pp. iii–iv.

64. [Hurd,] *Moral and Political Dialogues,* p. 383 (quoting [Yorke,] *Forfeitures for High Treason*). Also, see Jones, *Speech to Middlesex,* p. 11.

65. Bacon, *Discourse,* p. 100.

66. *Craftsman* 13, no. 440, 7 December 1734, p. 108.

67. [Bolingbroke,] *Dissertation,* p. 194. Also, see *Craftsman* 14, no. 466, 7 June 1735, p. 11; [Oldfield,] *History of the Boroughs* 1: 128–29; [Lyttelton,] *Persian Letters,* p. 186; [Tyrrell,] *Brief Enquiry,* pp. 34–35.

68. Speech of Lord Chatham, Lords Debates, 20 January 1775, *Hiberian Magazine* 5: 89. Also, see [Williams,] *Letters on Liberty,* p. 14.

69. Miller, "Glorious Revolution," p. 554.

70. Brand, *Defence of Reeves,* p. 63.

71. *Scots Magazine* 38 (1776): 15 footnote.

72. Goldie, "Roots of True Whiggism," pp. 208–9; Cherry, "Convention Parliament," p. 404; Thompson, "Reception of Locke," pp. 188, 190–91; Weston, "Ancient Constitution," p. 410.

73. Schwoerer, "Contributions of Declaration of Rights," pp. 112, 114, 113.

74. Pocock, *Politics,* p. 208.

75. Cherry, "Convention Parliament," p. 395; Ashley, *Magna Carta,* p. 58. But see Kenyon, *Revolution Principles,* p. 8.

76. Brand, *Defence of Reeves,* p. 66.

77. "Our Ancestors, whether *Saxons, Danes,* or *Normans* . . . disclaimed Submission to any Laws, but such as should be made by a full and free Representative of themselves in Parliament, the Members of which, qualified by their Possession of a competent Share in the common Stock." Charge of 1765, *Worcester Charges,* p. 10. Also, see Nasmith, *Grand Jury Charge,* pp. 6–7; Charges to the Westminster Grand Jury, 24 April 1728, 11 July 1728, 9 October 1728, 3 July 1729, Gonson, *Charges,* pp. 8, 44, 106–7, 129; Hare, *Grand Jury Charge,* p. 3.

78. Schwoerer, "Contributions of Declaration of Rights," p. 114.

79. Brand, *Defence of Reeves,* p. 63.

80. *Daily Gazetteer,* no. 36, 16 November 1734, p. 1, col. 1 and col. 2.

81. *London Journal* (#803), 16 November 1734, p. 1, col. 2; [Hervey,] *Ancient and Modern Liberty,* p. 40. Also, see *London Journal* (#765), 23 February 1733/34, p. 1, col. 1 and (#740), 1 September 1733, p. 1, col. 1.

82. Or, as sometimes put, before the Restoration. [Hervey,] *Ancient and Modern Liberty,* p. 5. On the Restoration as an alternative origin making the "new" constitution a continuation of the old, see Willman, "Blackstone and Caroline Law," pp. 39–70; Brand, *Defence of Reeves,* pp. 62–65.

83. "Debate in the Conway Resolutions, House of Lords, 10 February 1766, reprinted in *Debate on Revolution,* p. 115.

84. Letter from H. Hemersley to Governor H. Sharpe, printed in *Proceedings and Debates* 1: 570.

85. [Inglis,] *True Interest,* p. 15. But see Anon., *Remarks upon a Discourse,* p. 4.

86. [Stevens,] *Revolution Vindicated,* p. 3; Carysfort, *Thoughts on Constitution,* pp. 2–3; Cartwright, *Appeal Civil and Military,* pp. 31–32.

87. [Reeves,] *Thoughts, First Letter,* p. 45. "The name [that is, "Abdication"] contains a moral lesson of sufficient strength to any future Prince. . . . It likewise holds out no equivocal sense, like the term Revolution, which a pernicious demagogue can catch hold of, to subvert that very Constitution which the transactions of 1688 saved from subversion, intire and without change." Brand, *Defence of Reeves,* p. 67.

88. [Reeves,] *Thoughts, First Letter,* p. 53.

89. Entick *v.* Carrington, 19 *State Trials* 1030, 1067–68 (C.P., 1765); [1558–1774] *All English Reports* 41, 46 (C.P., 1765).

90. *London Journal* no. 768, 16 March 1733/34, p. 1, col. 1. The ancient constitution was then being argued by the opposition to Walpole's administration to demand annual elections and to decry "corruption." The *Journal,* speaking for the administration, and contending that the crown was too weak to rule without patronage, was saying that a new constitution had come into existence with the Glorious Revolution. That was why the ancient constitution was attacked.

91. *Daily Gazetteer,* #96, 18 October 1735, p. 1, col. 2.

92. *Daily Gazetteer,* #6, 5 July 1735, p. 1, col. 1. The *Gazetteer* was quoting [Lyttelton,] *Persian Letters,* p. 180. On the same page as that quotation Lyttelton also asked, "Is a long Prescription necessary to give Force to the Natural Rights of Mankind?"

93. [Lyttelton], *Persian Letters,* p. 180.

94. *Craftsman* 14, no. 466, 7 June 1735, p. 2.

95. *Craftsman* 11, no. 375, 8 September 1733, p. 145.

96. Kramnick, *Bolingbroke's Circle,* p. 136.

8: The Forensic History of Reform

1. Hill, "Norman Yoke," p. 116.

2. Bonwick, *English Radicals,* pp. 15–16. Also, see Royle and Walvin, *English Radicals,* pp. 27–29; Butterfield, *George III and People,* pp. 344–45.

3. Among other demands was one specifically asking that "the Ancient Constitution . . . of Parliaments be restor'd." Instructions of Stirling to its Representatives, 22 March 1742, *Great-Britain's Memorial* 2: 84.

4. Resolves of London Livery, 31 January 1782, reprinted in Sharp, *Legal Means,* p. 67 footnote (also, see pp. 49–50). Also, see Anon., *Conduct of Livery-Men,* p. 29.

5. Burgh, *Political Disquisitions* 3: 272. Similarly, see Williams, *Parliamentary Reformation,* p. 7.

6. *Craftsman* 12, no. 400, 2 March 1733/1734, p. 152. Also, see Speech of John Sawbridge, Commons Debates, 26 December 1772, *Gentleman's Magazine* 43 (1773): 109.

7. Anon., *Address to the Freeholders of Middlesex,* p. 20 footnote.

8. Sharp, *Circular Letter,* p. 8. Also, see Report of Westminster Sub-Committee, 19 March 1780, *Copy of Carysfort,* p. 13.

9. "A Real Friend to the People," *Declaration of those Rights of the Community of Great-Britain without which they cannot be Free* (broadside printed in London c. 1775, Huntington Library #141710).

10. Day, *Two Speeches,* p. 13. Similarly, see Batley, *Letter to Wyvill,* p. 21; Letter of 10 October 1782, Anon., *Enquiry into Legality and Expediency,* p. 41.

11. Young, *Example of France,* pp. 78–79.

12. [Basset,] *Equal Representation,* pp. 13–14.

13. Lofft, *Observations on Publication,* p. 6; [Almon,] *Free Parliaments,* pp. 9–15; Williams, *Parliamentary Reformation,* p. 19; Speech of Sir William Yonge, Commons Debates, 23 January 1745, *Parliamentary History* 13: 1089.

14. "We were so far from having *Annual Parliaments,* that is, Parliaments *chosen every year* by the *People,* either in the *Saxon Times,* or for a long Time after the Conquest, that we had *no Parliaments* at all in the *present Sense* of the Word, by which we mean, a *House of Commons . . . Chosen by the People." London Journal,* #768, 16 March 1733/34, p. 1, col. 3.

15. *London Journal,* #769, 23 March 1733/34, p. 1, col. 1.

16. *London Journal,* #740, 1 September 1733, p. 1, col. 1.

17. Stuart, *Historical Dissertation of Constitution,* p. 281. "How parliaments stood in British times I am not certain; but that there were parliaments then I am certain." Anon., *Defence of Magna Charta,* p. 262.

18. Hargrave, "Preface," p. lxxxii.

19. Johnson, *Concerning Parliaments,* p. 18.

20. Sharp, *Legal Means,* p. 33.

21. Squire, *Foundation,* pp. 179–80.

22. Sharp, *Legal Means,* p. 38.

23. Sharp, *Circular Letter,* p. 14. Also, see [Ramsay,] *Historical Essay,* pp. 130–31.

24. Sharp, *Circular Letter,* pp. 15–16.

25. Resolution of the Constitutional Society of Nottingham, 1780, printed in Wyvill, *Defence of Price,* p. 96.

26. Anon., *Letter on Corruption,* p. 45.

27. Instructions of Coventry, 2 March 1771, *Great-Britain's Memorial* 2: 35–36.

28. "In the Taught Tradition," pp. 647–61.

29. "[T]hey were unable to avoid carrying this [reformist] outlook back into the remotest centuries of the past, construing antiquity itself in terms of it." Butterfield, *George III and People,* p. 344. "Like men in all ages they did not realize that what they took out of the past was the very thing they had first put into it. By a piece of slight-of-hand . . . they pulled out of early history the shapes they had manufactured in their wishful thinking, and furnished their generation with just the type of anachronism that it required." Ibid.

30. Lofft, *Observations on Publication,* p. 6.

31. Day, *Two Speeches,* pp. 12–13; *Craftsman,* no. 470, 5 July 1735, p. 36.

32. Cartwright, *To Nottingham,* p. 3.

33. Sharp, *Legal Means,* pp. 51–52.

34. Speech of Edmund Burke, Commons Debates, 7 May 1782, Burke, *Works* 6: 148.

35. Carysfort, *Letter to Huntingdonshire,* pp. 3–4, 8.

36. Speech of Edmund Burke, Commons Debates, 7 May 1782, Burke, *Works* 6: 146.

37. *Remonstrance of Many Thousand,* pp. 4–5, 19; Pocock, "Origins of Study," pp. 233, 235; Skinner, "History and Ideology," p. 162.

38. Jefferson's dislike of the common law can be compared to that of the Levellers. Seaberg, "Norman Conquest," pp. 805–6. It is, however, misleading to say "Jefferson accepted without reservation the Leveller theory" of Saxonism. Dumbauld, *Jefferson and Law,* p. 155. He "accepted" the same tactics of forensic historical argument.

39. Pocock, "Machiavelli," pp. 572, 579.

40. [Basset,] *Equal Representation,* p. 14.

41. Christie, *Stress and Stability,* pp. 168–69.

42. Leder, *Liberty and Authority,* p. 119.

43. "Irrelevance of the Declaration," pp. 47–69; *Authority of Law; Authority to Legislate.*

44. Leder, *Liberty and Authority,* p. 93.

45. Grey, "Unwritten Constitution," p. 852; Hazeltine, "Influence," p. 6.

46. *Authority to Tax,* pp. 99–100.

47. See, e.g., Resolutions of the North Carolina Convention, 27 August 1774, *American Archives* 1: 733–35; Message from the Pennsylvania Assembly to Governor John Penn, 21 February 1767, *Pennsylvania Council* 9: 370; Instructions of Portsmouth, New Hampshire, *Boston Evening-Post,* 6 January 1766, p. 3, col. 1.

48. [Ruffhead,] *Considerations,* p. 15.

49. In one respect they did share a constitutional issue. Under both statutes, persons accused as violators were not tried by what was called "the right of trial by Juries, that pledge of Liberty, that inestimable inheritance, that free-born privilege of Englishmen." Address of the County of Devon to their Representatives in Parliament, 23 May 1763, *Gentleman's Magazine* 33 (1763): 300.

50. Representation of the Lord Mayor, Aldermen, and Commons of London to their Representatives, 23 March 1763, *Select Collection of Letters* 1: 70.

51. Petition of the Lord Mayor, Aldermen, and Commons of London to the King, *London Magazine* 32 (1763): 256.

52. "Conduct of Whigs and Tories," *Gentleman's Magazine* 33 (1763): 402. A petition to the House of Commons from the London Corporation complained that the excise "under any circumstances bear so hard on the liberty of the subject." *London Magazine* 34 (1765): 13.

53. [Lind,] *Answer,* p. 65.

54. *Monthly Review* 28 (1763): 397.

55. "A Freeholder," *Gentleman's Magazine* 34 (1764): 115.

56. *Monthly Review* 29 (1763): 397.

57. "A Freeholder," *Gentleman's Magazine* 34 (1764): 115. From the perspective of liberty, however, the amount of the tax could have a bearing. "Without the aid of sophistry, it is easy to demonstrate that all exorbitant impositions, especially on the necessaries of life, have a sure operation to the prejudice of public freedom. Tho' Liberty, as Montesquieu observes, gives occasion for excessive taxes, yet excessive taxes in return produce slavery." [Ruffhead,] *Considerations,* p. 22.

58. An example is [Oldfield,] *History of the Boroughs* 1: 15–16, 159.

59. *Concept of Liberty,* pp. 68–73; *Authority of Rights,* pp. 34–38.

60. The new jurisprudence developed over time, and like many constitutional theories it found full expression in the political and legal literature long before it was established. See, e.g., Young, *Example of France,* pp. 61–62, 241–42; Paley, *Principles of Philosophy,* pp. 461–70; [Keld,] *Polity of England,* p. 257. Also, see Pocock, *Virtue, Commerce, History,* p. 95.

61. Letters from John Adams to Thomas Jefferson, 15 July 1813 and 16 December 1816, *Adams-Jefferson Letters* 2: 357, 502. Among many other arguments, Hume contended that there had been public liberty under the Tudors, hence there had been no free constitution for the Stuarts to overthrow. Clive, *Not By Fact Alone,* p. 127.

62. Letter from Thomas Jefferson to John Adams, 25 November 1816, *Adams-Jefferson Letters* 2: 498–99.

63. Pocock, *Virtue, Commerce, History,* p. 309.

64. *Authority of Law,* pp. 85–99.

65. Gwillim, *Ely Grand Jury Charge,* p. 8. Also, see Anon., *Observations on Hurd's,* pp. 4–6 (but see p. 142); Worcestershire Grand Jury Charge, 1765, *Worcester Charges,* p. 10; Squire, *Foundation,* pp. 81–82; Gonson, *July Westminster Charge,* pp. 3–4.

66. Campbell, *Lives of the Chancellors,* 5: 256.

9: The Forensic History of Liberty

1. Pocock, *Machiavellian Moment,* pp. 340–41.

2. Laslett, "Book Review," p. 143.

3. Kelley, "English Law and Renaissance," p. 27.

4. Pocock, *Ancient Constitution Retrospect,* p. 302.

5. Pocock, *Ancient Constitution,* p. 17. It seems with some writers no credit is ever to be accorded to forensic argument. Every reference to the past is to be judged by the canons of scientific history: "The pattern in the early seventeenth century is a recurrent one: we find the common lawyers and the parliamentary Opposition appealing to a remote against a more recent past, as the Whig Reformers were to do two centuries later and as the Barons, so far as our evidence goes, had done, four centuries before." Styles, "Politics and Research," p. 53.

6. Styles, "Politics and Research," p. 53.

7. Brooks and Sharpe, "English Law and Renaissance," p. 142.

8. And recently it has been claimed that his influence, even over the law, has been overrated. Burgess, *Ancient Constitution,* pp. 58, 72; Sommerville, *Politics and Ideology,* p. 108.

9. "Coke can hardly be left out of an inquiry into the intellectual origins of the English Revolution, yet he presents difficulties. He was a lawyer, not an intellectual." Hill, *Intellectual Origins,* p. 227.

10. Pawlisch, "Davies and Ancient Constitution," p. 702.

11. Gray, "Reason, Authority, and Imagination," p. 35.

12. Bouwsma, "Lawyers and Culture," p. 327.

13. Coke, *Fifth Part,* "To the Reader" pp. [2–3, 4].

14. Gray, "Liberty and the Law," pp. 156–58, 162–63; Berman, "Origins of Jurisprudence," p. 1687.

15. Weston, "Diverse Viewpoints," p. 249.

16. Skinner, "History and Ideology," p. 178.

17. Klein, "Ancient Constitution," pp. 25–26; Vann, "Free Anglo-Saxons," p. 265.

18. Burgess, *Ancient Constitution,* pp. 72–73; Sommerville, *Politics and Ideology,* pp. 90–92; Berman, "Origins of Jurisprudence," p. 1680n75; Weston, "Ancient Constitution," p. 388. Also, see Tuck, "Ancient Law of Freedom," p. 139; MacKay, "Coke," p. 247. And as always, the scholar who stereotyped Coke as a "lawyer" has been misunderstood by his critics. Pocock, "Discourse of Sovereignty," pp. 385–86.

19. Kelley, "English Law and Renaissance," p. 33. Which does not mean one would agree with Kelley's explanation for that conclusion: "It is true that Coke himself did not hesitate to make use of historical writings, but this was merely because as a lawyer he believed the more arguments the better—there was no telling, he

remarked, what might persuade some people. But it was not in history that one learned about law; on the contrary, it was in the study of law that one found 'the faithful and true Histories of all Successive Times.'" Ibid., p. 32.

20. Sommerville, "History and Theory," p. 260.

21. Twiss, *Lawyers and Constitution,* p. 104.

22. *Commonwealth v. Chapman,* 13 *Metcalf* (*Mass.*) *Reports* 68, 73 (1847).

23. "'Lawyers' history,' . . . proceeds, generally speaking, on the assumption that anything said in a judicial decision which it is convenient to treat as authentic fact *is* authentic fact, whatever a competent historical scholar might have to say about the matter." Twiss, *Lawyers and Constitution,* p. 147.

24. *Van Ness v. Pacard,* 2 *Peters* (*U.S.*) 137, 144 (1829).

25. Levy, "Introduction," pp. xii–xiii.

26. Brady, *Introduction,* "Epistle" (n.p.).

27. Collier, "Historians Versus Lawyers," p. 140.

28. Hutson, "Creation of Constitution," p. 39.

29. It is not irrelevant that historians can conclude that sixteenth-century French law was *better law* than sixteenth-century English law because French lawyers were better historians. And that, no matter the substance, French law was more rational. Kelley, "English Law and Renaissance," p. 30.

30. Palmer, "Liberties as Provisions," p. 156.

31. Schauer, "Varied Uses," p. 7.

32. Kelley, "English Law and Renaissance," p. 30.

SHORT TITLES

Abingdon, *Dedication*
Willoughby Bertie, Earl of Abingdon, *Dedication to the Collective Body of the People of England, in which the Source of our present Political Distractions are pointed out, and a Plan proposed for their Remedy and Redress.* Oxford, England, 1780.

Abingdon, *Dedication to the People*
Willoughby Bertie, Earl of Abingdon, *Dedication to the Collective Body of the People of England, in which the Source of our present Political Distractions are pointed out, and a Plan proposed for their Remedy and Redress.* Oxford, England, 1780.

Abingdon, *Thoughts on Burke's Letter*
Willoughby Bertie, Earl of Abingdon, *Thoughts on the Letter of Edmund Burke, Esq.; to the Affairs of America.* 6th edition. Oxford, England, [c.1770].

Abridged Edition
John Phillip Reid, *Constitutional History of the American Revolution.* Abridged edition. Madison: University of Wisconsin Press, 1995.

Adair, *Fame*
Douglass Adair, *Fame and the Founding Fathers: Essays by Douglass Adair.* Edited by Trevor Colbourn. New York: Norton, 1974.

Adams, *Works*
The Works of John Adams, Second President of the United States. Edited by Charles Francis Adams. 10 vols. Boston: Little, Brown and Company, 1850–56.

Adams-Jefferson Letters
The Adams-Jefferson Letters: The Complete Correspondence Between Thomas Jefferson and Abigail and John Adams. Edited by Lester J. Cappon. Chapel Hill: University of North Carolina Press, 1959.

[Almon,] *Free Parliaments*
[John Almon,] *Free Parliaments: or, a Vindication of the Parliamentary Constitution of England; in Answer to Certain visionary of Plans of modern Reformers.* London, 1783.

American Archives
American Archives, Fourth Series. Containing a Documentary History of the English Colonies in North America From the King's Message to Parliament, of March 7, 1774, to the Declaration of Independence by the United States. Edited by Peter Force. Vols. 1 and 2. Washington, 1837.

American Gazette
The American Gazette. Being a Collection of all the Authentic Addresses, Memorials, Letters, &c. Which relate to the Present Disputes Between Great Britain and her Colonies. Containing also Many Original Papers Never Before Published. London, 1768.

American Revolution: The Critical Issues
The American Revolution: The Critical Issues. Edited by Robert F. Berkhofer, Jr. Boston: Little Brown, 1971.

Anon., *Address to the Freeholders of Middlesex*
Anonymous, *An Address to the Freeholders of Middlesex, Assembled at Free Masons Tavern, in Great Queen Street, Upon Monday the 20th of December 1779, Being the Day Appointed for a Meeting of the Freeholders, For the Purpose of Establishing Meetings to Maintain and Support the Freedom of Election.* 3d edition. London, [1779].

Anon., *Ancient and Modern Constitution*
Anonymous, *The Ancient and Modern Constituion of Government Stated and Compared. And also Some Remarks on the Controversy Concerning the Dependence of Members of Parliament on the Crown.* London, 1734.

Anon., *Animadversions on Discourse*
Anonymous, *Animadversions on a Discourse Entituted, God's Way of Disposing of Kingdoms.* London, 1691.

Anon., *Conduct of Livery-Men*
Anonymous, *The Conduct of the Livery-Men at the Late Election of a Lord-Mayor, and their Proceedings in the Common Hall Justified; with Some Cautions relating to their Future Conduct, and the Present State of the Nation.* London, 1739.

Anon., *Court of Star Chamber*
Anonymous, *The Court of Star Chamber, or Seat of Oppression.* London, 1768.

Anon., *Defence of English History*
Anonymous, *A Defence of English History, Against the Misrepresentations of M. de Rapin Thoyras, in his History of England, Now Publishing Weekly.* London, 1734.

Anon., *Defence of Magna Charta*
Anonymous, *A History and Defence of Magna Charta.* Dublin, 1769.

Anon., *Detector Detected*
Anonymous, *The Detector Detected; or, the Danger to Which our Constitution now lies exposed, Set in a True and Manifest Light.* London, 1743.

Anon., *Divine Rights*
Anonymous, *The Divine Rights of the British Nation and Constitution Vindicated.* London, 1710.

Anon., *Enquiry into Legality and Expediency*
Anonymous, *An Enquiry into the Legality and Expedienciency of Increasing the Royal Navy by Subscriptions for Building County Ships. Being the Correspondence on the Subject between Arthur Young & Capel Lofft.* Bury St. Edmund, England, 1783.

Anon., *Enquiry into Legal Rights*
Anonymous, *Enquiry into the Nature and Obligation of Legal Rights. With Respect to the Popular Pleas of the Late K. James's Remaining Right to the Crown.* London, 1693.

Anon., *Essay on the Constitution*

Anonymous, *An Essay on the Constitution of England.* London, 1765.

Anon., *Foundation of British Liberty*
Anonymous, *The Foundation of British Liberty; Proving the indisputable Right of every Englishman to the Common Laws of the Land, for the Protection of his Person and Property: In a Letter from a Gentleman in the Country to his Friend in London.* London, 1768.

Anon., *Judgment of Whole Kingdoms*
Anonymous [generally attributed to Lord Somers or to Daniel Defoe,], *The Judgment of Whole Kingdoms and Nations, Concerning the Rights, Power, and Prerogative of Kings, and the Rights, Privileges, & Properties of the People.* 12th edition. Newport, Rhode Island, 1774.

Anon., *Letter on Corruption*
Anonymous, *A letter to the People of Great Britain, on the present alarming Crisis. Pointing at the most eligible Means of limiting the Number of Place-Men and Pensioners, in Parliament, and putting an End to Bribery and Corruption; to obviate the dangers which now threaten this Kingdom.* London, 1771.

Anon., *Letter to Doctor Tucker*
Anonymous, *A Letter to Doctor Tucker on his Proposal of a Separation Between Great Britain and her American Colonies.* London, 1774.

Anon., *Liberty in Two Parts*
Anonymous, *Liberty in Two Parts.* London, 1754.

Anon., *Obedience to Government*
Anonymous, *Obedience to Civil Government Clearly Stated: Wherein the Christian Religion is rescu'd from the false Notions pretended to be drawn from it; and Mr. Hoadly's New Scheme, in his last Book of the Origin and Form of Government is Fully Considered.* London, 1711.

Anon., *Observations on Hurd's*
Anonymous, *Observations on the Reverend Doctor Hurd's, Two Dialogues, on the Constitution of the English Government. Address in a Letter to the Right Hon. Edmund Burke.* London, 1790.

Anon., *Old Constitution*
Anonymous, *The Old Constitution and Present Establishment in Church and State Honestly Asserted.* London, 1718.

Anon., *Political Disquisitions*
Anonymous, *Political Disquisitions Proper for Public Consideration in the Present State of Affairs in a Letter to a Noble Duke.* London, 1763.

Anon., *Reflections on Wilkes*
Anonymous, *Reflections on the Case of Mr. Wilkes, and on the Right of the People to Elect their own Representatives.* London, 1768.

Anon., *Remarks upon a Discourse*
Anonymous, [Henry Barry?], *Remarks upon a Discourse Preached December 15th 1774. Being the Day recommended by the Provincial Congress: And afterwards at the Boston Lecture. By William Gordon, Pastor of the third Church in Roxbury.* [New York], 1775.

Anon., *Representative of London*
Anonymous, *The Representative of London and Westminster in Parliament Examined and Consider'd.* London, 1702.

Anon., *Spirit and Principles*
Anonymous, *The Spirit and Principles of Whigs and Jacobites Compared. Being the Substance of a Discourse delivered to an Audience of Gentlemen at Edinburgh, December 22, 1745.* London, 1746.

Anon., *View of Internal Policy*
Anonymous, *A View of the Internal Policy of Great Britain.* London, 1764.

Anon., *Whigs and Tories*
Anonymous, *A Dissertation on the Rise, Progress, Views, Strength, Interests and Characters, of the Two Parties of the Whigs and Tories.* Boston, 1773.

Arbuthnot, *Freeholder's Catechism*
[John] Arbuthnot, *The Freeholder's Political Catechism. Written by Dr. Arbuthnot.* [London,] 1769.

Ashley, *Magna Carta*
Maurice Ashley, *Magna Carta in the Seventeenth Century.* Charlottesville: Published for the Magna Carta Commission of Virginia, University Press of Virginia, 1965.

Ashton, "Tradition and Innovation"
Robert Ashton, "Tradition and Innovation and the Great Rebellion," in *Three British Revolutions: 1641, 1688, 1776.* Edited by J. G. A. Pocock. Princeton, N.J.: Princeton University Press, 1980, pp. 208–23.

Atkyns, *Enquiry into Power*
Sir Robert Atkyns, *An Enquiry into the Power of Dispensing with Penal Statutes.* London, 1689.

Atkyns, *Power of Parliament*
Sir Robert Atkyns, *The Power, Jurisdiction and Priviledge of Parliament and the Antiquity of the House of Commons Asserted.* London, 1689.

Atkyns, *Tracts*
Sir Robert Atkyns, *Parliamentary and Political Tracts.* London, 1734.

[Atkyns,] *Treatise of Jurisdiction*
[Sir Robert Atkyns,] *A Treatise of the True and Ancient Jurisdiction of the House of Peers.* London, 1699.

[Atwood,] *Additions Answering Omissions*
[William Atwood,] *Additions Answering the Omissions of our Reverend Author.* London, 1681.

[Atwood,] *Answerer's Principles*
[William Atwood,] *A Speech, According to the Answerer's Principles, Made for the Parliament at Oxford.* London, 1681, printed with [Atwood,] *Jus Anglorum.*

[Atwood,] *Antiquity and Justice*
[William Atwood,] *The Antiquity and Justice of an Oath of Abjuration. In Answer to a Treatise Entituled The Case of an Oath of Abjuration Considered.* London, 1694.

[Atwood,] *Jus Anglorum*
[William Atwood,] *Jus Anglorum ab Antiquo; or, A Confutation of an Impotent Libel against the Government by King, Lords, and Commons. Under pretence of Answering Mr. PETYT, and the Author of Jani Anglorum Facies Nova. With a Speech, according the the Answerer's Principles, made for the Parliament at Oxford.* London, 1681.

Authority of Law
John Phillip Reid, *Constitutional History of the American Revolution: The Authority of Law.* Madison: University of Wisconsin Press, 1993.

Authority of Rights
John Phillip Reid, *Constitutional History of the American Revolution: The Authority of Rights.* Madison: University of Wisconsin Press, 1986.

Authority to Legislate
John Phillip Reid, *Constitutional History of the American Revolution: The Authority to Legislate.* Madison: University of Wisconsin Press, 1991.

Authority to Tax
John Phillip Reid, *Constitutional History of the American Revolution: The Authority to Tax*. Madison: University of Wisconsin Press, 1987.

[Bacon,] *Continuation*
[Nathaniel Bacon,] *The Continuation of the Historical & Political Discourse of the Laws & Government of England, Until the end of the Reign of Queen Elizabeth.* London, 1682.

Bacon, *Discourse*
Nathaniel Bacon, *An Historical and Political Discourse of the Laws and Government of England, from the First Times to the End of the Reign of Queen Elizabeth.* London, 1689.

Bailyn, *Ideological Origins*
Bernard Bailyn, *The Ideological Origins of the American Revolution.* Cambridge, Mass.: Harvard University Press, 1967.

Bailyn, *Pamphlets*
Pamphlets of the American Revolution: 1750–1776. Edited by Bernard Bailyn. Cambridge, Mass.: Belknap Press of Harvard University Press, 1965.

[Barrington,] *Observations on Statutes*
[Daines Barrington,] *Observations on the Statutes, Chiefly the more Ancient, from Magna Charta to the Twenty-First of James the First, Ch. XXVII. With an Appendix; Being a Proposal for New Modelling the Statutes.* London, 1766.

[Barrington,] *Revolution Principles*
[John Shute Barrington, First Viscount Barrington,] *The Revolution and Anti-Revolution Principles States and Compar'd, the Constitution Explain'd and Vindicated, And the Justice and Necessity of Excluding the Pretender, Maintain'd against the Book Entituled, Hereditary Right of the Crown of England Asserted.* 3rd edition. London, 1714.

[Basset,] *Equal Representation*
[Francis Basset, Baron Basset of Stratton,] *Thoughts on Equal Representation.* London, 1783.

Batley, *Letter to Wyvill*
Jeremiah Batley, *A Letter to the Revd Christopher Wyvill, Chairman of the Committee of the Yorkshire Association.* London, 1782.

Beloff, *Debate*
Max Beloff, "Introduction," to *Debate on Revolution,* pp. 1–40.

Berman, "Origins of Jurisprudence"
Harold J. Berman, "The Origins of Historical Jurisprudence: Coke, Selden, Hale," *Yale Law Journal* 103 (1994): 1651–1738.

Bever, *Discourse on Jurisprudence*
Thomas Bever, *A Discourse on the Study of Jurisprudence and the Civil Law; Being an Introduction to a Course of Lecture.* Oxford, England, 1766.

Blackstone, *Analysis of the Laws*
William Blackstone, *An Analysis of the Laws of England.* 6th edition. Oxford, England, 1771.

Blackstone, *Commentaries*
William Blackstone, *Commentaries on the Laws of England.* 4 vols. Oxford, England, 1765–69.

Blackstone, *Great Charter*
William Blackstone, *The Great Charter and Charter of the Forest, with other Authentic Instruments: to which is prefixed an Introductory Discourse containing the History of the Charters.* Oxford, England, 1759.

Blackstone, *Law Tracts*
William Blackstone, *Law Tracts in Two Volumes*. Oxford, England, 1762.

Blackstone, *Tracts*
William Blackstone, *Tracts Chiefly Relating to the Antiquities and Laws of England*. 3rd edition. Oxford, England, 1771.

Bland, *An Inquiry*
Richard Bland, *An Inquiry into the Rights of the British Colonies, Intended as as Answer to the Regulations lately made concerning the Colonies, and the Taxes imposed upon them considered*. Williamsburg, Virginia, 1766.

[Blount,] *William and Mary Conquerors*
[Charles Blount,] *King William and Queen Mary Conquerors: Or, a Discourse Endeavouring to prove that Their Majesties have on their Side, against the Late King, the Principal Reasons that make Conquest a Good Title*. London, 1693.

[Bohun,] *Non-Resistance*
[Edmund Bohun,] *The Doctrine of Non-Resistance or Passive Obedience No way concerned in the Controversies Now depending between the Williamites and the Jacobites*. London, 1689.

[Bolingbroke,] *Dissertation*
[Henry Saint John, Viscount Bolingbroke,] *A Dissertation Upon Parties; In Several Letters to Caleb D'Anvers, Esq*. 2nd edition. London, 1735.

Bolingbroke, *Political Writings*
Viscount Bolingbroke, *Political Writings*. Edited by Isaac Kramnick. New York: Appleton-Century-Crofts, 1970.

Bonwick, *English Radicals*
Colin Bonwick, *English Radicals and the American Revolution*. Chapel Hill: University of North Carolina Press, 1977.

Boston Evening-Post
The Boston Evening-Post (weekly newspaper).

Boston Gazette
The Boston Gazette and Country Journal (weekly newspaper).

Bouwsma, "Lawyers and Culture"
William J. Bouwsma, "Lawyers and Early Modern Culture," *American Historical Review* 78 (1973): 303–27.

Brady, *Complete History*
Robert Brady, *A Complete History of England, from the First Entrance of the Romans under the Conduct of Julius Caesar, Unto the End of the Reign of King Henry III*. London, 1685.

[Brady,] *Great Point*
[Robert Brady,] *The Great Point of Succession Discussed. With a Full and Particular Answer to a late Pamphlet, Intitled, A Brief History of Succession, &c*. London, 1681.

Brady, *Introduction*
Robert Brady, *An Introduction to the Old English History, Comprehended in three several Tracts*. London, 1684.

Brand, *Defence of Reeves*
John Brand, *A Defence of the Pamphlet Ascribed to John Reeves, Esq. and Entitled "Thoughts on the English Government."* London, 1796.

[Braxton,] *Address to the Convention*
[Carter Braxton,] *An Address to the Convention of the Colony and Ancient Dominion of Virginia; on the Subject of Government in general and recommending a particular Form to their Consideration*. Philadelphia, 1776.

Brooks & Sharpe, "English Law and Renaissance"
Christopher Brooks and Kevin Sharpe, "History, English Law and the Renaissance," *Past & Present* 72 (1976): 133–42.
Brown, "Norman Conquest"
R. Allen Brown, "The Norman Conquest," *Transactions of the Royal Historical Society* 17 (5th series) (1967): 109–30.
Browning, *Court Whigs*
Reed Browning, *Political and Constitutional Ideas of the Court Whigs*. Baton Rouge: Louisiana State University Press, 1982.
Burgess, *Ancient Constitution*
Glenn Burgess, *The Politics of the Ancient Constitution: An Introduction to English Political Thought, 1603–1642*. University Park: Pennsylvania State University Press, 1992.
Burgh, *Political Disquisitions*
J. Burgh, *Political Disquisitions; or, An Enquiry into public Errors, Defects, and Abuses. Illustrated by, and established upon Facts and Remarks, extracted from a Variety of Authors, Ancient and Modern*. 3 vols. Philadelphia, 1775.
Burke, *Works*
The Works of the Right Honourable Edmund Burke. London: Henry G. Bohn, 1856.
[Burnet,] *Submission to Supream Authority*
[Gilbert Burnet,] *An Enquiry Into the Measures of Submission to the Supream Authority: And of the Grounds upon which it may be lawful or necessary for Subjects, to defend their Religion, Lives, and Liberties*. n.i. [1688].
Butterfield, *Englishman and History*
H. Butterfield, *The Englishman and his History*. Cambridge, England; University of Cambridge Press, 1944.
Butterfield, *George III and People*
H. Butterfield, *George III Lord North and the People 1779–80*. London: G. Bell and Sons, 1949.
[Calef,] *Siege of Penobscot*
[John Calef,] *The Siege of Penobscot by the Rebels.... To which is subjoined a Postscript wherein a short Account of the Country of Penobscot is given*. [London?] 1781.
Campbell, *Duty of Allegiance*
George Campbell, *The Nature, Extent, and Importance, of the Duty of Allegiance: A Sermon Preached at Aberdeen, December 12, 1776, Being the Fast Day Appointed by the King, on Account of the Rebellion in America*. Aberdeen, 1777.
Campbell, *Duty Second Edition*
George Campbell, *The Nature, Extent, and Importance of the Duty of Allegiance: A Sermon Preached at Aberdeen, December 12, 1776, Being the Fast Day Appointed by the King, on Account of the Rebellion in America*. Second edition. Aberdeen, 1778.
[Campbell,] *Liberty and Right*
[John Campbell,] *Liberty and Right: Or, an Essay, Historical and Political, on the Constitution and Administration of Great Britain, Part I*. London, 1747.
Campbell, *Lives of the Chancellors*
John Lord Campbell, *The Lives of the Chancellors and the Keepers of the Great Seal of England, From the Earliest Times till the Reign of George IV*. Volume 5. London: John Murray, 1868.

Campbell, *Political Survey*
John Campbell, *A Political Survey of Britain: Being a Series of Reflections on the Situation, Lands, Inhabitants, Revenues, Colonies, and Commerce of this Island. Intended to Shew that we have not yet approached near the Summit of Improvement, but that it will afford Employment to many Generations before they push to their utmost Extent the national Advantages of Great Britain. In Two Volumes.* London, 1774.

Canning, *Letter to Hillsborough*
George Canning, *A Letter to the Right Honourable the Earl of Hillsborough, on the Present Situation of Affairs in America.* Boston, 1769.

Care, *English Liberties Providence Edition*
Henry Care, *English Liberties, or the Free-Born Subject's Inheritance. Containing Magna Charta, Charta de Foresta, the Statute De Tallagio non concedendo, the Habeas Corpus Act, and several other Statutes; with Comments on each of them.* 6th ediiton. Providence, Rhode Island, 1774.

Carlyle, *Justice and Necessity*
Alexander Carlyle, *The Justice and Necessity of the War with our American Colonies Examined. A Sermon Preached at Inveresk, December 12, 1776, Being the Fast-Day Appointed by the King, on account of the American Rebellion.* Edinburgh, 1777.

Cartwright, *Appeal Civil and Military*
John Cartwright, *An Appeal Civil and Military on the Subject of the English Constitution.* London, 1799.

Cartwright, *Constitution Produced*
John Cartwright, *The English Constitution Produced and Illustrated.* London, 1823.

Cartwright, *To Nottingham*
John Cartwright, *To the Gentlemen, Clergy, and Freeholders of the County of Nottingham,* 31 October 1778 (Three-page Huntington Library Rare Book #139401).

Carysfort, *Letter to Huntingdonshire*
John Joshua Proby, 1st Earl of Carysfort, *A Letter from the Right Honourable Lord Carysfort, to the Huntingdonshire Committee.* London, 1780.

Carysfort, *Thoughts on Constitution*
John Joshua Proby, 1st Earl of Carysfort, *Thoughts on the Constitution with a View to the Proposed Reform in the Representation of the People, and Duration of Parliaments.* London, 1783.

Cherry, "Convention Parliament"
George L. Cherry, "The Role of the Convention Parliament (1688–89) in Parliamentary Supremacy," *Journal of the History of Ideas* 17 (1956): 390–406.

Christianson, "Five Knights' Case"
Paul Christianson, "John Selden, the Five Knights' Case, and Discretionary Imprisonment in Early Stuart England," *Criminal Justice History* 6 (1985): 65–87.

Christianson, "Royal Voices"
Paul Christianson, "Royal and Parliamentary Voices on the Ancient Constitution c. 1604–1621," in *Mental World of the Jacobean Court.* New York: Cambridge University Press, 1991, pp. 71–95.

Christianson, "Young Selden"
Paul Christianson, "Young John Selden and the Ancient Constitution, ca. 1610–18," *Proceedings of the American Philosophical Society* 128 (1984): 271–315.

Christie, *Stress and Stability*
Ian R. Christie, *Stress and Stability in Late Eighteenth-Century Britain: Reflections on the British Avoidance of Revolution.* Oxford: Clarendon Press, 1984.

Churchill, *Divi Britannici*
Sir Winston Churchill, *Divi Britannici: Being a Remark Upon the Lives of all the Kings of this Isle, From the Year of the World 2855. Unto the Year of Grace 1660.* London, 1675.
Claeys, "Whigs, Liberals and Radicals"
Gregory Claeys, "Whigs, Liberals and Radicals," *Historical Journal* 33 (1990): 737–45.
Clanchy, "Remembering Past"
M. T. Clanchy, "Remembering the Past and the Good Old Law," *History* 55 (new series) (1970): 165–76.
Clive, *Not By Fact Alone*
John Clive, *Not By Fact Alone: Essays on the Writing and Reading of History*. New York: Alfred A. Knopf, 1989.
Coke, *Fifth Part*
The Fift[h] Part of the Reports of Sr. Edward Coke Knight, the Kings Attorney Generall: of divers Resolutions and Iudgements giuen vpon great deliberation in matters of great importance & consequence by the reuerend Iudges and Sages of the Law; together with the reasons and causes of their Resolutions and Iudgements. London, 1605.
Coke, "First Part"
Edward Coke, "The First Part of the Institutes," reprinted in *Magna Carta and the Idea of Liberty*. Edited by James C. Holt. New York: Wiley, 1972, pp. 17–18.
Colbourn, *Lamp of Experience*
H. Trevor Colbourn, *The Lamp of Experience: Whig History and the Intellectual Origins of the American Revolution*. Chapel Hill: University of North Carolina Press, 1965.
Collection in Favour of Liberty
A Collection of Letters and Essays in Favour of Public Liberty, First published in the News-Papers in the Years, 1764, 65, 66, 67, 68, 69, and 1770. 3 volumes. London, 1774.
Collier, "Historians Versus Lawyers"
Christopher Collier, "The Historians Versus the Lawyers: James Madison, James Hutson, and the Doctrine of Original Intent," *Pennsylvania Magazine of History and Biography* 112 (January 1988): 137–44.
[Collier,] *Vindiciae Juris Regii*
[Jeremy Collier,] *Vindiciae Juris Regii: Or Remarques Upon a Paper, Entitled an Enquiry into the Measures of Submission to the Supream Authority*. London, 1689.
Commager, "Enlightenment"
Henry Steele Commager, "America and the Enlightenment," in *The Development of a Revolutionary Mentality*. First Library of Congress Symposia on the American Revolution. Washington: Library of Congress, 1972, pp. 7–29.
Commager, *Jefferson*
Henry Steele Commager, *Jefferson, Nationalism, and the Enlightenment*. New York: George Braziller, 1975.
Complete Collection of Wilkes
A Complete Collection of the Genuine Papers, Letters, &c. in the Case of John Wilkes, Esq. Elected Knight of Shire of the County of Middlesex. Berlin, [1768].
Concept of Liberty
John Phillip Reid, *The Concept of Liberty in the Age of the American Revolution*. Chicago: University of Chicago Press, 1987.
Controlling the Law
John Phillip Reid, *Controlling the Law: Legal Politics in Early National New Hampshire*. DeKalb, Illinois: Northern Illinois University Press, 2004.

[Cook,] *Argumentum*
[Edward Cook,] *Argumentum Anti-Normannicum: or an Argument Proving, From Ancient Histories and Records, that William, Duke of Normandy Made no absolute Conquest of England, by the Sword; in the sense of our Modern Writers*. London, 1682.
Copy of Carysfort
Copy of a Letter from the Right Honorable Lord Carysfort to the Huntingdonshire Committee: to which is Added, the Report of the Westminster Sub-Committee, respecting the Duration of Parliament, and the Representation of this Country. [London, 1780].
Correspondence of Locke
The Correspondence of John Locke. Edited by E. S. De Beer. Volume 3. Oxford, England: Oxford University Press, 1978.
Craftsman
The Craftsman. Volumes 8 to 14. London, 1737.
The Crisis
Newspaper "Printed and published for the authors by T.W. Shaw." London, January 1775 to 6 October 1776.
Critical Review
The Critical Review: Or Annals of Literature by a Society of Gentlemen (monthly magazine, London, 1756–1817).
Daily Gazetteer
The Daily Gazetteer, London, 30 June 1735 to 27 October 1735.
Dalrymple, *Feudal Property*
John Dalrymple, *An Essay Towards a General History of Feudal Property in Great Britain*. 4th edition. London, 1759.
Day, *Two Speeches*
Thomas Day, *Two Speeches of Thomas Day, Esq. at the General Meetings of the Counties of Cambridge and Essex, Held March 25, and April 25, 1780*. n.i., 1780.
Debate on Revolution
The Debate on the American Revolution 1761–1783. A Sourcebook. Edited by Max Beloff. 2nd edition. New York, Harper & Row, 1960.
De Lolme, *Constitution: New Edition*
J. L. De Lolme, *The Constitution of England; or, an Account of the English Government; in which it is Compared Both with the Republican Form of Government, and the Other Monarchies in Europe*. New edition. London, Henry G. Bohn, 1853.
"Demophilus," *English Constitution*
"Demophilus," *The Genuine Principles of the Ancient Saxon, or English Constitution. Carefully collected from the best Authorities; With some Observations, on their peculiar fitness, for the United Colonies, in General, and Pennsylvania in particular*. Philadelphia, 1776.
Dickinson, "Debate on Sovereignty"
H. T. Dickinson, "The Eighteenth-Century Debate on the Sovereignty of Parliament," in *Transactions of the Royal Historical Society* 26 (5th series) (1976): 189–210.
Dickinson, *Liberty and Property*
H. T. Dickinson, *Liberty and Property: Political Ideology in Eighteenth-Century Britain*. New York: Holmes and Meier, 1977.
Dimwiddy, *Wyvill*
J. R. Dimwiddy, *Christopher Wyvill and Reform 1790–1820*. Borthwick Papers No. 39. York, England: St Anthony's Press, 1971.

Douglas, *Conquest and Historians*

David Douglas, *The Norman Conquest and British Historians*. Being the thirteenth Lecture on the David Murray Foundation in the University of Glasgow. Glasgow: Jackson, Son & Company, 1946.

Douglas, *English Scholars*

David C. Douglas, *English Scholars 1660–1730*. 2nd edition. London: Eyre & Spottiswoode, 1951.

[Dowdeswell,] *Sentiments of Freeholder*

[William Dowdeswell,] *The Sentiments of an English Freeholder, on the Late Decision of the Middlesex Election*. London, 1769.

Dugdale, *Origines Juridicales*

William Dugdale, *Origines Juridicales, or Historical Memorials of the English Laws, Courts of Justice, Forms of Tryal, Punishment in Cases Criminal, Law-Writers, Law Books, Grants and Settlements of Estates, Degrees of Sergeant, Innes of Court and Chancery*. 2nd edition, London, 1666.

Dumbauld, *Jefferson and Law*

Edward Dumbauld, *Thomas Jefferson and the Law*. Norman: University of Oklahoma Press, 1978.

[Dyson,] *Case of Middlesex*

[Jeremiah Dyson,] *The Case of the Late Election for the County of Middlesex, Considered on the Principles of the Constitution, and the Authorities of Law*. London, 1769.

Earbery, *Old Constitution*

Mathias Earbery, *The Old English Constitution Vindicated, And Set in a True Light*. London, 1717.

Earl, "Procrustean Feudalism"

D. W. L. Earl, "Procrustean Feudalism: An Interpretative Dilemma in English Historical Narration, 1700–1725," *Historical Journal* 19 (1976): 33–51.

Eliot, *Give Cesar His Due*

Jared Eliot, *Give Cesar his Due. Or, the Obligation that Subjects are under to their Civil Rulers, As was shewed in a Sermon Preach'd before the General Assembly of the Colony of Connecticut at Hartford, May the 11th, 1738. The Day for the Election of the Honourable the Governour, the Deputy-Governour, and the Worshipful Assistants*. New London, Connecticut, 1738.

Ellys, *Tracts on Liberty*

Anthony Ellys, *Tracts on the Liberty, Spiritual and Temporal, of the Subjects in England. Addressed to J.N. Esq; at Aix-la-Chapelle. Part II. [Of the Temporal Liberty of Subjects in England.*] London, 1765.

Elton, "Butterfield"

G. R. Elton, "Herbert Butterfield and the Study of History," *Historical Journal* 27 (September 1984): 729–43.

Elton, "Review Essay"

G. R. Elton, "Review Essay," *History and Theory* 20 (1981): 92–100.

Evans, "Antiquity of Parliaments"

E. Evans, "Of the Antiquity of Parliaments in England: Some Elizabethan and Early Stuart Opinions," *History* 23 (1938): 206–21.

Federalist

The Federalist. Edited by Jacob E. Cooke. Hanover, N.H.: Wesleyan University Press, 1961.

Ferguson, "Fortescue"
Arthur B. Ferguson, "Fortescue and the Renaissance: A Study in Transition" *Studies in the Renaissance* 6 (1959): 175–94.

[Ferguson,] *Remarks on a Pamphlet*
[Adam Ferguson,] *Remarks on a Pamphlet lately Published by Dr. Price, Intitled, Observations on the Nature of Civil Liberty, the Principles of Government, and the Justice and Policy of the War with America, &c. In a Letter from a Gentleman in the Country to a Member of Parliament*. London, 1776.

Fielding, *Grand Jury Charge*
Henry Fielding, *A Charge Delivered to the Grand Jury, at the Sessions of the Peace Held for the City and Liberty of Westminster, &c. on Thursday the 29th of June, 1749*. Dublin, 1749.

Fielding, *Increase of Robbers*
Henry Fielding, *An Enquiry into the Causes of the late Increase of Robbers, &c. With some Proposals for Remedying this Growing Evil*. 2nd edition. London, 1751.

Fine, "Rule of Law and Marxism"
Robert Fine, "The Rule of Law and Muggletonian Marxism: The Perplexities of Edward Thompson," *Journal of Law and Society* 21 (June 1994): 193–213.

"Forensic History"
John Phillip Reid, "Law and History," *Loyola of Los Angeles Law Review* 27 (November 1993): 193–223.

Fortescue, *De Laudibus*
Sir John Fortescue, *De Laudibus Legum Angliæ. By Sir John Fortescue, Lord Chief Justice, and Afterwards Lord Chancellor to King Henry VI*. New edition. London, 1775.

Fortescue-Aland, "Preface"
John Fortescue-Aland, "The Preface" to Sir John Fortescue, *The Difference Between an Absolute and Limited Monarchy; As it more particularly regards the English Constitution*. London, 1714.

[Fowle,] *Appendix to Eclipse*
[Daniel Fowle,] *An Appendix to the late Total Eclipse of Liberty*. Boston, 1756.

Fowle, *Total Eclipse*
Daniel Fowle, *A Total Eclipse of Liberty: Being a true and faithful Account of the Arraignment, and Examination of Daniel Fowle before the Honourable House of Representatives of the Province of the Massachusetts-Bay in New-England, Octob. 24th, 1756. Barely on Suspicion of his being concern'd in Printing and Publishing a Pamphlet, intitled, The Monster of Monsters*. Boston, 1755.

Frink, *Election Sermon*
Thomas Frink, *A King reigning in Righteous, and Princes ruling in Judgement. A Sermon Preached before His Excellency Thomas Pownall, Esq.; Governour, the Honourable His Majesty's Council, and House of Representatives, of the Province of the Massachusetts-Bay, in New England, May 31. 1758. Being the Anniversary for the Election of His Majesty's Council, for said Province*. Boston, 1758.

[Fullwood,] *Agreement Betwixt*
[Francis Fullwood,] *Agreement Betwixt the Present and the Former Government: Or, a Discourse of this Monarchy, whether Elective or Hereditary?* London, 1689.

Fussner, *Historical Revolution*
F. Smith Fussner, *The Historical Revolution: English Historical Writing and Thought 1580–1640*. London: Routledge and Paul, 1962.

[Galloway,] *Letter*
[Joseph Galloway,] *A Letter to the People of Pennsylvania; Occasioned by the*

Assembly's passing that Important Act, for Constituting Judges of the Supream Courts and Common-Pleas, During Good Behaviour. Philadelphia, 1760, reprinted in Bailyn, *Pamphlets,* pp. 257–72.

Gentleman's Magazine
The Gentleman's Magazine and Historical Chronicle (monthly magazine, London).

[Glover,] *Considerations*
[Richard Glover,] *Considerations on the Attorney-General's Proposition for a Bill for the Establishment of Peace with America*. London, 1782.

Goldie, "Roots of True Whiggism"
Mark Goldie, "The Roots of True Whiggism 1688–89," *History of Political Thought* 1 (June 1980): 195–236.

Gonson, *Charges*
Sir John Gonson's Five Charges to Several Grand Juries. . . . 4th edition. London, n.d.

Gonson, *July Westminster Charge*
Sir John Gonson, *A Charge to the Grand Jury of the City and Liberty of Westminster, &c. At the General Quarter-Sessions of the Peace, held the third Day of July, 1729, in Westminster-Hall*. London, 1729.

[Goodenough,] *Constitutional Advocate*
[Richard Goodenough,] *The Constitutional Advocate: By which, from the Evidence of History, and of Records, and from the Principles of the British Government, Every Reader may form his own Judgement concerning the Justice and Policy of the Present War with America. Addressed to the People at Large, And humbly submitted to the Consideration of their Representatives*. London, 1776.

Gottschalk, *Jean Paul Marat*
Louis R. Gottschalk, *Jean Paul Marat: A Study in Radicalism*. Chicago: University of Chicago Press, 1967.

Gough, *Fundamental Law*
J. W. Gough, *Fundamental Law in English Constitutional History*. Oxford: Clarendon Press, 1955.

Gough, "James Tyrrell"
J. W. Gough, "James Tyrrell, Whig Historian and Friend of John Locke," *Historical Journal* 19 (1976): 581–610.

[Grange,] *Late Excise*
[James Erskine, Lord Grange,] *The Late Excise Scheme Dissected: Or, an Exact Copy of the Late Bill, for Repealing several Subsidies, and an Impost, Now Payable on Tobacco, &c*. London, 1734.

Gray, "Liberty and the Law"
Charles M. Gray, "Parliament, Liberty, and the Law," in *Parliament and Liberty from the Reign of Elizabeth to the English Civil War*. Edited by J. H. Hexter. Stanford, Calif.: Stanford University Press, 1992, pp. 155–200.

Gray, "Reason, Authority, and Imagination"
Charles Gray, "Reason, Authority, and Imagination: The Jurisprudence of Sir Edward Coke," in *Culture and Politics from Puritanism to the Enlightenment*. Edited by Perez Zogorin. Berkeley: University of California Press, 1980, pp. 25–66.

Great-Britain's Memorial
Great-Britain's Memorial. Containing a Collection of the Instructions ... of the Freeholders and other Electors of Great-Britain, to their Representatives in Parliament, since the late Election. London, 1742.

Greenberg, "Confessor's Laws"
Janelle Greenberg, "The Confessor's Laws and the Radical Face of the Ancient Constitution," *English Historical Review* 104 (July 1989): 611–37.
Gregor, "Preface"
Francis Gregor, "The Preface" to Sir John Fortescue, *De Lauibus Legum Angliae*. New edition. London, 1775.
Grey, "Unwritten Constitution"
Thomas C. Grey, "Origins of the Unwritten Constitution: Fundamental Law in American Revolutionary Thought," *Stanford Law Review* 30 (1978): 843–93.
Guide to Rights
A Guide to the Knowledge of the Rights and Privileges of Englishmen. London, 1757.
Gwillim, *Ely Grand Jury Charge*
Henry Gwillim, *A Charge Delivered to the Grand Jury, at the Assizes Holden at Ely, on Wednesday the 27th Day of March 1799*. London, 1799.
Hale, *History of Common Law*
Matthew Hale, *The History of the Common Law of England*. Edited by Charles Gray. Chicago: University of Chicago Press, 1971.
Halifax, *Charles II*
George Savile, Marquis of Halifax, *A Character of Charles the Second: And Political, Moral and Miscellaneous Thoughts and Reflections*. London, 1750.
Hare, *Grand Jury Charge*
Hugh Hare, *A Charge Given at the General Quarter Sessions of the Peace for the County of Surrey Holden at Dorking on Tuesday the 5th day of April, 1692*. London, 1692.
Hargrave,"Preface"
Francis Hargrave, "Preface" to Sir Matthew Hale, *The Jurisdiction of the Lords House, or Parliament, Considered According to Antient Records*. London, 1796.
Hawles, *Englishman's Right*
Sir John Hawles, *The Englishman's Rights: A Dialogue Between a Barrister at Law, and a Juryman*. Philadelphia, 1798.
Hazeltine, "Influence"
H. D. Hazeltine, "The Influence of Magna Carta on American Constitutional Development," *Columbia Law Review* 17 (1917): 1–33.
Hedges, "Telling off the King"
William L. Hedges, "Telling off the King: Jefferson's *Summary View* as American Fantasy," *Early American Literature* 22 (Fall 1987): 166–74.
Herring, *Regicide Sermon*
Thomas Herring, *A Sermon Preached before the House of Lords, in the Abbey-Church of Westminster, on Wednesday Jan. 30, 1739–40. Being the Day appointed to be observed as the Day of the Martyrdom of King Charles I*. London, 1740.
[Hervey,] *Ancient and Modern Liberty*
[John Hervey, Lord Hervey of Ickworth,] *Ancient and Modern Liberty Stated and Compar'd*. London, 1734.
Heylyn, *Stumbling-Block*
Peter Heylyn, *The Stumbling-Block of Disobedience and Rebellion, Cunningly laid by Calvin in the Subjects way, Discovered, Censured and Removed*. London, 1658.
Hill, *Intellectual Origins*
Christopher Hill, *Intellectual Origins of the English Revolution*. Oxford: Oxford University Press, 1965.

Hill, "Norman Yoke"
Christopher Hill, "Norman Yoke," in Christopher Hill, *Puritanism and Revolution: Studies in the Interpretation of the English Revolution in the 17th Century*. London: Secker & Warburg, 1958, pp. 50–122.

Holdsworth, "Coke"
W. S. Holdsworth, "The Influence of Coke on the Development of English Law," in *Essays in Legal History Read Before the International Congress of Historical Studies Held in London in 1913*. Edited by Paul Vinogradoff. London, 1913, pp. 297–311.

Holliday, *Life of Mansfield*
John Holliday, *The Life of William Late Earl of Mansfield*. London, 1797.

Hulme, "Charles and Constitution"
Harold Hulme, "Charles I and the Constitution," in *Conflict in Stuart England: Essays in honour of Wallace Notestein*. Edited by William Appleton Aiken and Basil Duke Henning. Anchor Books, 1970, pp. 89–128.

Hulsebosch, "Ancient Constitution"
Daniel N. Hulsebosch, "The Ancient Constitution and the Expanding Empire: Sir Edward Coke's British Jurisprudence," *Law and History Review* 21 (Fall 2003): 439–82.

[Hurd,] *Moral and Political Dialogues*
[Richard Hurd,] *Moral and Political Dialogue Between Divers Eminent Persons of the Past and Present Age; with Critical and Explanatory Notes*. 2nd edition. London, 1760.

Hutson, "Creation of Constitution"
James H. Hutson, "The Creation of the Constitution: The Integrity of the Documentary Record," *Texas Law Review* 65 (November 1986): 1–39.

Ibbetson, *Folclande and Boclande*
James Ibbetson, *A Dissertation on the Folclande and Boclande of the Saxons*. London, 1778.

[Ibbetson,] *National Assemblies*
[James Ibbetson,] *A Dissertation on the National Assemblies Under the Saxon and Norman Governments*. London, 1781.

[Inglis,] *True Interest*
[Charles Inglis,] *The True Interest of America Impartially Stated in Certain Strictures on a Pamphlet Entitled Common Sense*. 2nd edition. Philadelphia, 1776.

"In Legitimate Stirps"
John Phillip Reid, "In Legitimate Stirps: The Concept of 'Arbitrary,' the Supremacy of the Parliament and the Coming of the American Revolution," *Hofstra Law Review* 5 (1977): 459–99.

"In the Taught Tradition"
John Phillip Reid, "In the Taught Tradition: The Meaning of Law in Massachusetts Bay Two Hundred Years Ago," *Suffolk University Law Review* 14 (Summer 1980): 931–74.

"Irrelevance of the Declaration"
John Phillip Reid, "The Irrelevance of the Declaration," in *Law in the American Revolution and the Revolution in the Law: A Collection of Review Essays on American Legal History*. Edited by Hendrik Hartog. New York: New York University Press, 1981, pp. 46–89.

[Jacob,] *Laws of Liberty*
[Giles Jacob,] *The Laws of Liberty and Property: Or, A Concise Treatise of all the Laws, Statutes and Ordinances, made for the Benefit and Protection of the Subjects of England*. 2nd edition. London, 1734.

Johnson, *Answer to the History*
Samuel Johnson, *An Answer to the History of Passive Obedience, just now reprinted under the Title of A Defense of Dr. Sacheverel.* London, 1709.
Johnson, *Argument Proving*
Samuel Johnson, *An Argument Proving, That the Abrogation of King James by the People of England from the Regal Throne and the Promotion of the Prince of Orange, one of the Royal Family, to the Throne of the Kingdom in his stead, was according to the Constitution of the English Government, and Prescribed by it.* London, 1692.
Johnson, *Concerning Parliaments*
Samuel Johnson, *An Essay Concerning Parliaments at a Certainty; or, the Kalends of May.* 2nd edition. London, 1694.
[Johnson,] *Defence of Magna Charta*
[Samuel Johnson,] *A History and Defence of Magna Charta.* London, 1769.
Johnson, *Notes on Pastoral*
Samuel Johnson, *Notes Upon the Phoenix Edition of the Pastoral Letter. Part I.* London, 1694.
Johnson, *Reflections on the History*
Samuel Johnson, *Reflections on the History of Passive Obedience.* London, 1689.
[Jones,] *Constitutional Criterion*
[William Jones,] *The Constitutional Criteria: By a Member of the University of Cambridge.* London, 1768.
Jones, *Country and Court*
J. R. Jones, *Country and Court: England, Sixteen Fifty-Eight to Seventeen Fourteen.* Cambridge, Mass.: Harvard University Press, 1978.
Jones, *Speech to Middlesex*
William Jones, *A Speech of William Jones, Esq. To the Inhabitants of the Counties of Middlesex and Surry, the Cities of London and Westminster, and the Borough of Southwark.* London, 1782.
Journals of Commons
Journals of the House of Commons. Printed by Order of the House of Commons, n.d.
Kammen, "Meaning of Colonization"
Michael Kammen, "The Meaning of Colonization in American Revolutionary Thought," *Journal of the History of Ideas* 31 (1970): 337–58.
Kantorowicz, *King's Two Bodies*
Ernst Kantorowicz, *The King's Two Bodies: A Study in Mediaeval Political Theology.* Princeton, New Jersey: Princeton University Press, 1957.
[Keld,] *Polity of England*
[Christopher Keld,] *An Essay on the Polity of England.* London, 1785.
Kelley, "English Law and Renaissance"
Donald R. Kelley, "History, English Law and the Renaissance," *Past & Present* 65 (1974): 24–51.
Kelley, "Rejoinder"
Donald R. Kelley, "A Rejoinder," *Past & Present* 72 (August 1976): 143–46.
Kelly, "Clio and the Court"
Alfred H. Kelly, "Clio and the Court: An Illicit Love Affair," *Supreme Court Review* 1965 (1965): 119–58.
Kenyon, *Revolution Principles*
J. P. Kenyon, *Revolution Principles: The Politics of Party 1689–1720.* Cambridge, England: Cambridge University Press, 1977.

Kern, *Kingship*
Fritz Kern, *Kingship and Law in the Middle Ages.* Translated by S. B. Chrimes. Oxford, England: Basil Blackwell, 1968.

King, *Essay*
Edward King, *An Essay on the English Constitution and Government.* London, 1767.

Kirtland, "Sobering Reflections"
Robert B. Kirtland, "Keep Your Eye on the Bastards! Or Sobering Reflections on the 150-Year Record of Early Virginia's Attitude Toward Lawyers," *Toledo Law Review* 14 (1983): 685–705.

Klein, "Ancient Constitution"
William Klein, "The Ancient Constitution Revisited," in *Political Discourse in Early Modern Britain.* Edited by Nicholas Phillipson and Quentin Skinner. Cambridge, England: Cambridge University Press, 1993, pp. 23–44.

Kliger, *Goths*
Samuel Kliger, *The Goths in England: A Study in Seventeenth and Eighteenth Century Thought.* Cambridge, Mass.: Harvard University Press, 1952.

Kramnick, "Augustan Politics"
Isaac Kramnick, "Augustan Politics and English Historiography: The Debate on the English Past, 1730–35," *History and Theory* 6 (1967): 33–56.

Kramnick, *Bolingbroke's Circle*
Isaac Kramnick, *Bolingbroke and His Circle: The Politics of Nostalgia in the Age of Walpole.* Cambridge, Mass.: Harvard University Press, 1968.

Kramnick, "Editor's Introduction"
Isaac Kramnick, "Editor's Introduction" to Henry St. John, Viscount Bolingbroke, *Historical Writings.* Edited by Isaac Kramnick. Chicago: University of Chicago Press, 1972, pp. xi-liii.

Lamont, *Prynne*
William M. Lamont, *Marginal Prynne, 1600–1669.* London: Routledge & Kegan Paul, 1963.

Laslett, "Book Review"
Peter Laslett, "Book Review," *History* 43 (1958): 143–44.

"Law and History"
John Phillip Reid, "Law and History," *Loyola of Los Angeles Law Review* 27 (November 1993): 193–223.

Lawson, *Politica Sacra*
George Lawson, *Politica Sacra & Civilis: Or, a Model of Civil and Ecclesiastical Government.* 2nd edition. London, 1689.

Leder, *Liberty and Authority*
Lawrence H. Leder, *Liberty and Authority: Early American Political Ideology 1689–1763.* Chicago: Quadrangle Books, 1968.

Lee, *Appeal to Justice*
[Arthur] Lee, *An Appeal to the Justice and Interests* of the *People of Great Britain, in the Present Dispute with America.* 4th edition. New York, 1775.

[Lee,] *Speech Intended*
[Arthur Lee,] *A Speech, Intended to have been Delivered in the House of Commons, in Support of the Petition from the General Congress at Philadelphia.* London, 1775.

[Leslie,] *Constitution, Laws and Government*
[Charles Leslie,] *The Constitution, Laws and Government of England, Vindicated in a Letter to the Reverend Mr. William Higden. On Account of his View of the English*

Constitution, with Respect to the Sovereign Authority of the Prince, &c. In Vindication of the Lawfulness of Taking the Oaths, &c. By a Natural Born Subject. London, 1709.

Levack, *Civil Lawyers*

Brian P. Levack, *The Civil Lawyers in England 1603–1641: A Political Study.* Oxford, England: Clarendon Press, 1973.

Levy, "Introduction"

Leonard Levy, "Introduction" to Charles Fairman and Stanley Morrison, *The Fourteenth Amendment and the Bill of Rights: The Incorporation Theory.* New York: Da Capo Press, 1970, pp. vii-xxv.

[Lind,] *Answer*

[John Lind,] *An Answer to the Declaration of the American Congress.* London, 1776.

Lloyd, *God's Ways*

William Lloyd, Bishop of S. Asaph, *A Discourse of God's Ways of Disposing of Kingdoms.* London, 1691.

Locke, *Two Treatises*

John Locke, *Two Treatises of Government: A Critical Edition with an Introduction and Apparatus Criticus.* 2nd edition. Edited by Peter Laslett. Cambridge, England: Cambridge University Press, 1967.

Lockwood, *Worth and Excellence*

James Lockwood, *The Worth and Excellence of Civil Freedom and Liberty illustrated, and a Public Spirit and the Love of our Country recommended. A Sermon Delivered before the General Assembly of the Colony of Connecticut, at Hartford, on the Day of the Anniversary Election. May 10th 1759.* New London, Connecticut, 1759.

Lofft, *Observations on Publication*

Capel Lofft, *Observations on a late Publication, entitled "A Dialogue on the Actual State of Parliament," and also on a Treatise Entitled "Free Parliaments."* London, 1783.

London Journal

London Journal (London newspaper).

Lowth, *Durham Assize Sermon*

Robert Lowth, *A Sermon Preached Before the Honourable and Right Reverend Richard, Lord Bishop of Durham, the Honourable Henry Bathurst, One of the Justices of the Court of Common Pleas, and the Honourable Sir Joseph Yates, One of the Justices of the Court of King's Bench; at the Assizes Holden at Durham, August 15, 1764.* 2nd edition. Newcastle, England, 1764.

Lucas, "Burke's Doctrine of Prescription"

Paul Lucas, "On Edmund Burke's Doctrine of Prescription: Or, an Appeal from the New to the Old Lawyers," *The Historical Journal* 11 (1968): 35–63.

[Lyttelton,] *Persian Letters*

[George L. Lyttelton, First Baron Lyttelton,] *Letters from a Persian in England, to his Friends at Ispahan.* 3rd edition. London, 1735.

[MacFarlane,] *History of George III*

[Robert MacFarlane,] *The History of the Second Ten Years of the Reign of George the Third, King of Great-Britain, &c.* London, 1782.

MacKay, "Coke"

R. A. MacKay, "Coke—Parliamentary Sovereignty or the Supremacy of the Law?" *Michigan Law Review* 22 (1924): 215–47.

Maitland, "Why History is Not Written"

Frederic W. Maitland, "Why the History of English Law is Not Written," in *The*

Collected Papers of Frederic William Maitland. Edited by H. A. L. Fisher. Cambridge: Cambridge University Press, 1911, pp. 480–97.

[Marat,] *Chains of Slavery*

[J. P. Marat,] *The Chains of Slavery. A Work Wherein the Clandestine and Villainous Attempts of Princes to Ruin Liberty are Pointed Out, and the Dreadful Scenes of Despotism Disclosed. To which is prefixed, An Address to the Electors of Great Britain in order to draw their timely Attention to the Choice of proper Representatives in the next Parliament.* London, 1774.

Maryland Gazette

The Maryland Gazette (weekly newspaper, Annapolis).

Massachusetts Gazette and Boston Post Boy

The Massachusetts Gazette and Boston Post Boy (weekly newspaper, Boston).

McDonald, *Novus*

Forrest McDonald, *Novus Ordo Seclorum: The Intellectual Origins of the Constitution.* Lawrence: University Press of Kansas, 1985.

McGowan, "Ethos in Law and History"

David McGowan, "Ethos in Law and History: Alexander Hamilton, *The Federalist,* and the Supreme Court," *Minnesta Law Review* 85 (2001): 755–898.

Millar, *Observations Concerning Ranks*

John Millar, *Observations Concerning Distinction of Ranks in Society.* 2nd edition. London, 1773.

Miller, "Glorious Revolution"

John Miller, "The Glorious Revolution: 'Contract' and 'Abdication' Reconsidered," *Historical Journal* 25 (1982): 541–55.

Miller, "Potential for Absolutism"

John Miller, "The Potential for 'Absolutism' in Later Stuart England," *History* 69 (1984): 187–202.

Missing, *Letter to Mansfield on Instructions*

John Missing, *A letter to the Right Honourable William Lord Mansfield Lord Chief Justice of the Court of Kings Bench: Proving that the Subjects of England, lawfully assembled to Petition their King, to Elect or Instruct their Representatives, are intitled to Freedom of Debate; and that all facts and Prosecutions for exerting that Right, are Unconstitutional and Illegal.* London, 1770.

[Molesworth,] "Preface"

[Robert, Viscount Molesworth,] "Preface" to Francis Holoman, *Franco-Gallia: Or a Account of the Ancient Free State of France and Most other Parts of Europe, before the Loss of their Liberties.* Translated by Robert, Viscount Molesworth. London, 1711.

Moore, "Comment on Pocock"

James Moore, "A Comment on Pocock," in *Theories of Property: Aristotle to the Present.* Edited by Anthony Pavel and Thomas Flanagan, Waterloo, Ontario: Wilfried Laurier University Press, 1979, pp. 167–75.

Morgan, *Prologue*

Prologue to Revolution: Sources and Documents on the Stamp Act Crisis, 1764–1766. Edited by Edmund S. Morgan. Chapel Hill: University of North Carolina Press, 1959.

Nasmith, *Grand Jury Charge*

James Nasmith, *A Charge Given to the Grand Jury, at the General Quarter Sessions of the Peace Holden for the County of Cambridge, the 15 Day of January, 1796.* Cambridge, England, 1796.

Neale, *Elizabeth I and Parliaments*

J. E. Neale, *Elizabeth I and Her Parliaments, 1559–1581*. Vol. I. London: Jonathan Cape, 1953.

[Neville,] *Plato Redivivus*

[Henry Neville,] *Plato Redivivus: or a Dialogue Concerning Government*. London, 1681.

Nicolson, *English Historical Library*

William Nicolson, *The English Historical Library. Part III. Giving an Account of our Records, Law-Books and Coins, from the Conquest to the End of Q. Elizabeth's Reign: So far as they are Serviceable to History*. London, 1699.

N. N., *Letter from Oxford*

N. N., *A Letter from Oxford, Concerning Mr. Samuel Johnson's Late Book*. Oxford, England, 1693.

Oaks, "Legal History"

Dallin H. Oaks, "Legal History in the High Court—Habeas Corpus," *Michigan Law Review* 64 (1966): 451–72.

[Oldfield,] *History of the Boroughs*

[T. H. B. Oldfield,] *An Entire and Complete History, Political and Personal, of the Boroughs of Great Britain, to which is Prefixed, an Original Sketch of Constitutional Rights, from the Earliest Period until the Present Time; and the Principle of our Ancient Representation Traced from the Most Authentic Records, Supported by Undeniable Testimonies, and Illustrated by a Variety of Notes and References, Collected from the Most Respectable, Legal, Political and Historical Authorities*. 3 volumes. London, 1792.

Otis, *Rights*

James Otis, *The Rights of the British Colonies Asserted and Proven* (1764), reprinted in Bailyn, *Pamphlets*, pp. 419–82.

Paley, *Essay upon the Constitution*

W. Paley, *An Essay Upon the British Constitution: Being the Seventh Chapter of the Sixth Book of the Principles of Moral and Political Philosophy*. London, 1792.

Paley, *Principles of Philosophy*

William Paley, *The Principles of Moral and Political Philosophy*. London, 1785.

Palmer, "Calling out the Troops"

Stanley H. Palmer, "Calling out the Troops: The Military, the Law, and Public Order in England, 1650–1850," *Journal for the Society for Army Historical Research* 56 (1978): 198–214.

Palmer, "Liberties as Provisions"

Robert C. Palmer, "Liberties as Constitutional Provisions 1776–1791," in William E. Nelson and Robert C. Palmer, *Liberty and Community: Constitution and Rights in the Early American Republic*. New York: Oceana Publications, 1987, pp. 55–148.

Parliament Debates

Proceedings and Debates of the British Parliaments Respecting North America 1754–1783. Edited by R. C. Simmons and P. D. G. Thomas. 6 volumes. Millwood, N.Y.: Kraus International Publications, 1982–1987.

Pawlisch, "Davies and Ancient Constitution"

Hans S. Pawlisch, "Sir John Davies, the Ancient Constitution, and Civil Law," *Historical Journal* 23 (September 1980): 689–702.

Pennsylvania Archives

Pennsylvania Archives: Eighth Series [Votes and Proceedings of the House of Representatives]. Volume 2. Pennsylvania Department of Property and Supply, 1931.

Pennsylvania Council

Minutes of the Provincial Council of Pennsylvania, From the Organization to Termination of the Proprietary Governor. Vol IX. Containing the Proceedings of Council From October 15th, 1762, to 17th of October, 1771, Both Days Included. Harrisburg, Pennsylvania: Theo. Fenn & Co., 1852.

Pennsylvania Gazette
Pennsylvania Gazette and Weekly Advertiser (weekly newspaper, Philadelphia).

Petyt, *Ancient Right*
William Petyt. *The Antient Right of the Commons of England Asserted; or, a Discourse Proving by Records and the best Historians, that the Commons of England were ever an Essential part of Parliament.* London, 1680.

Petyt, *Jus Parliamentarium*
William Petyt, *Jus Parliamentarium: or, the Ancient Power, Jurisdiction, Rights and Liberties, of the Most High Court of Parliament, Revived and Asserted.* London, 1739.

Plowden, *Rights of Englishmen*
Francis Plowden, *Jura Anglorum: The Rights of Englishmen.* London, 1792.

Pocock, *Ancient Constitution*
J. G. A. Pocock, *The Ancient Constitution and the Feudal Law: A Study of English Historical Thought in the Seventeenth Century.* Cambridge, England: Cambridge University Press, 1957.

Pocock, *Ancient Constitution Retrospect*
J. G. A. Pocock, *Ancient Constitution and the Feudal Law: A Study of English Historical Thought in the Seventeenth Century: A Reissue with a Retrospect.* Cambridge, England: Cambridge University Press, 1987.

Pocock, "Burke and Ancient Constitution"
J. G. A. Pocock, "Burke and the Ancient Constitution—A Problem in the History of Ideas," *Historical Journal* 3 (1960): 125–43.

Pocock, "Discourse of Sovereignty"
J. G. A. Pocock, "A Discourse of Sovereignty: Observations on the Work in Progress," in *Political Discourse in Early Modern Britain.* Edited by Nicholas Phillipson and Quentin Skinner. New York: Cambridge University Press, 1993, pp. 377–428.

Pocock, "Machiavelli"
J. G. A. Pocock, "Machiavelli, Harrington and English Political Ideologies in the Eighteenth Century," *William and Mary Quarterly* 22 (1965): 549–83.

Pocock, *Machiavellian Moment*
J. G. A. Pocock, *The Machiavellian Moment: Florentine Political Thought and the Atlantic Republican Tradition.* Princeton, N.J.: Princeton University Press, 1975.

Pocock, *Myth of Locke*
J. G. A. Pocock, *The Myth of John Locke and the Obsession with Liberalism.* William Andrews Clark Memorial Library Seminar. Los Angeles, 1980.

Pocock, "Origins of Study"
J. G. A. Pocock, "The Origins of Study of the Past: A Comparative Approach," *Comparative Studies in Society and History* 4 (1962): 209–46.

Pocock, "Political Thought"
J. G. A. Pocock, "The History of British Political Thought: The Creation of a Center," *Journal of British Studies* 24 (July 1985): 283–310.

Pocock, *Politics*
J. G. A. Pocock, *Politics, Language and Time: Essays on Political Thought and History.* New York: Atheneum, 1971.

Pocock, "Robert Brady"
J. G. A. Pocock, "Robert Brady, 1627–1700. A Cambridge Historian of the Restoration," *Cambridge Historical Journal* 10 (1951): 186–204.

Pocock, *Virtue, Commerce, History*
J. G. A. Pocock, *Virtue, Commerce, and History: Essays on Political Thought and History, Chiefly in the Eighteenth Century*. New York: Cambridge University Press, 1985.

Pole, *Gift of Government*
J. R. Pole, *The Gift of Government: Political Responsibility From the English Restoration to American Independence*. Athens: University of Georgia Press, 1983.

Pole, *Legislative Power*
J. R. Pole, *The Seventeenth Century: The Sources of Legislative Power*. Jamestown Essays on Representation. Charlottesville: University Press of Virginia, 1969.

Posner, "Blackstone"
Richard A. Posner, "Blackstone and Bentham," *Journal of Law and Economics* 19 (1976): 569–606.

Proceedings Against Manwaring
The Proceedings of the Lords and Commons in the Year 1628. Against Roger Manwaring Doctor in Divinity, [The Sachevell of those Days] For Two Seditious High-flying Sermons, intitled, Religion and Allegiance. London, 1709.

Proceedings and Debates
Proceedings and Debates of the British Parliaments Respecting North American 1754–1783. Edited by R. C. Simmons and P. D. G. Thomas. Millwood, N.J.: Kraus International Publications, 1983.

Proceedings in Parliament 1610
Proceedings in Parliament, 1610. 2 vols. Edited by Elizabeth Reid Foster. New Haven, Conn.: Yale University Press, 1966.

Prynne, *Plea for Lords*
William Prynne, *A Plea for the Lords, and House of Peers: Or, a full, necessary, seasonable, enlarged Vindication of the just, antient hereditary Right of the Lords, Peers, and Barons of this Realm to sit, vote, judge in all the Parliaments of England*. London, 1658.

Prynne, *Seasonable Chapter Three*
William Prynne, *A Seasonable, Legal and Historical Vindication of the Good old Fundamental Liberties, Rights and Laws of England, Chapter 3,4,5,6*. Printed as part of Prynne, *Seasonable Vindication*. 2nd edition. London, 1679.

Prynne, *Seasonable Vindication*
William Prynne, *The Works of William Prynne of Swainswick, Esquire since his last imprisonment, viz, the First and Second Part of a Seasonable, Legal, and Historical Vindication of the Fundamental Right and Laws of England, much enlarged: a Declaration and Protestation against Excise in General, and Hops a Native incertain commodity in Particular: a Polemicall Desertation, of the inchoation and determination of the Lordsday Sabbath: an Old Parliamentary prognostication, for the members there in consultation: Quakers unmasked, and clearly Detected to be the Spawn of Romish Frogs &c*. London, 1655.

Prynne, *Second Part*
William Prynne, *The Second Part of a Seasonable Legal and Historical Vindication, and Chronological Collection of the Good old Fundamental Liberties, Franchises, Rights, Lawes, Government of all English Freemen*. . . . London, 1655.

Prynne, *Truth Triumphing over Falsehood*
William Prynne, *Truth Triumphing over Fals[e]hood, Antiquity over Novelty*. London, 1645.

Pudsey, *Constitution and Laws*

William P[udse]y, *The Constitution and Laws of England Consider'd.* London, 1701.

[Ramsay,] *Historical Essay*

[Allan Ramsay,] *An Historical Essay on the English Constitution: Or, An impartial Inquiry into the Elective Power of the People, from the first Establishment of the Saxons in this Kingdom. Wherein the Right of Parliament, to Tax our distant Provinces, is explained, and justified, upon such constitutional Principles as will afford an equal Security to the Colonists, as to their Brethren at Home.* London, 1771.

[Ramsay,] *Right of Conquest*

[Allan Ramsay,] *An Essay on the Right of Conquest.* Florence, 1783.

[Reeves,] *Thoughts, First Letter*

[John Reeves,] *Thoughts on the English Government. Addressed to the Quiet Good Sense of the People of England. In a Series of Letters. Letter the First.* London, 1795.

[Reeves,] *Thoughts, Second Letter*

[John Reeves,] *Thoughts on the English Government. Addressed to the Quiet Good Sense of the People of England. In a Series of Letters. Letter the Second.* London, 1799.

Remonstrance of Many Thousand

A Remonstrance of Many Thousand Citizens, and other Free-born People of England, To their owne House of Commons. Occasioned through the illegal and Barbarous Imprisonment of that Famous and Worthy Sufferer for his Countries Freedoms, Lieutenant Col. John Lilburne. n.i. [1646].

Resnick, "Locke and Ancient Constitution"

David Resnick, "Locke and the Rejection of the Ancient Constitution," *Political Theory* 12 (February 1984): 97–114.

Revolutionary Virginia

Revolutionary Virginia, The Road to Independence. Volume 1: *Forming Thunderclouds and the First Convention, 1763–1774.* Compiled by William J. Van Schreeven, edited by Robert J. Scribner. [Charlottesville]: Published for Virginia Independence Bicentennial Commission, University Press of Virginia, 1973.

Richards, "Interpretation and Historiography"

David J. Richards, "Interpretation and Historiography," *Southern California Law Review* 58 (January 1985): 489–549.

[Robinson,] *Political Catechism*

[Robert Robinson,] *A Political Catechism.* London, 1782.

Roche, "Convention as Case Study"

John P. Roche, "The Convention as a Case Study in Democratic Politics," reprinted in *Essays on the Making of the Constitution.* Edited by Leonard W. Levy. 2nd edition. New York: Oxford University Press, 1987, pp. 175–212.

[Rokeby,] *Further Examination*

[Matthew Robinson-Morris, Second Baron Rokeby,] *A Further Examination of Our Present American Measures and of the Reasons and the Principles on which they are founded.* Bath, England, 1776.

Royle and Walvin, *English Radicals*

Edward Royle and James Walvin, *English Radicals and Reformers, 1760–1848.* Lexington: University of Kentucky Press, 1982.

[Ruffhead,] *Considerations*

[Owen Ruffhead,] *Considerations on the Present Dangerous Crisis.* Edinburgh, 1763.

Rule of Law

John Phillip Reid, *Rule of Law: The Jurisprudence of Liberty in the Seventeenth and*

Eighteenth Centuries. DeKalb, Illinois: Northern Illinois University Press, 2004.

Rushworth, *Historical Collections*
John Rushworth, *Historical Collections: The Third Part; in Two Volumes*. Volume 1. London, 1692.

Rutherforth, *Natural Law*
T. Rutherforth, *Institutes of Natural Law Being the substance of a Course of Lectures on Grotius de Jure Belli et Pacis Read in S. Johns College Cambridge*. 2 vols. Cambridge, England, 1754.

[Rymer,] *Prospect of Government*
[Thomas Rymer,] *A Prospect of Government in Europe, and Civil Policy. Shewing the Antiquity, Power, Decay of Parliaments*. London, 1681.

St. Amand, *Historical Essay*
George St. Amand, *An Historical Essay on the Legislature Power of England* ... [1725], reprinted in *A Complete Collection of the Lords' Protest, from the First upon Record, in the reign of Henry the Third, to the present time; with a Copious Index. To which is added, An Historical Essay on the the Legislative Power of England, their Ancient Constitution, and the Changes that have happened in the Persons that composed them ... Volume the Second*. London, 1767.

Saltern, *Of Antient Lawes*
George Saltern, *Of the Antient Lawes of Great Britaine*. London, 1605.

Schauer, "Varied Uses"
Frederick Schauer, "The Varied Uses of Constitutional History," in William E. Nelson and Robert C. Palmer, *Liberty and Community: Constitution and Rights in the Early American Republic*. New York: Oceana Publications, 1987, pp. 1–13.

Schoeck, "Elizabethian Society"
R. J. Schoeck, "The Elizabethian Society of Antiquaries and Men of Law," *Notes and Queries* 199 (1954): 417–21.

Schuyler, *Empire*
Robert Livington Schuyler, *Parliament and the British Empire: Some Constitutional Controversies Concerning Imperial Legislative Jurisdiction*. New York: Columbia University Press, 1929.

Schwoerer, "Contributions of Declaration of Rights"
Lois G. Schwoerer, "The Contributions of the Declaration of Rights to Anglo-American Radicalism," in *The Origins of Anglo-American Radicalism*. Edited by Margaret and James Jacob. London: George Allen & Unwin, 1984, pp. 105–24.

Scots Magazine
The Scots Magazine (monthly magazine, Edinburgh).

Seaberg, "Norman Conquest"
R. B. Seaberg, "The Norman Conquest and the Common Law: The Levellers and the Argument from Continuity," *Historical Journal* 24 (1981): 791–806.

Second Address
A Second Address to the Public from the Society for Constitutional Information. n.i., n.d.

Select Collection of Letters
Select Collection of the Most Interesting Letters on the Government, Liberty, and Constitution of England; Which have appeared in the different News-papers from the elevation of Lord Bute, to the death of the Earl of Egremont. Volume 1. 2nd edition. London, 1763.

[Seller,] *History of Passive Obedience*
[Abednego Seller,] *The History of Passive Obedience Since the Reformation*. Amsterdam, 1689.

[Seward] *Rights of the People*

[William W. Seward,] *The Rights of the People Asserted, and the Necessity of a More Equal Representation in Parliament Stated and Proven*. Dublin, 1783.

Sharp, *Circular Letter*

Granville Sharp, *A Circular Letter to the Several Petitioning Counties, Cities, and Towns, Addressed to their respective general Meetings, against the late Proposition for the triennial Election of Representatives*. 2nd edition. Reprinted in Sharp, *Defence*.

Sharp, *Defence*

Granville Sharp, *A Defence of the Ancient, Legal, and Constitutional Right of the People, to elect Representatives for every Session of Parliament; viz. Not only "every year once," but also "More often if need be."* London, 1780.

Sharp, *Legal Means*

Granville Sharp, *The Legal Means of Political Reformation, Proposed in Two Small Tracts*. 8th edition. London, 1797.

Sharpe, *Sir Robert Cotton*

Kevin Sharpe, *Sir Robert Cotton, 1586–1631: History and Politics in Early Modern England*. Oxford: Oxford University Press, 1979.

Shelton, *Charge to Suffolk Grand Jury*

Maurice Shelton, *A Charge Given to the Grand-Jury, at the General Quarter-Sessions of the Peace, Holden at St. Edmunds-Bury for the Liberty thereof; In the County of Suffolk: On the 11th of October, An. Dom. 1725*. London, 1726.

[Sheridan,] *Observations on the Doctrine*

[Charles Francis Sheridan,] *Observations on the Doctrine laid down by Sir William Blackstone, Respecting the extent of the Power of the British Parliament, Particularly with relation to Ireland. In a Letter to Sir William Blackstone, with a Postscript Addressed to Lord North*. Dublin, 1779.

Sidney, *Discourses Concerning Government*

Algernon Sidney, *Discourses Concerning Government*. London, 1698.

Siegel, "Aristotelian Basis of Law"

Stephen A. Siegel, "The Aristotelian Basis of English Law," *New York University Law Review* 56 (1981): 18–59.

[Sinclair,] *Considerations on Proceedings*

[Sir John Sinclair,] *Considerations on Proceedings by Information and Attachment. Addressed to the Members of the House of Commons. By a Barrater at Law*. 2nd edition. London, 1768.

Skinner, "Conquest and Consent"

Quentin Skinner, "Conquest and Consent: Thomas Hobbes and the Engagement Controversy," in *The Interregnum: The Quest for Settlement, 1646–1660*. Edited by G. E. Aylmer. [Hamden, Conn.]: Archon Books, 1972, pp. 79–98.

Skinner, "History and Ideology"

Quentin Skinner, "History and Ideology in the English Revolution," *Historical Journal* 8 (1965): 151–78.

Smith, *Gothic Bequest*

R. J. Smith, *The Gothic Bequest: Medieval Institutions in British Thought, 1688–1863*. Cambridge, England: Cambridge University Press, 1987.

Society for Constitutional Information

Two publications distributed by the Society for Constitutional Information, both without title, imprint, or binding. The copies at the Huntington Library, San Marino, California, are in the rare book collection and are numbered (for 1782) 310802 and (for 1783) 305204.

[Somers,] *Brief History*
[John Somers, Baron Somers,] *A Brief History of the Succession, Collected out of the Records, and the most Authentick Historians. Written for the Satisfaction of the Nation.* London, 1689.

Sommerville, "History and Theory"
Johann P. Sommerville, "History and Theory: The Norman Conquest in Early Stuart Political Thought," *Political Studies* 34 (1986): 249–61.

Sommerville, *Politics and Ideology*
J. P. Sommerville, *Politics and Ideology in England, 1603-1640.* London: Longman, 1986.

Squire, *Foundation*
Samuel Squire, *An Enquiry into the Foundation of the English Constitution; Or, An Historical Essay upon the Anglo-Saxon Government both in Germany and England.* London, 1745.

[Squire,] *Historical Essay on Ballance*
[Samuel Squire,] *An Historical Essay Upon the Ballance of Civil Power in England, From its first Conquest by the Anglo-Saxons, to the Time of the Revolution; in which is introduced a new Dissertation upon Parties: With a proper Dedication to the Freeholders and Burgesses of Great Britain.* London, 1748.

[Stevens,] *Revolution Vindicated*
[William Stevens,] *The Revolution Vindicated, and Constitutional Liberty Asserted. In Answer to the Revered Dr. Watson's Accession Sermon, Preached before the University of Cambridge, on October 25th, 1776. In a Letter to a Friend. By the Author of Strictures on Dr. Watson's Restoration Sermon.* Cambridge, England, 1776.

[Stewart,] *Letter to Dr. Price*
[James Stewart,] *A Letter to the Rev. Dr. Price, F.R.S. Wherein his Observations on the Nature of Civil Liberty, the Principles of Government, &c. Are Candidly Examined; His Fundamental Principles refuted, and the Fallacy of his Reasoning from these Principles delected. Also the True Principles of Liberty, Explained and Demonstrated, the Constitutional Authority of the Supreme Legislative of Great Britain, Over every Part of the British Dominions, Both in the Matter of Legislation and Taxation, and in every Act of Legal Authority, Asserted and Fully Vindicated.* London, 1776.

Straka, "Sixteen Eighty-Eight"
Gerald M. Straka, "Sixteen Eighty-eight as the Year One: Eighteenth-Century Attitudes Towards the Glorious Revolution," *Studies in Eighteenth-Century Culture* 1 (1971): 143-67.

Stuart, "Discourse"
Gilbert Stuart, "A Discourse Concerning the Laws and Government of England," in Sullivan, *Lectures on the Constitution,* pp. i-xxxii.

Stuart, *Historical Dissertation of Constitution*
Gilbert Stuart, *An Historical Dissertation concerning the Antiquity of the English Constitution.* 2nd edition. London, 177O.

Styles, "Politics and Research"
Philip Styles, "Politics and Historical Research in the Early Seventeenth Century," in *English Historical Scholarship in the Sixteenth and Seventeenth Centuries.* Edited by Levi Fox. Published for the Dugdale Society. London: Oxford University Press, 1956, pp. 49–72.

Sullivan, *Lectures on the Constitution*
Francis Stoughton Sullivan, *Lectures on the Constitution and Laws of England: With*

a Commentary on Magna Carta, and Illustrations of Many of the English Statutes. To which Authorities are added, and a Discourse is prefixed, concerning the Laws and Government of England by Gilbert Stuart, LL.D. 2nd edition. London, 1776.

Sutherland, "Conquest and Law"
Donald Sutherland, "Conquest and Law," *Studia Gratiana* 15 (1972): 35–51.

Tarlton, "Rulers now on Earth"
Charles D. Tarlton, "'The Rulers now on Earth': Locke's Two Treatises and the Revolution of 1688," *Historical Journal* 28 (1985): 279–98.

Thompson, "Fundamental Law"
Martyn P. Thompson, "The History of Fundamental Law in Political Thought from the French Wars of Religion to the American Revolution," *American Historical Review* 91 (December 1986): 1103-28.

Thompson, "Idea of Conquest"
M. P. Thompson, "The Idea of Conquest in Controversies over the 1688 Revolution," *Journal of the History of Ideas* 38 (1997): 33-46.

Thompson, "Reception of Locke"
Martyn P. Thompson, "The Reception of Locke's Two Treatises of Government 1690–1705," *Political Studies* 24 (1976): 184–91.

Thompson, "Significant Silences"
Martyn P. Thompson, "Significant Silences in Locke's *Two Treatises of Government:* Constitutional History, Contract and Law," *Historical Journal* 31 (1987): 275–94.

Thomson, *Constitutional History*
Mark A. Thomson, *A Constitutional History of England 1642 to 1801*. London: Methuen & Co., [1938].

Towers, *Vindication of Locke*
Joseph Towers, *A Vindication of the Political Principles of Mr. Locke: In Answer to the Objection of the Rev. Dr. Tucker, Dean of Glocester*. London, 1782.

Trumbull, *Discourse at New Haven*
Benjamin Trumbull, *Discourse, Delivered at the Anniversery Meeting of the Freeman of the Town of New Haven, April 12, 1773.* New Haven, Conn., 1773.

Tuck, "Ancient Law of Freedom"
Richard Tuck, "'The Ancient Law of Freedom': John Selden and the Civil War," in *Reactions to the English Civil War 1642–1649*. Edited by John Morrill. London: Macmillan, 1982, pp. 138–61.

Tuck, *Natural Rights Theories*
Richard Tuck, *Natural Rights Theories: Their Origin and Development*. Cambridge, England: Cambridge University Press, 1979.

Tucker, *Letter to Burke*
Josiah Tucker, *A Letter to Edmund Burke, Esq.; Member of Parliament for the City of Bristol, and Agent for the Colony of New York, &c. In Answer to His Printed Speech, Said to be Spoken in the House of Commons on the Twenty-Second of March, 1775.* 2nd edition. Glocester, England, 1775.

Tucker, *Treatise*
Josiah Tucker, *A Treatise Concerning Civil Government, In Three Parts*. London, 1781.

Twiss, *Lawyers and Constitution*
Benjamin Rollins Twiss, *Lawyers and the Constitution: How Laissez-Faire Came to the Supreme Court*. New York: Russell & Russell Inc., 1962.

Twysden, *Certaine Considerations*
Sir Roger Twysden, *Certaine Considerations Upon the Government of England.*

Volume 45. Camden Society, London, 1849.

[Tyrrell,] *Brief Enquiry*

[James Tyrrell,] *A Brief Enquiry into the Ancient Constitution and Government of England.* London, 1695.

Vann, "Free Anglo-Saxons"

Richard T. Vann, "The Free Anglo-Saxons: A Historical Myth," *Journal of the History of Ideas* 19 (April 1958): 259–72.

[Vincent,] *Letter to Dr. Richard Watson*

[William Vincent,] *A Letter to the Reverend Dr. Richard Watson, King's Professor of Divinity in the University of Cambridge.* London, 1780.

Warren, "Introduction"

Earl Warren, "Introduction" to *American Journal of Legal History* 1 (1957): 1.

Warrington, *Works*

Henry Booth, Earl of Warrington, *The Works of the Right Honourable Henry late L[ord] Dalamer and Earl of Warrington.* London, 1694.

Weston, "Ancient Constitution"

Corinne C. Weston, "England: Ancient Constitution and Common Law," in *The Cambridge History of Political Thought 1450–1700.* Edited by J. H. Burns. Cambridge, England: Cambridge University Press, 1991, pp. 374–410.

Weston, "Diverse Viewpoints"

Corinne Comstock Weston, "Diverse Viewpoints on Ancient Constitutionalism," in *The Roots of Liberty: Magna Carta, Ancient Constitution, and the Anglo-American Tradition of Rule of Law.* Edited by Ellis Sandoz. Columbia: University of Missouri Press, 1993, pp. 232–51.

Weston, "Legal Sovereignty"

Corinne Comstock Weston, "Legal Sovereignty in the Brady Controversy," *Historical Journal* 15 (1972): 409–31.

Weston and Greenberg, *Grand Controversy*

Corinne Comstock Weston and Janelle Renfrow Greenberg, *Subjects and Sovereigns: The Grand Controversy over Legal Sovereignty in Stuart England.* New York: Cambridge University Press, 1981.

Wilkes, *English Liberty*

John Wilkes, *English Liberty: Being a Collection of Interesting Tracts, From the Year 1762 to 1769. Containing the Private Correspondence, Public Letters, Speeches and Addresses, of John Wilkes, Esq. Humbly Dedicated to the King.* London, [1770].

[Wilkes,] *Letter to Johnson*

[John Wilkes,] *A Letter to Samuel Johnson, L.L.D.* [London,] n.d.

[Williams,] *Essential Rights*

[Elisha Williams,] *The Essential Rights and Liberties of Protestants. A Sensible Plea for the Liberty of Conscience and the Rights of private Judgement, In Matters of Religion, Without any Controul from human Authority. Being a Letter from a Gentlemen in the Massachusetts-Bay to his Friend in Connecticut.* Boston, 1744.

[Williams,] *Letters on Liberty*

[David Williams,] *Letters on Political Liberty. Addressed to a Member of the English House of Commons, on his being Chosen into the Committee of an Associating County.* London, 1782.

Williams, *Parliamentary Reformation*

Joseph Williams, *Parliamentary Reformation: Examined under the Following Articles: Extending the Right of Election. Abolition of Boroughs. Qualification of Members. Abridging the Duration of Parliament.* London, 1782.

Willman, "Blackstone and Caroline Law"
Robert Willman, "Blackstone and the 'Theoretical Perfection' of English Law in the Reign of Charles II," *Historical Journal* 26 (1983): 39–70.
Wilsher, "Power Follows Property"
J. C. Wilsher, "'Power Follows Property'—Social and Economic Interpretations in British Historical Writing in the Eighteenth and Early Nineteenth Centuries," *Journal of Social History* 16 (Number 3) (1983): 7–26.
Withers, *Whigs Vindicated*
John Withers, *The Whigs Vindicated, the Objections that are commonly brought against them Answer'd, and the Present Ministry Prov'd to be the best Friends to the Church, the Monarchy, the Lasting Peace, and real Welfare of England.* 5th edition. London, 1715.
Witmer, *Property Qualifications*
Helen Elizabeth Witmer, *The Property Qualifications of Members of Parliament.* New York: Columbia University Press, 1943.
Wood, *Creation*
Gordon Wood, *The Creation of the American Revolution 1776–1787.* Chapel Hill: University of North Carolina Press, 1969.
Wooddeson, *Jurisprudence*
Richard Wooddeson, *Elements of Jurisprudence Treated of in the Preliminary Part of a Course of Lectures on the Law of England.* Dublin, 1792.
Wooddeson, *Laws of England*
Richard Wooddeson, *A Systematical View of the Laws of England; as Treated in a Course of Vinerian Lectures, Read at Oxford, During a Series of Years, Commencing in Michaelmas Term, 1777.* Volume 1. Dublin, 1792.
Worcester Charges
Charges to Grand Juries, Delivered at the Quarter Session of the Peace for the County of Worcester, from the Year 1760 to 1776. Worcester, England, 1780.
Works of Algernon Sydney
The Works of Algernon Sydney, a new edition. London, 1772.
Wright, *Grand Jury Speech*
John Wright, *The Speech of John Wright, Esq; One of the Magistrates of Lancaster County, to the Court and Grand-Jury, on his Removal from the Commission of the Peace at the Quarter-Session held at Lancaster for the said County in May 1741.* [Philadelphia, 1741].
Wright, *Law of Tenures*
Sir Martin Wright, *Introduction to the Law of Tenures.* 4th edition. London, 1792.
Wynne, *Eunomus*
Edward Wynne, *Eunomus: or, Dialogues Concerning the Law and Constitution of England with An Essay on Dialogue.* 2nd edition. London, 1785.
Wyvill, *Defence of Price*
Christopher Wyvill, *A Defence of Dr. Price and the Reformers of England.* London, 1792.
Yale, "Hobbes and Hale"
D. E. C. Yale, "Hobbes and Hale on Law, Legislation and the Sovereign," *Cambridge Law Journal* 31 (1972): 121–56.
[Yorke,] *Forfeitures for High Treason*
[Charles Yorke,] *Considerations on the Law of Forfeitures, for High Treason. With an Appendix concerning Estates-Tail in Scotland.* 4th edition. London, 1775.
Young, *Example of France*
Arthur Young, *The Example of France. A Warning to Britain.* 4th edition. London, 1794.

ACKNOWLEDGMENTS

Leave from teaching responsibilities at New York University School of Law was provided by the Filomen D'Agostino Greenberg and Max E. Greenberg Faculty Research Fund at New York University School of Law, and by John Sexton, dean of the School of Law. The index is the work of Barbara Wilcie Kern of Greenwich Village, and the cite and substance checking was performed by Brian L. Frye in the summer, between his second and third year as a student at New York University School of Law.

Many people aided me in researching and writing this book. A very special debt of thanks is owed to Paul Langford of Lincoln College, Oxford University. Professor Langford one day came over to my desk in the rare-book reading room of the Huntington Library and said he had just read something that he was certain I could use. He had discovered the *Seize of Penobscot* pamphlet with the proclamations of the British and American commanders at the battle of Castine, each appealing to the people to support the ancient constitution, which are quoted at the first paragraph of Chapter One.

Research was made both easier and more pleasant by the professional competence of the staff of the Huntington Library, most particularly Fred Perez and Alan Jutzi. As always, the librarians at New York University School of Law were just as professional. Gretchen Feltes went on line to locate rare books, Radu Popa took me to the right floor, and Terry Ballard made the entire writing easier by transforming the printed word onto a disk. It does not seem likely, but perhaps in some inexplicable fashion this study profited by being read and discussed in part by the premier group of American legal historians, members of the New York University School of Law Colloquium in Legal History: R. B. Bernstein, Gerald Giannattosio, William LaPiana, Martin S. Flaherty, and William E. Nelson.

Research on the ancient constitution and Magna Carta was first undertaken for a conference on "Magna Carta, the Ancient Constitution, and the Anglo-American Tradition of Rule of Law," sponsored by the Liberty Fund of Indianapolis, Indiana, and conducted in St. George's House of Windsor Castle, in June 1988, in observance of the 773rd anniversary of the signing of Magna Carta. The conference was under the direction of Professor Ellis Sandoz of Louisiana State University. He edited the conference papers, which were published by the University of Missouri Press in a volume entitled *The Roots of Liberty: Magna Carta, Ancient Constitution, and the Anglo-American Tradition of Rule of Law* (1993). This is where the germinal ideas for this monograph first appeared. My thanks to the University of Missouri Press for allowing me to expand upon that article.

A serious error was prevented when Shirley Gray pointed out that it was not Sir Edward Coke but Franklin Pierce who wrote: "Dedicated and scholarly writers of history, my advice is, do not confuse what you do with what lawyers do, and do not judge lawyers by how well they master petty tasks when their eye is on liberty, and not on telling tales." Pierce wrote this in his annual Christmas message, and it was Leila Nelson who pointed out that he may have borrowed the thought from Coke. What Coke wrote, Leila discovered, was "To the grave and learned writers of histories my advice is, that they meddle not with any point or secret of any art or science, especially the laws of the realm, before they confer with some learned in that profession." As always, Coke gave good advice.

INDEX

www.ingramcontent.com/pod-product-compliance
Ingram Content Group UK Ltd.
Pitfield, Milton Keynes, MK11 3LW, UK
UKHW030915290525
459016UK00004B/31